How did British Jewry respond to the Holocaust, how prominent was the Holocaust on the communal agenda and what does this response tell us about the values, politics, fears and identity of the Anglo-Jewish community? This book studies the priorities of that community, and thereby seeks to analyse the attitudes and philosophies which informed actions. It paints a picture of Anglo-Jewish life and its reactions to a wide range of matters in the external, Gentile world.

Richard Bolchover charts the transmission of the news of the European catastrophe and discusses the various theories which have thus far been posited regarding reactions in these exceptional circumstances. He investigates the structures and political philosophies of Anglo-Jewry during the war years and covers the reactions of Jewish political and religious leaders as well as prominent Jews acting outside the community's institutional framework. Various co-ordinated responses, political and philanthropic, are studied, as are the issues which dominated the community at that time, namely internal conflict and the fear of increased domestic anti-semitism: these preoccupations inevitably affected responses to events in Europe. The latter half of the book looks at the ramifications of the community's socio-political philosophies including, most radically, Zionism, and their influence on communal reactions. This is the first and only published work on this subject, and it raises major questions about the structures and priorities of the British Jewish community.

BRITISH JEWRY AND THE HOLOCAUST

BRITISH JEWRY
AND THE HOLOCAUST

RICHARD BOLCHOVER

CAMBRIDGE
UNIVERSITY PRESS

Published by the Press Syndicate of the University of Cambridge
The Pitt Building, Trumpington Street, Cambridge, CB2 1RP
40 West 20th Street, New York, NY 10011–4211, USA
10 Stamford Road, Oakleigh, Victoria, 3166, Australia

Richard Bolchover 1993

First published 1993

Printed in Great Britain at the University Press, Cambridge

A catalogue record for this book is available from the British Library

Library of Congress cataloguing in publication data
Bolchover, Richard.
British Jewry and the Holocaust / Richard Bolchover.
p.   cm.
Includes bibliographical references.
ISBN 0 521 43234 0
1. Jews – Great Britain – Politics and government. 2. Holocaust,
Jewish (1939–1945) – Public opinion, 3. Public opinion – Jews.
4. Public opinion – Great Britain. 5. Zionism – Great Britain.
6. Great Britain – Ethnic relations. 1. Title.
DS 135.E8B65   1993
305.892´4041 – dc20   92–20409   CIP

ISBN 0 521 43234 0 hardback

74847

To my parents and brothers.
With love.

Contents

Preface

This book is the published version of an earlier dissertation. In that work I thanked all who had helped me in those original endeavours and I most sincerely reiterate my gratitude now. As regards the transition to publication I must thank my good friend Mark Phillips who has been an invaluable source of guidance and advice. Dr Tony Kushner of the University of Southampton and Dr David Cesarani of the Wiener Library have both assisted me greatly by reading and commenting on my text. Richard Fisher, editor at Cambridge University Press, has been a considerable help in all matters practical and I thank him again for recommending the work to the Syndicate. Last but by no means least I must also restate my sincerest appreciation to Professor Steven Zipperstein of Stanford University. It was he who guided me through the first tentative steps towards this publication and without him it simply would not have been possible.

My most profound thanks must go to my family who have supported me wholeheartedly in this and in all my endeavours. I have dedicated this book to my three brothers and to my parents. Their love and affection has been constant and unfailing. My mother and father guided and advised me in the production of this book with their customary wisdom and patience. It is an almost unbearable sadness to know that my beloved father did not see its final publication. He was involved in every stage of its production. His judgment and his humour never failed to steer me on to the right course. Though the pain of grief is now intense I know that his example and his humanity remain a beacon of light and inspiration to those who loved him.

Introduction

This book analyses Anglo-Jewish responses to the Holocaust. This community was unique in that it was the only Jewry in a democratic country which, while actively engaged in and physically close to the war, was never occupied by the Germans. It is important to explore the nature of this community's response against this distinctive background. The emphasis here will not be on the influence, or lack of it, that Anglo-Jewry had on events. Rather the book examines what the community's response to this historical experience reveals about its own organisational structure and socio-political philosophy. The book is, in other words, a contribution to the understanding of Anglo-Jewry, not the Holocaust.

Much of the existing historical work on diasporic Jewish reactions to the Holocaust is narrative. This book takes a different approach, one which focusses on the attitudes and philosophies which informed actions. Whilst I shall not overlook the deviation of segments of the community or individuals, it is normative responses that will be the subject of this study, responses that were on the surface frequently inconsistent or contradictory.

Despite the considerable growth in interest in the field of 'bystander' or 'onlooker' response to the Holocaust this is the first book which concerns itself with the British Jewish response. American Jewish response has been the subject of numerous books, articles and reports and has consequently been the focus of considerable debate and discussion. The British Jewish response has, in contrast, been sadly neglected.[1]

I have surveyed most of the relevant sources, including memoirs, biographies, archives of Jewish organisations and Government archives. Newspapers are a major source for this book, and in particular the *Jewish Chronicle*. It reported almost all public matters of Jewish concern and its reportage, notwithstanding the Revisionist outlook of its editor Ivan Greenberg, was on the whole impartial and comprehensive. So much so indeed that even dissident and provincial Jewish journals paid deference to it (see the Glasgow *Jewish Echo* editorials on 19 June 1942 and 21 August 1942 and the Agudist *Di Vochenzaitung* on July 1943, p. 4). As its pages are not dominated by partisan or parochial concerns its coverage gives a good assessment of the community's moods and priorities. It is undoubtedly the most widely read Jewish publication of the time.[2]

The book hardly touches on the historical East End/West End divide in the London Jewish community. Despite the militancy of East End groups such as the Jewish Friendly Societies and Trade Unions, the Workers' Circle (Arbeter Ring) and Jews in the Communist Party who forced the pace on anti-Nazi protest rallies and the anti-German boycott between 1933 and 1939, these groups had faded from view by 1942.[3] The outbreak of war had proved a watershed in the history of the East End as a focus of Anglo-Jewish life. The move to leafier suburbs, promoted by economic forces, had already begun in the 1920s and 1930s and was well under way. The battering taken by the East End in the Blitz and the evacuation which followed exacerbated the trend, so much so that one contemporary could write that by 1945 'the Whitechapel district which had already begun before the war to give place to other neighbourhoods as Jewish centres, may now be regarded as on the very verge of disappearance as a place of Jewish residence'.[4] The Friendly Societies, Trades Unions and Workers' Circles saw their membership decline considerably during the war. The movements' constituent groups were largely disbanded. Many of the young who had been prominent in the campaigns of the 1930s were now on active service. The same was true of activist Jewish youth groups. The Communist Party remained strong but its concern was mainly with the general struggle against Fascism, and, after 1941, it laid particular emphasis on support for the Soviet war effort. For the Party the Jews of Europe were only an indirect issue. Consequently for the duration of the war the East End did not play a particularly independent or distinctive part in the response of Anglo-Jewry to the Holocaust.[5] Refugee Jews similarly had little impact. As I will show, the indigenous community had placed them under severe constraints, and moreover many had at first been interned and later conscripted. This rendered them a marginal factor.

I have not dealt with Anglo-Jewish views of Nazism before the War because both the outbreak of hostilities in 1939 and the systematic policy of extermination of the Jews of Europe pursued by the Nazis after 1941 mark two very significant discontinuities in the response of Anglo-Jewry. The wartime response can legitimately and, in my view, should properly be examined separately.

The book deals exclusively with the internal dynamics of the Anglo-Jewish community. The reader will not find much discussion of the nature of the actions of the external Gentile world including those of the government or of anti-semitic groups. I am interested here solely in Anglo-Jewry's perceptions of these groups, not in the groups themselves.

I have tried to examine any public statement or publication of a British Jew which might have a bearing on response to the Holocaust. Many, though not all, of those individuals turned out to be involved somehow in Anglo-Jewish institutions. Within these circles there was some diversity, however, and these individuals can be said to have articulated all those socio-political philosophies present within the community at large.

The public nature of the statements and actions I have studied is crucially important. Meetings behind closed doors, conversations and letters do not have the same wide impact on attitudes and opinions. Public statements, however, can be amplified, retracted or openly challenged. It is only by a study of what British Jews were prepared to say and do in public that we can determine the contours on the map of Anglo-Jewish attitudes regarding the outside, non-Jewish world.

This book shares the assumption held by most Jewish historians that the Jews constituted a people who, even after emancipation, remained united by strong cultural bonds. These bonds, based on common heritage and religion, produced strong feelings of solidarity and unity which extended beyond national boundaries. Since the establishment of the State of Israel, of course, there has been clear evidence of such solidarity in strong diasporic support for Israel. But in the first half of this century, many examples of transnational Jewish solidarity are also to be found, as are institutions that expressed it. These included political unions (the Zionist movement and the World Jewish Congress), religious organisations (the World Agudist Organisation), representative bodies (the foreign committees of the Board of Deputies and the Anglo-Jewish Association), newspapers such as the *Jewish Chronicle* and a host of philanthropic bodies. This book assumes the existence of a strong and abiding sense of communal loyalty among the Jews of Europe. What I will investigate is how it was manifested and in what ways it was affected by competing Anglo-Jewish interests and ideologies in the period 1942–5.

PART I

Knowing and believing

Knowing and believing

When did the news of the mass murder of European Jewry reach Britain? What facts were known, how did they come to be known and who knew them? Detailed research on these questions has already been undertaken in other works,[1] but it is important that this book too should detail the information on the European atrocities that was available to Britain's Jewish community from the day war was declared on 3 September 1939.

The first part of this book, therefore, outlines the context of British Jewry's response to the Holocaust. It examines the information that was available to the Anglo-Jewish community about events behind Nazi lines and summarises the main conclusions of the existing body of scholarly literature on diasporic response to the Holocaust.

In order to assess the response of Britain's Jewish community, we need to ask what actual facts were known to the community at the time. In the years since the Holocaust mountains of documentary and photographic historical evidence have emerged. But we must make the huge mental leap to ask what was known to those who could have only second-hand information at the time.

I

The main conduit of information was, of course, the press. Andrew Sharf, in his work *The British Press and Jews under Nazi Rule*, states categorically that 'on the whole question of atrocity and extermination, the Press knew well and printed accurately exactly what was happening ... few facts of Nazi anti-semitism were left unstated by the British press'.[2] Indeed one could go further and suggest that in Britain's newspapers one finds as firm a grasp of the motivations behind Nazi policy as was available anywhere. The newspapers indicated trends in German actions earlier than others and reported them accurately and swiftly.

As early as 16 December 1939 the *Times* published an article indicating the murderous intent of the Nazis, headlined 'A Slow Road to Extermination'. The aim of the Nazi scheme was to set up 'a place for gradual extermination, and not what the Germans would describe as a Lebensraum or living space'.[3] The first reports on the mass killings by the *Einsatzgruppen* on Soviet territory were printed in December 1941, the most famous of which, the Babi-Yar massacre, was marked by a report of the Joint Foreign Committee of the Board of Deputies of British Jews and the Anglo-Jewish Association released to the press on 17 December, and stating that 52,000 people, Jews and non-Jews, had been murdered by the Nazis after the German occupation of Kiev.[4]

The use of gas as a weapon of mass extermination was first mentioned in a 9 January 1942 *Jewish Chronicle* report that poison gas experiments had been conducted at Mauthausen concentration camp.[5] As details of the massacres flowed into London, those with an intimate knowledge of events occurring within Nazi-occupied territory became convinced of the radical nature of Hitler's solution to the 'Jewish Problem'. On 9 June 1942 General Sikorski, the Polish Prime Minister, broadcast from London on the BBC European Services: 'The Jewish population in Poland is doomed to annihilation in accordance with the maxim "Slaughter all the Jews regardless of how the war will end."'[6] The *Daily Telegraph* began a despatch on 25 June as follows: 'More than 700,000 Polish Jews have been slaughtered by the Germans in the greatest massacre in the world's history.' The report reviewed the mass exterminations in East Galicia and Lithuania and revealed for the first time the use of 'travelling gas chambers' in Chelmno concentration camp. The newspaper declared that the Germans had 'embarked on the physical extermination of the Jewish population'. The article continued to state that these facts were 'wholly in keeping with Hitler's many times avowed policy'.[7] Five days later, on 30 June 1942, the same newspaper included a report under the headline 'More Than 1,000,000 Jews Killed in Europe'. This story made one further point of great importance which had not been clearly spelled out previously – that it was the aim of the Nazis 'to wipe the race from the European continent'.[8]

The fact of a systematic extermination of Jews was now widely accepted in newspaper columns. On the same day as this second *Daily Telegraph* report appeared, most British newspapers carried stories with headlines such as 'Massacre of Jews: Over 1,000,000 Jews Dead Since War Began' (*Times*), '1,000,000 Jews Die' (*Evening Standard*), 'Million Jews Die' (*News Chronicle*), 'Bondage in Eastern Europe – A Vast Slaughterhouse of Jews' (*Scotsman*), 'Great Pogrom – 1 Million Jews Die' (*Daily Mail*) and 'Jewish War Victims – More Than 1 Million Dead' (*Manchester Guardian*).[9]

Details of gas killings were now commonplace. The weekly magazine *News Review* told in July 1942 of the 'large gas stations' which had been set up in Poland 'to kill off Jews ... No sleeping-drugs were wasted on them. They were just trussed up and finished off.'[10]

In tandem with these press reports, the British Foreign Office received a telegram on 10 August 1942 which many historians consider a turning-point in British response. What it said was not in fact new but its impact, particularly on British government and Jewish organisational circles, was great. The telegram, sent by the Geneva representative of the World Jewish Congress, Dr Gerhart Riegner, contained a message for Sidney Silverman MP: 'Received alarming report stating that, in the Fuehrer's Headquarters, a plan has been discussed and is under consideration, according to which all Jews in countries occupied or controlled by Germany numbering 3½–4 millions should, after deportation and concentration in the East, be at one blow exterminated, in order to resolve, once and for all, the Jewish question in Europe.'[11] At the end of the same month, another Jewish official in Geneva, Richard Lichtheim of the Jewish Agency, wrote to London in more concrete as well as resigned fashion: 'This process of annihilation is going on relentlessly and there is no hope left to save any considerable number ... Therefore it is no exaggeration to say that Hitler has killed or is killing 4 million Jews in Continental Europe and that no more than 2 million have a chance of surviving.'[12]

As information from Europe built up, the response of British institutions, both Jewish and non-Jewish, became more organised. The first major rally held in Britain to protest against the German extermination programme was held in the Caxton Hall under the auspices of the British Labour Party on 2 September 1942. The Home Secretary, Herbert Morrison, told the meeting that 'the mounting tale of atrocity and horror was no surprise to the people of this country'.[13] On 8 September the Prime Minister, Winston

Churchill, made the first government statement in the House of Commons specifically referring to the Jews. In a speech on German atrocities he described those committed against the Jews as 'the most bestial, the most squalid and most senseless of all their offences'.[14]

Reports from Europe became increasingly desperate. The Jewish Telegraphic Agency carried a despatch on 20 September from 'a point at the border of Axis-held territory'. The report ended with a terse invocation: 'Pogroms on unprecented scale in Poland. The Nazis have begun the extermination of Polish Jews. Save Us.'[15]

No newspaper doubted the Nazis' intent to destroy physically Europe's Jews, nor the centrality of this aim in Nazi policy. The Riegner telegram, originally sent on 8 August, was published (without attribution) in the *Jewish Chronicle* on 2 October 1942 under the headline 'Nazis' Master Plan for Jews'.[16] On 27 October the *Manchester Guardian* commented on a speech by Hitler (presumably that delivered on 30 September 1942 at the Berlin Sports Palace) which had threatened the annihilation of the Jews of Europe. The *Guardian* warned its readers not to take Hitler's claim 'as just another wild and whirling threat'; Hitler 'aims literally at the extermination of the Jews in Europe so far as his hand can reach them'. Between one and two million Jews 'are believed to have already been destroyed', it stated, and perhaps four and a half million remained to be killed 'if Hitler had his way'.[17]

This murder of Europe's Jews was seen as a distinct and unique phenomenon. In a three-page bulletin of 1 December 1942 the World Jewish Congress British Section reported on the 'annihilation of European Jewry'. Hitler's policy was 'total destruction'. Two million Jews at least had already been 'murdered, tortured and deliberately starved to death in Eastern Europe'. The number was probably 'much greater'. Using for the first time the word that has since come to refer to the systematic murder of European Jewry, the bulletin stressed that in March 1942 'the holocaust took on a formal design under an explicit policy'.[18] The *Times* in an article of 4 December under the title 'Deliberate Policy for Extermination' referred to a total of 1,700,000 Jews 'liquidated'. The newspaper commented that 'all other war crimes of Nazism will fail in the end – and the defeat of German Fascism is inevitable – but this particular aim, a complete extermination of Jews, is already being enforced'.[19]

11 December 1942 marked another important watershed in the flow of information to Anglo-Jewry. The *Jewish Chronicle*, collating

earlier reports from Europe, appeared with a black border on its front page and a headline 'Two Million Jews Slaughtered; Most Terrible Massacre of All Time: Appalling Horrors of Nazi Mass Murders'.[20] Another attempt to raise people's consciousness took place on 13 December 1942, when the Chief Rabbi, J. H. Hertz, declared a day of fasting and mourning for the victims of the Nazis, and a service was held at the Bevis Marks synagogue in London. The effect was maintained and emphasised when four days later, on 17 December, Anthony Eden, the Foreign Secretary, made a detailed declaration on the extermination of European Jewry to the House of Commons issued in the name of eleven Allied Governments and of the French National Committee. The House rose and stood in silence for two minutes following the declaration.[21]

The beginning of 1943 saw important articles on the subject of European Jewry published prominently. The *New Statesman and Nation* printed on 9 January a major article entitled 'Our Part in Massacre'. Hitler 'is engaged in exterminating the Jews of Europe, not metaphorically, not more or less, but with a literal totalitarian completeness, as farmers try to exterminate Californian beetles'.[22]

Allied Government reaction to the news from Europe was now also the subject of comment. The *Manchester Guardian* on 22 April saw the Bermuda Refugee Conference as a 'side-stepping of the Jewish problem. The facts remain, the extermination goes on.'[23] On the same day *The Times* reported on a UP despatch from Sweden on 'secret Polish radio' containing the first news of the Warsaw ghetto uprising.[24] The story of the Warsaw ghetto continued to unfold and on 23 May the *Manchester Sunday Chronicle* published a detailed account under the headline 'Warsaw Jews Defy Nazis' Might in Last Stand Against Mass Murder. Pitched Battle Rages in Ghetto.'[25] As the toll of destruction mounted the *People* published a statement of the Institute of Jewish Affairs in New York on 17 October which declared that 'Hitler has Murdered Three Million Jews in Europe.'[26]

The pattern of the Nazi extermination was clearly set by the time the Germans occupied Hungary on 19 March 1944. The Board of Deputies held an emergency meeting two days later to discuss the situation. The fate of Hungarian Jewry was in no doubt as the *Jewish Chronicle* headlined its story on 14 June 1944: 'Hungarian Jews Doomed. Planned Extermination'.[27] As reports of the deportations of Hungarian Jews to the death camps reached London Sidney

Silverman spoke in the House of Commons of 'the total annihilation of European Jewry by Hitlerite Germany'.[28]

As the war drew slowly to its close and death camps were liberated, photographic evidence became available. The first pictures of the gas ovens and skeletons of Majdanek were published in the *Jewish Chronicle* on 18 August 1944.[29] The flow of information continued to the very end. The World Jewish Congress British Section received news in February 1945 of the Nazi order to liquidate concentration camp occupants before their imminent Allied capture.[30]

Though emphasis on the Final Solution had declined since its peak in December 1942, Sharf concludes that 'there can therefore be no doubt that, at each stage of the disaster very full information was available and was used by the British Press. Nor can there be any doubt that the majority was willing to accept that information as true ... [The Press] went on telling the British people almost precisely what was happening.'[31] This assessment, as the above testifies, is wholly correct. What I have detailed here are only the salient turning-points in the coverage and public analysis of Nazi intent on the Jewish question. However it should be stressed that every turn and every stage of the Nazi extermination was reported in Britain. Details of massacres and deportations from all the centres of Jewish population, large and small, were included almost daily in Britain's newspaper columns. Information, then, was abundant and accurate, and it is against this background that Anglo-Jewish response must be placed.

II

It has been going on, this sin against humanity – this sin so great that even to speak of it, even to think of it, makes one ashamed to be a man – it has been going on ever since Hitler came to power in the early weeks of 1933. There has never been the slightest excuse for anyone to plead ignorance of it. In that very first year I published 'The Brown Book of Hitler Terror', in which the first stages of the terror were exposed with a wealth of documentary and photographic evidence which allowed of no denial. Or should have allowed ... [These] are no revelations at all to those who have lived in an agonised consciousness of them, day after day, for twelve long years.[32]

So wrote Victor Gollancz, the English-Jewish left-wing publisher and author, in his blistering indictment following the liberation of Buchenwald in 1945. In stark contrast, the wartime President of the Board of Deputies of British Jews, Selig Brodetsky, in his memoirs written in 1954 claimed that

We still did not realise the terrible extent of the annihilation of the Jewish populations of Europe carried out systematically and in cold blood by the Nazis, till it all came out at the Nuremberg Trials of the chief war criminals, when the war was over, and we discovered that more than 6 million Jews had been murdered or deliberately starved to death by the Nazis, under the direction of Himmler, the Archbutcher of History. The World was shocked by the revelation.[33]

And the *Jewish Year Book*, the Anglo-Jewish community's compendium of facts on the Jewish world, still listed in its 1948 'Table of the Jewish Population of the Chief Jewish Centres' the population figures for Prague in 1930, for Vilna, Lublin, Lodz, Lwow and Cracow in 1931, Leipzig and Hamburg in 1933, Berlin in 1939 and Vienna and Warsaw for 1940.[34] The figures were accompanied by the rider that 'in view of the large movements of population in recent years and in particular the considerable reductions in the Jewish figures for several countries, Jewish population statistics, always largely a matter for approximation, must necessarily be less reliable than ever'.[35]

How are we to account for this contradiction? The 'inveterate British inability to grasp imaginatively what could happen on the continent of Europe'[36] certainly played a part in obscuring comprehension – George Steiner calls it a 'debilitating provinciality'. At one point in 1942 Brodetsky, in a lecture, warned, 'Let us not make the mistake of thinking of the Jews in Europe as being ruined Jews of Whitechapel or of Bayswater.' But for many historians, the key problem in this regard is 'more cognitive than affective, the ostensible existence of a gap between information and knowledge which prevented news of the Holocaust from being believed and internalised even after it had been reliably reported and confirmed'.[37] Yehuda Bauer observes that the Jews of the Free World seemed, at the time, unable to comprehend that the Nazis were bent on a programme of total biological annihilation of the Jewish people, even though from June 1942 they 'had all the information ... that was needed to establish the facts'.[38] For such historians, whose explanations are widely accepted, the apparent blindness demonstrated by figures like Brodetsky resulted from a failure of imagination, an inability to piece together or evaluate what was known or to grasp its full meaning. For them the slaughter of European Jewry took place in a different mental world. The agony was enacted, as Wasserstein states, in 'a separate moral arena, a grim twilight world where the conventional ethical code did not apply'.[39] 'The whole scheme', says Laqueur, 'was beyond human imagination'; and 'the idea of genocide seemed ... far fetched ... The evil nature of Nazism was beyond their comprehension.'[40] 'Its enormity', Katz writes, 'put it beyond belief.'[41] 'The fact that millions were killed was more or less meaningless. People could identify perhaps with the fate of a single individual or a family but not with the fate of millions. The statistics of murder were either disbelieved or dismissed from consciousness.'[42] Arthur Koestler, in an oft-quoted comment of 1944, said that 'a dog run over by a car upsets our emotional balance and digestion; 3,000,000 Jews killed in Poland cause but a moderate uneasiness. Statistics don't bleed; it is the detail which counts. We are unable to embrace the total process with our awareness, we can only focus on little lumps of reality.'[43] Though the evidence was plentiful and definitive, belief in it did not naturally follow.

In their subsequent reflections on this period, Diaspora Jewish figures constantly refer to this gulf. The American Jewish Labour Zionist leader Marie Syrkin, reflecting on her and her colleagues' reactions to the news from Europe, speaks of 'numb disbelief'. 'We could not take on what we heard', and were 'unable to assimilate'[44] it. Irving Howe, looking back, says, 'to be human meant to be unequipped to grapple with the Holocaust'.[45]

Evidence for this phenomenon is not merely *ex post facto*, but was expressed during the war itself. The *Jewish Chronicle*, in an editorial of 3 July 1942 entitled 'Massacre' which commented on its first reports of a systematic extermination of Jewry, alluded to this conceptual problem. 'The average mind simply cannot believe the reality of such sickening revelations, or that men, even the vilest and most bestial, could be found to perpetrate such disgusting orgies of sadistic mania.'[46]

This problem, some historians argue, reflected not only the inability of the human intellect to come to terms with evil, but also the novelty of the act. 'When the waves of persecution mounted,' writes Katz, and especially when frightful information about the ghettos and death camps reached the world from behind the borders of the warring Third Reich, the events transcended *all* the wonted concepts derived from historical experience. For Auschwitz and Treblinka there was no earlier historical analogy and there was no philosophical, or for that matter theological, frame of mind that could possibly integrate them into any system of thought. The Holocaust was an absolute *novum* lacking accountability in any rational terms at the disposal of the generation that experienced it ... For the generation that lived through it, [it] can only be characterised as a trauma, a wounding experience beyond the reach of intellectual conceptualisation.[47]

For Bauer, in this case discussing American Jewish response, the problem has the following solution:

People were aware that something terrible was going on, did not dare to disbelieve openly, but could not bring themselves to lend credence to information that the total Jewish population of Nazi Europe was being murdered. The reason for this is not really difficult to understand. Jews were being killed in Europe for no other reason than that they had been born Jews (by Nazi definitions). The crime they were being accused of was one which quite literally had no precedent; they were accused of living, of having been born. This was stated repeatedly and openly in various Nazi documents. 'Criminals' were accused of various transgressions, but in the case of Jews, it was simply stated that they had been killed or punished because they were Jews. Raised and educated in an American society based on certain elemental values that originally derived from Jewish moral concepts, American Jews were singularly unprepared to adapt quickly to the thought that they were living in a different century from the one they had imagined.[48]

The fact that the Nazi decision and its efficient execution lacked historical precedent is certainly an important factor in explaining British Jewish response. As the *Jewish Chronicle* wrote on 3 July 1942, 'All history provides no precedent ... It is murder as a fine art, such as the blackest of barbarisms have never dreamed of ... It is of the utmost importance to emphasise that all these devilries are not performed in heat or passion or panic. They are conceived in furtherance of high Nazi policy.'[49]

Moreover, we must be wary of the mistake of imposing hindsight on our deliberations. Wasserstein comments, 'What appears in retrospect as a logical progression could not be forecast in advance ... At any rate such forecasts were not made by any responsible Jewish leaders in Britain.'[50] Hugh Trevor-Roper speaks to the same theme:

Nothing in the previous history either of Germany or of anti-semitism pointed to so horrible a conclusion. It was not merely a reversion to barbarism. It was not a sudden, spasmodic pogrom such as had happened in the Middle Ages. In its careful planning and systematic execution, it showed a hideous scientific rationality which pointed ominously forward to a new, not an old, Dark Age.[51]

Many onlookers allude to the problems they had at the time due to their interpretation of Nazi killings in light of past persecution and pogroms. Along those lines Marie Syrkin records that 'reports of wholescale massacres in particular communities were interpreted as pogroms, more terrible than any in the course of Jewish history but still to be viewed as savage aberrations rather than as evidence of a master plan'.[52]

Some historians have also pointed to other reasons for the gap between knowing and believing. Friedman refers to the 'legacy of skepticism towards "atrocity stories" and disillusionment with humanitarian causes in general left by the experience of World War I'.[53] Others point to a general inurement to suffering left in the wake of the First World War; in the view of these historians, nothing could shock. Some, extrapolating from Hannah Arendt, assume that 'an initial explanation of the general passivity of the onlookers may be sought precisely in the most banal behaviour . . . pure self-interest at the individual or group level'.[54] This, suggests Penkower, is reflective of a more general 'abdication of moral responsibility'.[55]

Moreover Britain, it is argued, was particularly desensitised during the war. Hunger for news from the fronts and the concern for serving relatives both put considerable strain here on the capacity for comprehension. The sheer anomie of war took its toll. After all, it was not until the battle of Stalingrad in February 1943 that the British could be more or less certain that they too would not become Hitler's victims. 'In wartime, when so much is uncertain – when hatred breeds passion and passion is exploited by propaganda – it is prudent to suspend judgement',[56] writes Trevor-Roper. The Jewish community was no exception to the general rule. Eva, Marchioness of Reading and President of the World Jewish Congress British Section, admits that 'we were borne hopelessly on the tide of war'.[57] Moreover, the community had its own exclusively domestic concerns relating to the war: caring for German refugees, education for evacuated children and chaplaincy for Jewish servicemen.

Insensibility also derived from the Jews' feelings of powerlessness, for 'belief merely advertised impotence'.[58] Hitler, by showing that a country could function well without Jews, exposed the myth of Jewish power which had given substance to Jewish diplomacy since the First World War, if not before. More than this, 'the whole Jewish people now supported the Allied cause unquestioningly. Nothing had to be done to capture Jewish good will. In the arena of power politics no greater misfortune can befall a group than being taken for granted.' As Kushner caustically observes, the British government knew that 'philosemitism, even in a rampant form, offered no threat to law and order'.[59]

This perception of Jewish powerlessness was a fair representation of reality and it resulted from several factors. Jewish influence on the British government was limited by more than numerical weakness. Anti-semitism in the corridors of power was undoubtedly one reason; British policy in Palestine was another. Anti-alienism along with the unlikelihood of an easing of domestic immigration quotas in a wartime economy must also be considered. The need to defeat Hitler's armies prevented consideration of Nazism's non-military implications. It was not only Jews who were ignored. The Polish government-in-exile made repeated requests of the British and American governments that German cities be bombed in retaliation for atrocities committed against Polish citizens, yet these, like those from Jewish sources, were denied. The Allied armies made no visible attempt to interfere with the 'death marches' of concentration camp prisoners in the winter of 1944–5 (the majority of those involved were non-Jews) despite their ability to do so with little difficulty.

This powerlessness bred despair. 'There is something that is even more appalling in this tragedy than Nazi hypocrisy, sacrilege and sadism,' wrote Chief Rabbi J. H. Hertz in 1938, 'and that is, *our* helplessness to provide a comprehensive remedy for the injustice and inhumanity; the consciousness of our impotence effectively to deal with the immeasurable suffering consequent upon that injustice and inhumanity.'[60] The news from Europe caused widespread paralysis and despair. Bauer states that there was a sense of hopelessness: 'The general assumption ... was that nothing could be done, that European Jewry was lost.'

This hopelessness took its toll on Anglo-Jewish leaders. Julia Namier, in her biography of her husband the historian and Zionist Lewis Namier, writes that 'in a state of abiding grief, he froze into the stance of an observer meticulously attentive to humanity's murderous antics'.[61] As war went on, 'life went on, despair giving way to resignation'.[62]

Furthermore, historians suggest that while many had the capacity to comprehend, to do so would have been catastrophic. 'Thinking in terms of millions was a way for many people to escape the reality of murder of countless individual human beings, a way in which sanity could be preserved in the midst of unthinkable disaster.'[63] Theirs was the 'reaction of sanity; had ... they grasped what was happening ... [they] might well have lost their capacity to do anything'.[64] As proof of this Wasserstein points to the suicide in April 1943 of Shmuel Zygielbojm, the representative of the Bund in the Polish government-in-exile in London. 'Here was the ultimate in activism. But like the Warsaw Ghetto revolt, it was a glorious but hopeless gesture of moral defiance: it changed nothing.'[65]

Many historians have thus placed Diaspora Jewish response entirely in a psychological context. Bauer speaks of a 'mixture of incredulity, hope that this might turn out to be a nightmare from which the Jewish people might one day mercifully wake up, utter despair resulting from an accurate appreciation of what was happening, a desire for immediate action, a terrible feeling of helplessness, and even a desire to escape responsibility and hide behind words or meaningless actions'.[66]

There are, however, indications that such psychological explanations are not a wholly adequate guide to explaining the range of Anglo-Jewish (and, for that matter, Diaspora Jewish) response. As early as 1933 Jewish leaders spoke openly of their fear of the destruction of Jewry. Hertz warned in 1933 that 'nothing less than extermination of the Jews would, it seems, satisfy the wilder spirits among the Nazis'.[67] Throughout the war itself the community did make formal centralised responses to the events in Europe – delegations, memoranda, speeches and meetings – as well as considerable philanthropic efforts on behalf of Europe's Jews, through the Central Council for Jewish Refugees, the Central British Fund for Jewish Relief and Rehabilitation, and through the Hatzalah Rescue work of the Jewish Agency among others. Such actions, it is true, were typically unconnected and limited in character. They did not form part of a continuous organised campaign. The Holocaust was not high on the Anglo-Jewish agenda, but it was there.

Evidence that at least some British Jews both knew and believed

the information emanating from Europe is available. Victor Gollancz wrote in his pamphlet *Let My People Go*, published in December
1942:

Apart altogether from the immense mass of evidence of Hitler's actions in
Europe not only from Poland but from every European country, consider
the following. Anyone who has studied Hitler's mind, as revealed both in
his acts and in his utterances, cannot fail to be aware that for this pitiful
paranoic there is one supreme *idée fixe*; namely, that the Jews are a sub-race,
that they are the cause of all the ills of Germany and Europe, and that it is
his, Hitler's, literally divine mission to exterminate them. This is his belief:
it is an absolutely genuine belief, in so far as a madman's belief can be
called genuine, and perhaps the greatest of all the mistakes that have been
made in dealing with Hitler is not to understand that when he says that he
believes something, and that he intends to do something, however incredible, he *does* believe it and he *will* do it if he can. When, therefore, Hitler
announced in February of this year that 'the Jews will be exterminated',
and when on November 8th 1942 he said:

On September 1st 1939 I said ... that if Jewry started this war in order
to overcome the Aryan people, then it would not be the Germans who
would be exterminated. The Jews laughed at my prophecies in Germany.
I doubt if they are laughing now. I can assure them that they will lose all
desire to laugh wherever they may be, and I shall be right in this
prophecy too.

– when he said this he was not 'making propaganda': he was stating a
plain intention which, in his certainty of being right, he was determined to
carry out with all the force of his demonic will.[68]

Gollancz was undoubtedly influenced by many more intellectual
currents than most in the British Jewish community. His relationship with Judaism and the community's normative socio-political
philosophy was certainly unconventional – both his religion and
politics were too quixotic for most. Nevertheless he was by no means
marginalised at this time. He served on the Board of Deputies and
was very active on its Publications Committee, and his views were
widely reported in the Jewish Press.

But it may be that Gollancz's unconventionality itself gives us a
clue to a fuller understanding of Anglo-Jewish response than those
explanations which historians have thus far suggested. It could be
that it was 'the mentality derived from education, religiosity, and
social and political aspirations that made the difference'.[69] Anglo-
Jewish response was inevitably influenced by the way the community

saw itself and its position in Britain, and by the way in which it conceived of its Jewishness, organised its institutions and conducted its affairs. It is within this context that the response of Anglo-Jewry to the slaughter of European Jewry must be understood.

PART II

The institutions

Introduction: the Anglo-Jewish community

Anglo-Jewry, like other post-emancipatory Western Jewish communities, defined itself almost exclusively as a religious community. Its central institutions were voluntary and reflected this formal religious definition. The most basic, local level of affiliation was the synagogue, to which members paid annual dues. The synagogues, which exhibited a considerable level of internal religious differentiation, divided themselves into a number of religious groupings, including the Ashkenazi Orthodox, Sephardi (these two groupings viewed themselves as traditional elements), Reform and Liberal (these latter two viewed themselves as progressive elements). The essential theological demarcation between the traditional and the progressive groupings lay in their claimed relationship to *halakhah*, the Jewish legal code, and its practical application. In essence, however, the actual difference in thought or observance between members of different groupings was often blurred. Though formal affiliation and self-definition divided the community into groupings, a spectrum would probably be more an accurate description, with the Union of Orthodox Hebrew Congregations standing at one religious extreme and the rather small Liberal Movement at the other. Membership of a synagogue was often determined by the country of origin of the immigrant ancestors (Germans tended toward Reform; Russians toward Orthodox) although many other factors existed, including proximity to a particular synagogue. The traditional grouping overwhelmingly predominated, accounting for some eighty per cent of synagogue members. In addition to the sheer demographic majority of East European immigrants and their descendants, who mainly joined Orthodox synagogues, this also reflected the strong centralising force operating within Anglo-Jewry which derived from its propensity to perceive itself as a counterpart

to the established Church. The Sephardim, or Spanish and Portu-
guese community, was the oldest existent part of Anglo-Jewry and
represented the traditions of those who claimed descent from the late
fifteenth-century exiles from the Iberian peninsula.

Most provincial synagogues operated independently, without any
formal organisational affiliation, but in London, where sixty per
cent of British Jewry lived, two major umbrella organisations of
Orthodox synagogues existed: the Federation of Synagogues, and
the larger and richer United Synagogue which accounted for some
forty per cent of the synagogue affiliation of the metropolis. The
United Synagogue dominated the Anglo-Jewish religious structure.
This was partly due to its size and partly due to the community's
tendency towards centralisation, a tendency which gained its
impetus from the elite but had the full support of the folk. The
United Synagogue, or at least its lay leaders, effectively controlled
the appointment of Anglo-Jewry's most important office, the Chief
Rabbinate. The occupant of this office was, by far, the most important and best known communal leader – the apotheosis of the
centralising force.

The Chief Rabbi throughout this period, indeed the occupant of
the position since 1913, was the energetic J. H. Hertz. In many ways
Hertz, whose leadership was marked by conflict, was emblematic of
the community he represented. He had no difficulty in holding
opposing views simultaneously. For instance, at times he saw history
as merely the manifestation of the divine will, while at others he held
that man's fate was entirely in his own hands. He criticised his own
flock for their disunity and contention, yet he even more than most
in the Anglo-Jewish leadership was never happier than when spoil-
ing for a fight. As the *Dictionary of National Biography* observes, 'he
never despaired of finding a peaceful solution to any problem when
all other possibilities had failed'. His conflict with Sir Robert Waley
Cohen, President of the United Synagogue, was fabled throughout
the community. Though superficially concerned with the primacy of
the rabbinate as opposed to lay leadership, the argument was in fact
the battleground for two insatiable egos. Despite this disagreement
and his own powerful advocacy of Zionism, Hertz sided with the
non-Zionist establishment (of which Waley Cohen was an important
member) in the battle for hegemony at the Board of Deputies.
Whilst Hertz's publications included the most widely produced
apologetic work in the Jewish Anglo-Saxon world, his *Book of Jewish*

Thoughts, as well as patriotic statements of almost embarrassing lyricism, he was more critical than most in Anglo-Jewry of British government (or at least Foreign Office) policies concerned with the Middle East or the situation of Jews in Europe. As we shall see later, such inconsistencies were thoroughly in keeping with the tenor of Anglo-Jewish life.

The Chief Rabbi's authority centred mainly on his role as the acknowledged representative of the Anglo-Jewish community on state, public and ceremonial occasions. All synagogue organisations acknowledged the Chief Rabbi as the representative head of the Anglo-Jewish community on such occasions. Most of Anglo-Jewry's provincial Orthodox synagogues, as well as all those of the United Synagogue, sought his guidance on questions of ecclesiastical law and religious life, although others did not acknowledge his religious jurisdiction. Apart from the Chief Rabbinate the United Synagogue also controlled general communal religious functions such as prison visiting and army chaplaincy.

Synagogues perceived themselves exclusively as places of religious worship, which effectively prevented them from confronting issues outside the religious sphere. The *Jewish Chronicle* reports on only one synagogue general meeting between 1942 and 1945 which discussed the European situation at all (Brixton Synagogue; 28 May 1943, p. 6). According to the general rule of the United Synagogue, 'it is not in order to allow any discussion on any subject which is outside the conduct of the affairs of the synagogue'. There was to be no discussion on 'extraneous matters',[1] a ruling which, due to the centrality of the religious definition to Anglo-Jewish thinking, was never challenged. Hence in the institution that most immediately affected the lives of most British Jews the European Jewish situation could not be considered.

The main lay institution of Anglo-Jewry, the Board of Deputies of British Jews, was also primarily synagogue-based. The vast majority of its deputies represented synagogues (although there were exceptions for friendly and other societies), thus preserving the religious basis of community organisation. This body had come into existence in 1760 and since then it had developed a committee structure to deal with all civil matters affecting Anglo-Jewry. By 1942 the Board had established the Law, Parliament and General Purposes, Foreign Affairs, Jewish Defence, Finance, Palestine, Aliens, Charities, Registration and Education committees. The

Board held plenary sessions monthly and was presided over by a President elected on a four-year term who chaired the Executive and plenary sessions and represented the Board at public occasions. In 1940 the Board had 387 deputies representing 235 synagogues, twelve colonial communities and sixteen institutions (including the Anglo-Jewish Association, the Federation of Synagogues, the Union of Orthodox Hebrew Congregations and the United Synagogue). By 1945 this had grown to 459 deputies, representing 241 synagogues, six colonial communities and twenty-seven institutions.

Aside from the synagogue-based institutions, two other important organisations pertain to the topic of this book. The first, the Anglo-Jewish Association, founded in 1871, lay firmly in the tradition started by the Alliance Israelite Universelle, namely of philanthropic help to Jews abroad. Its constitution stated its aims as firstly 'to obtain protection for Jews abroad who may suffer in consequence of being Jews', and secondly 'to advance the social, moral and intellectual welfare of the Jews in backward lands'.[2] Membership of the Association was open to all British Jews upon payment of a subscription. The Association had a distinguished membership which included most of the established wealthy families of Anglo-Jewry, and its prestige derived from this factor rather than from the size of its membership, which in fact was relatively small.

The second was the British section of the World Jewish Congress, a New York-based body adhering to the following platform:

(a) the recognition of the collectivity of the Jewish people as a whole;

(b) the belief in its collective destiny;

(c) the realisation of the necessity to co-ordinate activities on behalf of its various sections.[3]

The World Jewish Congress was founded in Geneva in 1936 and reflected a need for centralised action by Jewish communities throughout the world. It sought to challenge what it saw as the 'pusillanimous doctrine of splendid isolation' adopted by the various national Jewish organisations. The establishment of the World Jewish Congress British Section resulted from the perception of some that the representations to the Government by the Board of Deputies on the fate of Jewish communities abroad were feeble and ineffective.

The corporate membership of the British section of the World Jewish Congress comprised the Zionist Federation, the Mizrahi

(Orthodox Zionist) Federation and other smaller societies. However the Congress was made up mainly of individuals joining in a personal capacity as opposed to institutional affiliation. They were mostly of intellectual bent and, by implication of their membership of the Congress, had Jewish interests above and beyond the parochial concerns directly affecting the British Jewish community. Such individuals included Sidney Silverman MP, Eva Marchioness of Reading, Noah Barou, Lord Melchett, Philip Guedalla, Rabbi Dr Abraham Cohen, Alex Easterman and Rebecca Sieff. Here refugee Jews could have formal representation, in contrast to other Anglo-Jewish institutions. Thus the World Jewish Congress was the only forum for contact between British Jews and the exiled leaders of the Polish, Czechoslovakian, Austrian and other European Jewish communities resident in London during the war.

Relationships between the various institutions were often stormy, as they frequently felt challenged by one another. However, it would be wrong to identify Anglo-Jewish history solely, or even predominantly, with the history of its institutions, as so often has been done. Many Jews did not formally belong to any of the above institutions. Furthermore, power and status within the community were more often than not completely unrelated to the formal organisational structure. Wealth and position in the general society were much more likely determinants of someone's communal authority and prestige.

There were thus two separate power systems. One derived from the community's own institutional structure and a person's position within it, and the other from general British society and a British Jew's status therein. However, many of the organisations sought to buttress their power by recruiting members of the Anglo-Jewish aristocracy as patrons and leaders. Thus many of the official offices of the community were occupied by such Anglo-Jewish grandees on a principle of *noblesse oblige*.

Illustrative of these two co-existent power structures is the list of Jewish Members of Parliament printed in the *Jewish Year Books* of 1940 and 1945–6. Listed are eleven Jewish Members of the House of Lords: the Marquess of Reading, Viscounts Bearsted and Samuel (the latter also a Privy Councillor and Leader of the Liberals in the Lords from December 1944; Deputy Leader before that), Barons Hirst (died 22 January 1943 with no heir), Jessel, Mancroft (2nd Baron succeeded 1st on 17 August 1942), Melchett, Rothschild,

Southwood, Swaythling, with the addition of Lord Nathan of Churt (formerly Labour MP for Wandsworth; see below), elevated to the Lords during the war itself, and acting as Leader of the Labour Party in the Upper House. Of these the *Year Book* lists seven as holding some formal office within the organised community, namely Lords Reading, Bearsted, Samuel, Melchett, Rothschild, Swaythling and Nathan. Lord Melchett and his sister Eva Marchioness of Reading, though brought up as Christians (their mother was not Jewish), both converted to Judaism upon the rise of Hitler, both playing significant roles in the Zionist Movement.

In the House of Commons, the *Year Book* lists sixteen Jewish Members: Daniel Frankel (Labour, Mile End), Col. L. H. Gluckstein (Conservative, E. Nottingham), Sir Percy A. Harris Bart. (Liberal, S. W. Bethnal Green, Leader of the Liberals in the Commons and a Privy Councillor), Leslie Hore-Belisha (Liberal National, Devonport, Privy Councillor and Secretary of State for War 1940–1), Thomas Levy (Conservative, Elland), Daniel L. Lipson (Conservative, Cheltenham), A. M. Lyons KC (Conservative, E. Leicester), Col. Harry L. Nathan (Labour, Wandsworth; see above), James Armand de Rothschild (Liberal, Isle of Ely), M. R. A. Samuel (Conservative, Putney; died 3 March 1942), Emanuel Shinwell (Labour, Seaham), Lewis Silkin (Labour, Peckham), S. S. Silverman (Labour, Nelson), George R. Strauss (Labour, N. Lambeth), H. G. Strauss (Conservative, Norwich), and John David Mack (Labour, Newcastle-under-Lyne; elected during the war on 11 March 1942 upon the elevation of Josiah Wedgwood to the Lords). Of these the *Jewish Year Book* listed eight as holding offices within the community (Gluckstein, Hore-Belisha, Lyons, Nathan, Rothschild, Samuel, Silverman and Mack). The ranks of the Privy Councillors were joined by one non-parliamentary Jew, the athlete and colonial Chief Justice Sir Sidney Abrahams.

The community, as will be seen later, was, of course, eager to avoid giving the impression of any sort of Jewish political interest as represented by Jewish MPs or others in public life. Thus there was never the suggestion of any informal lobby of Jewish parliamentarians. However any Jew in Parliament (however previous distant from Jewish affairs) who wished to associate with Jewry's organisations was almost automatically granted influence and office.

Undoubtedly the liveliest forum for debate available to the Jewish community was the *Jewish Chronicle*. The newspaper was owned by a limited company whose Board of Directors appointed the editor. The Directors, apart from Leonard Stein (then President of the Anglo-Jewish Association), were almost all unconnected with the other main central institutions of the community.[4] Whilst the paper did not seem to lead Jewish opinion it certainly reflected it. News items covered all the formal organisations of the community and there was extensive coverage of news of Jewish interest from Britain and overseas. Its letters page attracted all manner of correspondents, notwithstanding their disagreements with editorial slants, and a weekly copy of the *Jewish Chronicle* provided the best picture of news and views on the Anglo-Jewish community.

One mode of affiliation which cannot be underestimated is that of philanthropic donations. A large number of British Jews, both synagogue-affiliated and unaffiliated, contributed to one or more of the many charities and benevolent societies which abounded within the community (of which only a few were represented on the Board of Deputies). This philanthropic endeavour, which amounted to a considerable annual sum, assumed an almost ritualistic or symbolic value. The donation was seen as an act, possibly the primary act, of affiliation to the community – the choice of recipient often had no significance. The act of giving itself seemed all-important. This 'philanthropic' approach to problems was seen by the community as non-political, even when the beneficiaries were immigrants or Jewries overseas. Certainly the community preferred the philanthropic approach to the problems it confronted to other more political strategies.

In terms of social identification at this time, most British Jews, though their language and dress were thoroughly modelled on their English surroundings, did not opt out of being Jewish. Indeed conversions to Christianity were very rare. Anglo-Jewry considered that having a religious affiliation gave a person status in society. The Anglo-Jewish leadership was not made up of assimilationists, and it prided itself on the fact that it achieved a balance between the two worlds, remaining fully loyal to Judaism. Many Jews, even those who maintained little formal contact with the Jewish community, mixed in an overwhelmingly Jewish social circle. They were, in short, acculturated, not assimilated.

The Anglo-Jewish community, like its Western counterparts, struggled to define its identity within the post-medieval, post-corporate centralised state. It was tied institutionally to a predominantly synagogal structure, and philanthropy provided its major focal point for activism. Its structure testified to and fortified an almost universally accepted Anglo-Jewish socio-political philosophy stemming from a perception of emancipation, liberalism, patriotism and the Jews' relation to the state in which they lived. Despite some differences in organisation and style there were many underlying assumptions and concerns which characterised the English Jew. It is by way of an exploration of these, as much as an examination of the activities of communal institutions, that this book attempts to study Anglo-Jewry's response to the catastrophe of European Jews under Nazism.

CHAPTER I

Communal priorities: conflict and domestic anti-semitism

Throughout the period of the Second World War, the Anglo-Jewish community was mainly preoccupied with internal conflict, particularly over Zionism, and domestic problems, the most pressing of which was British anti-semitism. The primary concern of this book is to study perceptions of Nazi atrocities, and it is fundamental to an understanding of these that we set them firmly within the context of British Jewish life at that time. Such an approach will go a considerable way in explaining how and why Anglo-Jewry responded as it did. To understand this we must examine the major concerns of Anglo-Jewish life at this time, particularly those connected with conflict and the fear of anti-semitism in Britain.

CONFLICT

Conflict, to paraphrase Henry Feingold, is the *sine qua non* of Jewish communal life.[1] Never was this more apparent than in Anglo-Jewry and its 'tangled web of communal politics during the Second World War'.[2] During this time the central institutions and personalities of the organised community were racked by internecine battles. One of these, over the definition and goals of Zionism, can safely be described as the greatest conflict the community had ever seen. This issue dominated the meetings of the Board of Deputies and the Anglo-Jewish Association from 1942 to 1944, embroiled the World Jewish Congress British Section in 1943 and 1944 and continued to simmer below the surface until the establishment of the State of Israel in 1948. It thus enveloped the three main organisations whose constitutions referred to responsibilities to Jews abroad and thereby also involved the major *dramatis personae* on the Jewish communal stage at a time when most of European Jewry was being killed. Though the argument between the rival groups centred on the existence of a

Jewish nation and the desirability of a post-war Jewish state, the
debate was dominated by a larger contest for communal control and
power. In effect, it was a conflict between two social groups.

To understand the nature of the conflict, some historical background is required. The leadership of the Board of Deputies and of
the Anglo-Jewish Association had until 1939 been in the hands of
the so-called 'Grand Dukes' or 'Cousinhood' of Anglo-Jewry –
richer Jewish families who had originally arrived in Britain before
the mass immigration of the 1880s and who were now often titled
and linked by marriage.[3] Representatives of the families deemed it
their duty to serve as the communal leaders of Anglo-Jewry. The
lists of Presidents of the Board, the Association and the United
Synagogue are, from the early nineteenth century onward, pep-
pered with such names as Rothschild, Montagu, Montefiore and
Waley Cohen. These families, originating entirely in Central or
Western Europe, were the very embodiment of a philosophy of
denationalising Jewry, and they defined their Jewishness in terms of
a purely religious affiliation. However, they had spent a great deal of
time helping their co-religionists who were in less fortunate circumstances than themselves both through philanthropic endeavour and
through direct intercession. (In particular one could cite Moses
Montefiore's activities during the Damascus Affair in 1840 and the
representations made by the Anglo-Jewish leadership during the
Russian pogroms of the late nineteenth and early twentieth centuries.) But members of the Cousinhood, along with almost all
British Jewry, strenuously avoided the notion that this activity
expressed a worldwide Jewish national solidarity. The Anglo-Jewish
leadership sought to educate foreign Jews to be loyal citizens of the
countries in which they dwelt. In this way, the Anglo-Jewish leadership acted much like its counterparts elsewhere in the West: its
diplomatic intercession was designed to preserve the religious rights
and freedoms of co-communicants overseas.

The first major challenge to the leadership of the Cousinhood had
come during the First World War, following the British Government's November 1917 Balfour Declaration on a Jewish National
Home in Palestine. The leading families, given their understanding
of the emancipation as a contract under whose terms Jews
renounced all claims to a separate nationality, opposed the establishment of a Jewish national entity which they feared would put
into question their loyalty and the loyalty of Anglo-Jewry as a

whole. The President of the Board of Deputies, D. L. Alexander, and the President of the Anglo-Jewish Association, Claude G. Montefiore, in their joint capacities as the Conjoint Foreign Committee's co-presidents, wrote to the *Times* on 17 May 1917 expressing their opinion that 'Zion' was a term reserved purely for a religious idea and could not be deemed a political objective. Although they supported Jewish settlement in Palestine, this, they argued, did not imply that Jews belonged in Zion alone and were homeless aliens everywhere else.[4] Alexander, however, had not consulted the members of the Board before sending the letter, and following a response by the Chief Rabbi, J. H. Hertz, published in the *Times* declaring that the views of the two men were unrepresentative of Anglo-Jewry, and an unfavourable Board of Deputies vote (55–51), Alexander resigned from the Board's Presidency.

This episode surrounding the Balfour Declaration, however, cannot be seen as the ultimate downfall of the leading families. They continued to control the Board of Deputies until 1939, and both the Anglo-Jewish Association and the United Synagogue well beyond that. Moreover, at this embryonic stage of the battle over Zionism, the existence of two opposing camps divided by origin and social status, which was so clearly to emerge in the 1930s, was not yet in evidence. After all, the Declaration itself was addressed to Lord Rothschild, obviously a member of one of the pre-eminent families of the Cousinhood and yet one identified with the Zionist cause.

In the inter-war years, however, two distinct camps did appear with differing views over the Zionist issue. The conflict, if seen from an ideological perspective, is a very odd one. It cannot even be said to have divided into groups of Zionist and non-Zionists (let alone anti-Zionists), although one camp (with Lenin-like adroitness) styled itself the 'Zionist Caucus'. Few in either camp ever felt Zionism constituted a personal imperative for themselves. Many of those outside the Zionist Caucus described themselves as Zionists, including Leonard Stein (who had been the Political Secretary of the Jewish Agency), A. M. Hyamson and Chief Rabbi Hertz. Both sides agreed that Palestine should serve as the premier place of refuge for Jews exiled or persecuted, and all sought the abrogation of the 1939 White Paper which restricted Jewish immigration into Palestine. Even over the semantic definitions of nation and state, differences were not clear cut, with many outside the Caucus arguing for a Jewish Commonwealth – a 'self-governing territory' –

which amounted in all but name to a state but with a sanitised British term. As Brodetsky recalls in his memoirs, 'each Jewish body used words which meant that Jews should be allowed to immigrate into Palestine'.[5] Leonard Stein was at pains to point out that the majority outside the Zionist Caucus, 'far from being lukewarm or indifferent about Jewish aspirations in Palestine, was warmly and actively sympathetic'.[6] The leaders of the Anglo-Jewish Association, which eventually became the refuge of most of those outside the Zionist Caucus, stood 'unequivocally for the abrogation of the White Paper, for the opening of Palestine to the fullest Jewish immigration, and the development by Jews of its economic resources under conditions which would permit them to build up a national home'.[7]

Hence ideology was not the *casus belli* and the factors promoting the dispute are to be found elsewhere: firstly, in the political strategy of the Zionist Caucus; secondly, in the fact that the period under discussion coincided with a shift in the managerial equilibrium of the Jewish community, with the turn-of-the-century immigration wave from Eastern Europe now reaching that stage of organisation and ambition which enabled it to seek communal office. With regard to the first factor, that of political strategy, we must evaluate how the Zionist Caucus pursued a policy of infiltration and communal conquest. This was a programme of electoral management and displacement which would ultimately ensure the presence of a majority of Zionist sympathisers on the leading councils of the major Anglo-Jewish bodies, particularly the Board of Deputies.[8] The Caucus pursued this course without diversion, spearheaded in this period by the Secretary of the Zionist Federation, Lavy Bakstansky. (According to Cohen, he possessed a 'quick clear mind, staccato speech, a decisive and forceful manner and steely determination' that 'overwhelmed whoever he dealt with'.[9]) In 1943 Bakstansky characterised the conflict thus: 'We have not undertaken our campaign of opposition ... by accident, or merely on the caprice of any individual, it was the result of years of study and accumulated bitterness.'[10] By prompting its members and supporters to secure election as Deputies to the Board, the Caucus was able to elect Professor Selig Brodetsky to the Presidency on 17 December 1939, only two months after he had attended his first meeting at the Board on 15 October 1939.

Throughout the early years of the war differences between those in and outside the Caucus bubbled beneath the surface, and in the triennial elections held in June 1943 the Zionist Caucus was able to secure a majority on the Board's Executive Committee. The Caucus at once fixed its attention on the issue of the stewardship of the Joint Foreign Committee. The Committee was jointly chaired by the Presidents of the Board and of the Anglo-Jewish Association, and membership was divided equally between representatives of the two bodies. The Caucus objected strongly to this arrangement. They depicted the Anglo-Jewish Association as the undemocratic bulwark of the non-Zionist establishment, an organisation which derived its power solely from the positions of its members in general society – in effect, a body limited exclusively to members and supporters of the Cousinhood. Thus the Caucus determined to remove the Anglo-Jewish Association representation from the Joint Committee and form a new committee solely under the Board's own jurisdiction. To effect this change on 4 July 1943, at the largest gathering in the history of Board, the Caucus was able to vote for the effective dissolution of the Joint Foreign Committee. The Anglo-Jewish Association, now ousted from the Joint Committee, was equally determined to maintain its voice on matters concerning Jews abroad and formed its own General Purposes and Foreign Committee in October 1943. Thus there were now two committees both claiming to represent Anglo-Jewry on events affecting Jewry overseas.[11]

The meetings of the Board, the largest and most acrimonious it had ever seen, were almost totally dominated by this issue between 1942 and 1944, as were those of the Association. Eventually an unsteady compromise between the two sides was arrived at in 1944, when the Anglo-Jewish Association and the Board agreed to consult one another on matters affecting Jews abroad. However, even this modest concord was jeopardised when, in January 1944, leaders of the Zionist Caucus publicised their discussions with the World Jewish Congress British Section (itself an offshoot of the American-based organisation) – negotiations which had begun three years before agreement was finally concluded in March 1944. Many British Jews feared that an alliance with the Section would give the impression that the opinions of Anglo-Jewry were being dictated by a body based in New York. Many viewed the very notion of an international Jewish body – such as the World Jewish Congress, which posited that the Jews were a unified national entity rather than merely co-religionists of various citizenships – as anathema. In their eyes it by far exceeded the dangers of Zionist notions, which, at least, had the saving grace of limiting full Jewish nationhood to the entity in process of formation in Palestine.[12] This dangerous stress which the World Jewish Congress placed on a supra-national Jewish bond naturally challenged much of the community's socio-political philosophy. Early in the history of the Congress Neville Laski, President of the Board of Deputies between 1933 and 1939, had privately approached a Foreign Office official and informed him that mistaken 'conceptions of the Jewish people as a united national organisation' and 'ideas of Jewish nationhood' were a danger to the civic rights of Jews in all countries. He requested that access to the Foreign Office should be confined solely to the Joint Foreign Committee.[13] For its part, the Congress had been set up to oppose what its leaders saw as the weak stances of the Board on Foreign Affairs and was therefore predisposed to conflict with the Board. At the initial Congress in 1936, Maurice Perlzweig from Britain declared in barely veiled reference to traditional Anglo-Jewish politics: 'We who are in this Congress would have the world know that we have forever put behind us the pusillanimous doctrine of splendid isolation. We believe in the principle of collective security for the Jewish people.'[14] At the height of the negotiations with the Board in October 1943 the British Section's Executive declared that the community's traditional 'philanthropic approach' to foreign affairs was 'wholly inapposite and valueless'.[15]

Accord between the three bodies – namely the Board, the World Jewish Congress British Section and the Anglo-Jewish Association – whose constitutions demanded they deal with the condition of Jewries abroad was thus not going to be easy. As the *Contemporary Jewish Record* reported in 1944:

To avoid a complete rift with the Anglo-Jewish Association, which had objected to the proposed agreement between the Board of Deputies and the … World Jewish Congress for the establishment of a liaison committee on foreign affairs, the Board voted (19th March) to replace the plan with an arrangement providing merely for exchange of information and consultation between the two bodies, each retaining its complete freedom of action. A similar agreement for an exchange of views between the Board and the Association was accepted by the Board at the same session and ratified on 21st April by the council of the A.J.A.[16]

As to the second factor which promoted the dispute – the demographic changes in Anglo-Jewry at this time – the battle over

Zionism has been seen as 'the triumph of the immigrants of 1881'[17] over the older established English Jews, the culmination of a 'contest between the old community and the new, between the East and the West'.[18] The period of the Second World War coincided with a shift in the demographic, economic and managerial equilibrium that had previously characterised Anglo-Jewry, causing, as Cohen points out, the 'liquefaction of the Anglo-Jewish political system'.[19] The East European immigrants for whom the Zionist Caucus was the political anchor were now far more numerous than their opponents and it was only a matter of time before they managed to turn this fact to political advantage. That time arrived during the years of the Second World War and the success it gave the Zionist Caucus only increased their confidence, confirming their belief in the tactics of conquest.

The conflict over Zionism was by no means the only one to occupy the time and energy of British Jews. The activities of the Agudist Rabbi Dr Solomon Schonfeld were also a focus of strife. In January 1943, the month following the Allied Declaration, Schonfeld personally lobbied MPs and Peers promoting a parliamentary motion regarding the condition of the Jews in Europe and the British response to it. Brodetsky and the Board were displeased, seeing Schonfeld's action as a challenge to their authority as the representative organs of Anglo-Jewry, and strenuous efforts were made to restrain him. Schonfeld wrote to the *Jewish Chronicle* on 29 January 1943 explaining himself.

In the face of such a calamitous situation, together with a few leading Churchmen and Parliamentarians, I undertook to rouse and organise wide support for a Motion to be tabled in both Houses of Parliament, asking His Majesty's Government to declare its readiness to find temporary refuge in its own territories, or in territories under its control, for endangered persons. Support for the Motion was widespread. Within ten days, two Archbishops, eight Peers, four Bishops and forty-eight members of all parties had signed notice of meeting to consider the Motion. This effort was met by a persistent attempt on the part of Professor Brodetsky and some of his colleagues to sabotage the entire move. Without even full knowledge of the details, his collaborators asked members of the House to desist from supporting the new effort.[20]

Brodetsky defended his position, stating that 'the intervention of an unauthorised individual, however well-intentioned, in a situation of this sort, naturally brings confusion and may have damaging effects'.[21] He used an analogy to illustrate the Board's authority:

'Each individual citizen of a country might think he could run the country better than the Prime Minister ... but no citizen had the right to set up his own War Cabinet and run the War as he thought fit.'[22] The power and prestige of the Board were paramount, for both the Board and its representative committee 'have enjoyed the advantage of accessibility to the British Government and the power of representation to the Government on matters affecting Jews inside and particularly outside this country. Any interference with this power would mean the diminution of the power of British Jewry to act on behalf of Jews and would be a crime against Jewish interests.'[23] It was unlikely that Schonfeld's rather modest intervention could damage the Board's power of representation, let alone have damaging effects on the British response to the situation in Europe. In a letter to the *Jewish Chronicle* appearing on 5 February 1943, a correspondent, Mr A. Dolland, deplored 'at this grave crisis in our history any attempt to sabotage, in an effort of face-saving, this important move, designed to help'.[24] Such appeals were to no avail, and Schonfeld's efforts, which quite possibly would have had some impact on British government policy, were effectively scuppered.

Another conflict, which directly pertained to the European situation, concerned the Anglo-American Committee for a Jewish Army. This committee was an offshoot of an American organisation promoting the establishment of a Jewish fighting force to fight Hitler under a Jewish flag. The organisation was led in America by a Revisionist Zionist leader, the charismatic Hillel Kook (known also as Peter Bergson). A full-time organiser, US Captain Jeremiah Helpern, was sent to Britain to muster support. Although many of the campaign's underlying motives reflected the belief that the presence of a Jewish flag amidst the Allied forces would give Jewry more muscle in negotiations regarding Palestine after the war, the Committee nonetheless was sincere in its persistent calls for a more activist stance to help Jews in Europe.

The General Zionist Jewish Agency, to which the Zionist Federation of Great Britain and Ireland was allied, and which had its own campaign for a fighting force, saw the Committee as spearheaded by Revisionists whose strident nationalism they not only opposed but saw as very dangerous for the Jewish people. Furthermore, many non-Zionists saw an identifiable Jewish fighting force as highlighting Jewish nationality, with all of its dire implications. The Committee was ostracised largely for these reasons by many communal organisations. However, the campaign was supported by many within Anglo-Jewry, both Zionists and non-Zionists, as well as by some non-Jews (Lord Strabolgi being particularly prominent). The *Jewish Chronicle*, edited at the time by the Revisionist Ivan Greenberg, was the Anglo–American Committee's major institutional supporter in Britain. The *Chronicle*'s coverage ensured that news of its activities would be widespread, and consequently the Committee attracted much more support than the mainstream Jewish leadership liked to admit. However Field-Marshal Sir Philip Chetwode, a prominent non-Jewish supporter of the Committee, spoke of 'internal Jewish differences which have hampered the work of getting forward with the Jewish Army project' and further commented that 'the tragic irony of it is that my regrets are shared by the vast majority of the Jews in the world today'.[25] The 'differences' Chetwode spoke of never vanished, and when, in August 1944, the British Government finally did form a Jewish Brigade, a fierce controversy broke out between the Agency and the Committee as to who had influenced the decision the most.[26]

There were many other wider intra-Zionist conflicts conducted by representatives in Britain with as much ferocity as in Palestine itself, as each organisation and group of individuals sought to preserve its autonomy and prestige. The Revisionists and 'Old' Zionists constantly quarrelled over the division of money received from the Zionist Federation and the Keren Hayesod.[27] The religiously Orthodox and non-Zionist Agudah fought with the Agency over the education of refugee children in Palestine[28] and further opposed the World Jewish Congress because of the participation of American Reform Rabbis within it.[29]

And this was not all. Unconnected entirely with international Jewish politics, the personal animosity between Sir Robert Waley Cohen, President of the United Synagogue, and the Chief Rabbi, J. H. Hertz, was well known and of considerable importance. Though there were substantive differences between their conceptions of Orthodox Judaism, the most important factor was their difference of temperament, with neither willing to accord to the other the position of paramount authority in Anglo-Jewry. The subject of yet another conflict undertaken with great vigour was the Movement for Refugee Children which oversaw the placing of refugee Jewish children from Germany in homes in Britain and whose officers included many of the women of the Cousinhood. A synagogue body, the Union of Orthodox Hebrew Congregations, distributed booklets accusing the Movement of placing these Jewish children in non-Jewish homes and thereby 'Child Estranging'.[30] Contention also surrounded the Joint Emergency Committee's provision of Jewish input into the Butler Education Act. The Committee was originally set up to provide for the education of Jewish children evacuated from London and was subsequently used as a co-ordinating body for London Jewish education. The Chief Rabbi, among others, objected to its composition because of the participation of Liberal and Reform Rabbis.[31] There was even a dispute amongst the Jewish Army Chaplains. When the Senior Chaplain Dayan Gollop became ill in March 1944 he appointed a Liberal Rabbi, Dr Leslie Edgar, as his temporary replacement, overlooking an obvious candidate, the Orthodox Rabbi Dr Louis Rabinowitz, whom Gollop disliked. This appointment caused a deep rupture, and eventually Rabbi Israel Brodie was appointed as permanent replacement.

The list of conflicts is a long one and prompts questions about the more general causes of communal dispute in this period, particularly as the conflicts seem to lack any great ideological dimension. It would seem that it stemmed primarily from the lack of an established political hierarchy within Anglo-Jewry's organisational structure. It was unclear for instance whether or not the President of the United Synagogue was subordinate to the Chief Rabbi. Similarly the relationship between the Board of Deputies and the Chief Rabbi was undefined and likewise subject to many different interpretations. Thus there were no strict rules as to what should occur if the Chief Rabbi and the President of the Board or the President of the United Synagogue were in conflict. Furthermore, the degree to which those who held communal office but had no status in English Gentile society should be beholden to those whose status derived wholly from their wealth or position in general society was much open to dispute. Often those who derived power from the general society were given office within the Jewish community, but this usually exacerbated the instability and contentiousness of the community.

Because of this lack of definition in authority structure great emphasis was placed on the search for honour, or rather prestige (*koved* in Yiddish), and this became the determining power-giving factor over which disputes were fought. Most of the communal conflicts can be reduced to battles of honour between personalities or groups of personalities. Conflicts rarely ended in communal fission. Seldom were new organisations formed. (Indeed it is remarkable that the great immigration of 1881 to 1914, the largest the community has seen, has created so few organisations of its own.)[32] Rather, conflicts were over position – they were between community leaders rather than between leaders and members, or amongst members. Issues were often used as focal points for communal visibility. This emphasis on prestige was an established and universal feature of Jewish culture, due particularly to the relatively small size and self-enclosed nature of Jewry. It littered the community scene with various feuds and vendettas. As Brodetsky noted in his memoirs, 'It was very difficult to get any kind of unity in Jewish life, often for prestige reasons, not because of any real difference of opinion.'[33] 'Koved-hunting', as the *Chronicle* was frequently to call it, was the over-riding feature of the battles, and this central theme was highlighted in a *Jewish Chronicle* editorial of 11 August 1944 with that heading. It describes its effects on new ideas and institutions:

As soon as a new organisation pokes its mushroom head above the green it is at once treated as suspicious; within two days it is proclaimed poisonous; and by the end of a week it is regarded as the enemy whose destruction ranks second in importance only to that of Nazism itself. The closer the aims of the mushroom approximate to those of the established movement, the more bitterly does the latter assail it.[34]

Arguments even occurred as to which Jewish organisation was largely responsible for the 17 December 1942 Allied Declaration made by Eden in the House of Commons concerning the Nazi extermination plan. As the *Chronicle* editorialised on 5 March 1943:

The clash between rival Jewish organisations pursuing very similar ends is, of course, an old story. What is, perhaps, not so old is the reckless and competitive Koved-hunting which now accompanies it. It might, for instance, tax the most retentive memories among us to say how many Jewish organisations have claimed the sole credit for bringing about the memorable denunciation by Parliament of Hitler's Jew-massacres, still more to name them. 'Alone we did it' has been the refrain of so many, sometimes varied by 'Alone I did it!'[35]

Conflict driven by the competition of egos was thus the major theme of Anglo-Jewry during this period. Indeed it was the major focus of internal Jewish creativity in England. Though the polemics were often ferocious, they were, at heart, part of a larger family quarrel. The ideological content of the struggles was of limited importance; it was the jockeying for position which was crucial. Though vociferous, the arguments were regarded as neither serious threats nor serious contributions to Jewish life in England. British Jewry considered that only Gentiles could seriously affect the rhythms and patterns of Anglo-Jewish existence.

FEAR OF DOMESTIC ANTI-SEMITISM

Of all issues concerning the Gentile world, it was concern over anti-semitism which most occupied the mind of Anglo-Jewry. But the preoccupation was with the anti-semitism found within British shores rather than that occurring on the continent of Europe.

On this issue two views of emancipation often produced contradictory results. Liberal politics suggested that anti-semitism was an anachronism which could be eradicated by the education of the non-Jews. A rival philosophy which I have styled the politics of fear, and which saw the emancipation as a contract between the state and the Jews, suggested to Anglo-Jewry that anti-semitism was at least partly its own fault. As a result British Jews, fearful of any anti-semitic resurgence caused by some Anglo-Jewish abrogation of the contract, paid considerable attention to specific accusations that they were too rich, too powerful, sly in business, un-English and clannish. The community strenuously attempted to address these problems through education and other strategies involving, among other things, some significant internalisation of anti-semitic accusations.

Anglo-Jewry's understanding of the emancipation as a contract and the inherent threat of anti-semitism upon its abrogation led it to maintain a low-profile political strategy. Its frantic desire to counter anti-semitic accusations was a major influence on all its dealings. British Jews bent over backwards to prove that they conformed to none of the prevalent anti-semitic stereotypes, to the extent that their attempts circumscribed positive action in other areas. The fear of anything which they imagined might threaten the safety or status of Anglo-Jewry acted as a severe constraint on the community. Like most people, British Jews were primarily concerned with their own fate, even if it was relatively unthreatened compared with the fate of distant Jewry.

The intense anxiety over anti-semitism was, in part, due to the difficulty the community had in understanding the phenomenon. In the eyes of Anglo-Jewry, Britain was a model, perhaps the exemplary model, of enlightened tolerance. Anti-semitism, in the form of direct physical and verbal attacks or discrimination against Jews in and out of work, was therefore portrayed as a marginal phenomenon. It was the product of poor education, economic rivalry or one uncharacteristically bad experience with a Jew. As a result the continued existence, even strengthening, of anti-semitic sentiment in the 1930s and 1940s did not fit in at all with Anglo-Jewish thoughts of progress and its supposedly beneficial effects on British society. Indeed it presented the community with an unexplored – and from their vantage-point unexplorable – phenomenon. Such anxiety was accentuated at a time when Hitler was demonstrating the strength of anti-semitic feelings in a country once considered as civilised as England. It was a situation profoundly at variance with Anglo-Jewish liberal understanding.

The community naturally did have views about the nature and causes of anti-semitism. Liberalism had taught British Jews to interpret it as a sporadic resurgence of medieval hatred often promoted by economic stress. Differences in anti-semitism were unrecognised; all were explained as having the same general cause. The roles of different political and religious cultures in fashioning hatred of the Jews were unexplored. British Jewry viewed anti-semitism as identical wherever it occurred and whatever form it took. For instance, until 1941 the Soviet Union and Nazi Germany were equal *bêtes noires* for many leading figures in the community. Chief Rabbi Hertz in his *Book of Jewish Thoughts*, published and widely circulated in 1941, recalled his own statement at the 1938 Albert Hall Protest Meeting: 'Nazism, like Communism, is a persecuting paganism; and the Brown Bolshevism of Berlin, as its Red variety in Moscow is the negation of God erected into a system.'[36] This depiction of Soviet Russia as an equal partner with Nazism in the attack on Jewry was commonplace. Hertz was frequently to refer to Nazism as the 'Brown Bolshevism of Berlin' when discussing the fate of Polish Jews, and in doing so collapsed the distinction between the Soviets and the Nazis, despite the fact that in Russia, as opposed to Germany, Jews, while perhaps considered citizens of a second order, were at least accepted as human beings.[37]

The analysis of British anti-semitism was similarly informed by those Anglo-Jewish socio-political philosophies which originated in the emancipation. British Jews had the emancipation contract very much in their minds. The blame for anti-semitism lay just as much at the feet of Jews as of non-Jews. Hertz's *Book of Jewish Thoughts* cited Claude Montefiore's comment of 1897: 'Ten bad Jews may help to damn us; ten good Jews may help to save us; which *minyan* will you join?'.[38] Consistent with the resultant widespread internalisation of anti-semitic accusations particularly concerning Jews in business, and in tune with Anglo-Jewish apologia of the time, Brodetsky seemingly felt obliged to assert in 1942 that the Jew 'has not been characterised by the millionaires flying across the Atlantic hugging bags of precious stones, but by the nameless Jew, walking through sand and storm, and carrying in his arms the Jewish Law'.[39] In retrospect his protestations seem absurd.

Consequently the Jewish businessman was frequently targeted for advice. Rabbi Dr I. Mattuck of the London Liberal Synagogue, echoing both Montefiore's and Brodetsky's comments, stated in December 1944 that 'one Jew could ruin the good name of all Jews. Particularly the Jew in business, continually brought into close contact with non-Jews, bore a greater share of responsibility than ever before in our history.'[40] All these statements reflected the widespread Anglo-Jewish belief that the Jew was profoundly vulnerable.

If the emancipation contract had taught that anti-semitism was, in part, the Jew's fault, then liberalism had explained that it was the preserve of the poorly-educated, the immoral, the sick and the anarchic. The Anglo-Palestinian Club debated the motion 'That anti-semitism is a phenomenon in British life which can be combatted by effective propaganda'. At this debate Victor Mishcon stated that anti-semitism 'had its roots in wrongful education',[41] and Rabbi Dr Alexander Altmann, then Communal Rabbi of Manchester, explained that domestic anti-semitism was 'a symptom of moral insanity and a prelude to social disintegration'.[42]

Domestic anti-semitism was therefore to be combated by educative measures designed for either Jewish or non-Jewish consumption. For the non-Jews, numerous examples of apologetic literature were published in this period. These enumerated the virtues and contributions of Jews to society and 'exposed' the myths and canards of anti-semitic accusations. For instance, Cecil Roth's three main works, *The Jewish Contribution to Civilisation, A Short History of the Jews* and *A History of the Jews in England,* all much in the vain of apology, were published in the 1930s and early 1940s and were widely reprinted. Numerous other works of apologia were published. Above all, Hertz's *Book of Jewish Thoughts* exemplified the trend. This book was a revised edition of one he had compiled during the First World War and intended for soldiers at the front (where many British non-Jews came into contact with Jews for the first time). The importance of this book on the British Jewish scene reflected Anglo-Jewry's grave concerns and fears concerning domestic anti-semitism. For compiling the volume the *Jewish Chronicle* hailed Hertz as 'one of the greatest vindicators of Jews and Judaism that the records of our history have to show'.[43] It was referred to as 'a beloved work', even 'an immortal work'.

It has warmed the heart of the non-Jew in all stations of life towards our people and among all classes and creeds, including notably a former Archbishop of Canterbury. It has been a vindication not only of Judaism but of truth. It has been ever a source of encouragement for our people in the midst of all their trials, for its wide welcome carries the cheering message that there are thousands of Gentiles ready to listen to the truth ... Many of us can still recall the thrill we had when we were first handed this miniature masterpiece by our Chaplains, how all the occasional annoyances at what Jews sometimes did were thrust back into their proper perspective ... Which of us has been able to restrain ourselves from lending it to Gentile acquaintances, as the best of all anti-defamation propaganda?[44]

In a review of a work on a similar theme, *The Jews – Some Plain Facts,* published by the Board of Deputies in April 1942, the *Jewish Chronicle* suggested: 'Read it, if possible pass a copy to your Jew-baiter. If he is fair and honest you may not remove his dislike of Jews, but you will cure his anti-semitism. If you cannot by this means, he is neither fair nor honest, so let him be an anti-semite, for the greater glory of Israel.'[45]

The politics of liberalism proclaimed that the eradication of anti-semitism was possible if the right administrative measures were taken. Anti-semitism, declared Brodetsky in his lecture on 'Jews in the Post-War Settlement',

must be once and for all eliminated from the world. Perhaps the future international authority which will guarantee the world settlement will set up an international commission to deal with the problem of education; if so, it will be part of the business of this commission to deal also with the

question of the Jewish people in the educational systems in various countries of the world. Anti-semitism should become as internationally forbid-
den as any other international disease ... like white slave traffic.[46]

Indeed it was not only possible but inevitable. The war itself would
speed the process as Jewish and non-Jewish soldiers fought side by
side.

Jews who in Britain, in the U.S.A., or in the U.S.S.R., are joining their
fellow-citizens in a common struggle against the common disease of
Nazism, cannot but find in this experience something which unites them
with their non-Jewish fellow-citizens more strongly than ever before. It is
not impossible that after the war there will be some anti-semitism in Britain,
and in other Allied lands, but Jews who have fought for the same aim
together with their non-Jewish fellows will not, when this fight is successful,
find it easy to look upon these colleagues as strangers with whom they have
nothing in common.[47]

Despite such optimistic prophecies, Anglo-Jewry had still to face
British realities such as Oswald Mosley's British Union of Fascists,
which was seen as part of an anti-semitic international with links
throughout Europe. In fighting this fascism, however, the Jewish
community was anxious not to promote an openly Jewish political
interest. Throughout this period the Board of Deputies Defence
Committee did unofficially supply leaflets exposing fascist tactics to
election candidates of the major political parties, who then distributed them in the constituencies as their own. There was, however,
nothing to connect the publication of these leaflets with the Defence
Committee.[48]

The increasing worry of domestic anti-semitism, already rising in
the 1930s with the emergence of fascism, thus became a dominant
theme in Anglo-Jewish thinking during the War years, and the
period saw the establishment of two main defence organisations, the
Council of Christians and Jews and the Trades Advisory Council.
The Council of Christians and Jews, which reflected the optimistic
politics of Anglo-Jewish liberalism, was founded in October 1942 'to
fight the spirit of Nazism'.[49] The body, a combined Jewish and
non-Jewish vehicle for attacking anti-semitism, conformed entirely
with the community's self-perception as an equal and similar
partner with other religious denominations. The organisation
included a pillar of the English Establishment, the Archbishop of
Canterbury, who, with the Cardinal Archbishop of Westminster,

the Moderator of the Free Church Federal Council and the Chief
Rabbi, was a Joint President. Even here, however, Anglo-Jewish
fears of highlighting the Jewish aspects of any issue, including
anti-semitism, are evident. Brodetsky's memoirs, for example,
record nonsensically that 'In October 1942 the Council of Christians
and Jews was formed, based on the view that anti-semitism is as bad
for Christians as it is for Jews.'[50]

As for the Jews themselves, they were to be 'educated' in better
public behaviour, particularly when it concerned business. Allegations that Jews were prominent in black-market activity particularly
preoccupied the community, and led the Board of Deputies to create
the Trades Advisory Council in 1940, with Sir Robert Waley Cohen
as President. The body was specifically designed to counter these
charges. Its aim was to remove what it called 'the economic causes of
anti-semitism, which were manifest in friction between Jewish
manufacturers and traders on the one hand, the Gentile businessman and the public on the other'.[51] Its Secretary, Maurice Orbach,
declared in January 1942 that it was 'the first organisation in the
world formed with the object of dealing with defamers outside and
the delinquents inside the trading community'.[52] The Council's
motives lay firmly within the general political philosophy of Anglo-
Jewry, and in the community's eyes it was a great success. Maurice
Orbach declared in February 1944 that 'In twelve months they had
settled almost 200 different issues which were not only possible
breeding-grounds for anti-semitism, but whose settlement secured as
friends for the T.A.C. and for Jewry, hundreds of thousands of non-
Jews who might otherwise have become their enemies. This figure
did not include arbitrations which they had each month.'[53]

Nevertheless, Waley Cohen's biographer complained that
'although the Council had effectively prevented the misconduct that
lay at the root of not more than 10 percent of anti-Jewish feelings,
the Board and its Defence Committee were making no appreciable
headway in curing the other 90 percent which stemmed from ignorance and prejudice'.[54] Educating the Jews against anti-semitism, it
seems, was an easier task than educating the Gentiles. Nonetheless
Waley Cohen continued to maintain that anti-semitism was 'merely
a symptom of a deeper-seated ill, and its eradication could best be
achieved as part of a campaign to inculcate the positive virtues of
tolerance and true religion'.[55]

However, the Trades Advisory Council's campaign often

backfired. Newspaper articles depicted the Jewish community as having set up a body to combat Jewish black-marketeering and thus as implicitly acknowledging the existence of the misdemeanours. John Goodenday, Chairman of the Textile Section of the Council, incurred much disfavour in the *Jewish Chronicle* for referring at a public meeting to the 'many weak and wicked Jewish traders attracted to the Black Market'.[56] Moreover, many in the community tried to avoid the description of anti-semitism as a specifically Jewish issue and they opposed the establishment of the Council, precisely because it was an exclusively Jewish body.

On the issue of anti-semitism, dissenting voices were occasionally heard, however. Harold Laski, the LSE academic and socialist theorist with an abiding interest in Jewish matters, saw anti-semitism in broader structural terms, as a product of the class struggle. He saw it as a tool of aristocratic privilege, the product of 'ancient memories', and observed, 'It is therefore natural enough that in an epoch when privilege has used, in men like Hitler and Mussolini, the outlaws of civilisation, to stay by counter-revolution the expansion of the democratic idea, the rights of the Jew should be the first sacrifice to be exacted.' As for other British Jews, the condition of Jewry was a barometer, but for Laski it was a barometer not of liberalism but of liberty: 'the moral stature of a nation is set by its recognition that the claim of the Jew to freedom is the claim of its own people to strike off its chains'.[57] For Laski it was not education but some form of social revolution that was required to eradicate anti-semitism.

His views however, were the exception not the rule. The fear that Jewish action might promote anti-semitism, illustrated by the establishment of the Trades Advisory Council, was a result of the community's understanding of the emancipation as a contract. This severely constricted Anglo-Jewry. British Jews felt that any overt expression of Jewish 'nationality', or rather 'internationality', would upset the balance of the contract and possibly even promote an anti-semitic backlash. Tolerance of the Jew resulted from his keeping the contract. Breaking the contract by the Jews might result in a mutual abrogation by Gentile society. This anxiety was only enhanced by Anglo-Jewish fears of the uneducated masses, and what they might do if unchecked.

This constant and preoccupying worry about anti-semitism had been particularly noticeable in Anglo-Jewish attitudes towards

Jewish refugees. 'Anti-alienism' had been common within the Jewish community both during the great Eastern European immigration of the turn of the century and during the immigration of German Jews in the 1930s. The uncomfortable thought of a conspicuous, alien and obviously Jewish element in society was a distinct factor in the formulation of the community's policy. As a result of the well-entrenched fear of arousing anti-semitism the community attempted to restrict the number of Jews entering the country, and it was clear that the Anglo-Jewish community would only pursue a policy which might have resulted in the influx of large numbers of Jews to Britain with great reluctance. Many considered Hitler's strategy to be to deprive Europe's Jews of all their possessions, and, having turned them into paupers, to force them upon countries where they would become a burden on the local resources and thus cause anti-Jewish feelings. Consequently the community's leadership tried to exercise considerable selectivity regarding Jewish immigrants to Great Britain – they were preferably to be young, self-supporting, able-bodied, skilled and assimilated.[58] In his book *Britain and Refugees from the Third Reich, 1933–1939*, A. J. Sherman cites Sir Samuel Hoare's assessment that Jewish leaders were

averse from allowing very large numbers of Jews to enter this country or from allowing the entry of Jews whom they had not themselves approved, since they were afraid of an anti-Jewish agitation in this country. For the same reason they were unwilling to give definite figures as to the number of Jews admitted, since they were afraid that any number published would be attacked from both sides as being too big or too little.[59]

Once refugees did arrive, the community's attitude was ambivalent. Although the great majority of those interned in the spring and summer of 1940 were Jewish refugees, the *Jewish Chronicle* in an editorial on 17 May expressed approval of the extension of internment, declaring that the argument in its favour could not 'be resisted, least of all at this juncture when the very life of the nation is at issue'. In its issue of 24 May, the newspaper published on its front page a report from its Amsterdam correspondent which stressed the supposed role of fifth columnists in the German conquest of the Netherlands and vehemently urged that 'the most rigorous steps' be taken against all refugees in Britain.[60]

Complaints against the refugees continued. Otto Schiff, a patron of the Council for German Jewry, forwarded to the Board of Deputies a report on increased anti-semitism in Cardiff which remarked that 'from the sparse contact I have had with my co-religionists in Cardiff, I must admit that the majority of them are not a very likeable lot', and stressed the 'typically continental and Jewish outlook' of many Jewish refugees in the area.[61]

The Anglo-Jewish Community went to great lengths to disperse the refugees around the country and advised them to keep a low profile, so as to avoid the impression of a substantial and menacing Jewish body within England. The Board of Deputies appointed a Public Relations Officer whose main job was to monitor and, if necessary, correct the public behaviour of refugees in London. She approached people in the street who spoke German too loudly, she remonstrated with café-owners who displayed German language newspapers and she arranged for vigilante committees to be formed by the Jewish communities in the provincial centres to keep watch on their refugees. Newspapers were carefully scrutinised for reports of any refugee who had drawn unfavourable comments. A handbook entitled 'Helpful Information and Guidance for Every Refugee', issued in English and German, and published jointly by the Board of Deputies and the German Jewish Aid Committee in June 1939, adjured each refugee to regard himself as 'in honour bound' to start immediately to learn English and its correct pronunciation, and to refrain from speaking German or reading German newspapers in public, or indeed from speaking in a loud voice altogether. The refugee was also urged not to criticise Government regulations, nor the way things were done in Britain, and not to make himself conspicuous by his manner and dress.

Keenly felt and firmly internalised anti-Jewish stereotypes were much in evidence, and refugees were informed that 'The Englishman attaches very great importance to modesty, understatement in speech rather than over-statement, and quietness of dress and manner. He values good manners far more than he values the evidence of wealth.' Other instructions to the refugee were not to take part in any political activities, and especially not to 'spread the poison of "It's bound to come in your country."' Prevailing Anglo-Jewish political philosophies were much to the fore when in conclusion the pamphlet requested each refugee to 'be loyal to England, your host'.[62]

Anglo-Jewish perceptions of the causes of anti-semitism lay behind the anxiety displayed by Anglo-Jewish agencies. The Chairman of the Defence Committee of the Board of Deputies expressed st..ong concern during the war at what he described as 'the thoughtless behaviour of so many of them [the refugees] in areas where they are concentrated namely Golders Green, Hampstead, North London etc.'[63] These tensions meant that there was a great danger that the 'refugees' would become the scapegoat of 'English' Jewry, being blamed for all the misfortunes befalling the latter.[64]

The refugees, who had directly suffered from Hitlerian persecution and who still had relatives and friends in Nazi-occupied Europe, were thus not afforded much welcome by the Anglo-Jewish community. None of them rose into the hierarchy of British Jewry's institutions despite the high intellectual calibre, professional stature, creativity and vigour of many of them. Indeed they were discouraged from pursuing political activity of any sort. As a result a considerable source of anti-Nazi Jewish politics, the most informed body within the community, played no part in the Anglo-Jewish response to the events of Europe.

When refugees did wish to set up separate organisations, the *Jewish Chronicle* suggested, 'with all good feeling, that our refugee friends are best located in the British Jewry organisations already provided, and in which they have full liberty to make their voices heard. Moreover, such an attitude of confidence would be at least a fitting return for the prolonged work which these bodies have performed on their behalf.'[65] When a refugee Zionist society, the Jacob Ehrlich Society, sought representation at the Board of Deputies, the newspaper reported that the Board represented 'the Jewish permanents as against the foreign birds of passage. To dilute the Board's composition is to do more injury to our foreign co-religionists themselves than any advantage that might accrue to them.'[66] On the rare occasions when a German Jew did achieve a position of importance he was subjected to harrassment by British Jews. A correspondent in the *Jewish Chronicle* in January 1942 wrote on the young Immanuel Jakobovits's appointment as Minister of Brondesbury Synagogue:

Your readers must have read – as I did – with incredulity and indignation of the appointment which those responsible ... have thought fit to make at Brondesbury Synagogue. A youth, barely 20, of German nationality, who only came to this country as a refugee 5 years ago, is appointed to the ministry of a synagogue ... His experience has been limited to six months as a Reader in an evacuee community – he was until comparatively recently living in a country which will be, quite properly, abhorrent to all

right-thinking people for generations to come, and, I repeat, he is barely 20
years of age, an age when, it seems to me, with the incessant and crying
demand for man-power he might have considered interrupting his career
for some more active contribution to the War effort.[68]

Certainly the government, aware of Anglo-Jewish anxiety on the
refugee issue, used it to rebuff Jewish delegations. According to
Harold Laski in the *Daily Herald*, and reported in Victor Gollancz's
Let My People Go, 'It was whispered that a Minister of the Crown
lectured a deputation ... who thought that Britain might provide a
refuge for children, for whom, otherwise, there is little hope or none.
He warned them that these victims might, if British generosity were
to save them, provoke an outburst of anti-semitism in Britain.'[68] The
government itself was by no means immune from anti-semitism. As
Wasserstein and Gilbert have shown, Britain's immigration laws
had been informed by considerable anti-Jewish and 'anti-alien'
sentiment. It was the government alone which had the power to
admit the refugees, and fault for the failure so to do lies primarily
with it. Without the existence of anti-semitism in Britain the Jewish
community's attitude toward the refugees would have been very
different. Nevertheless, other attitudes existed in Britain alongside
anti-semitism, namely traditions of liberalism and tolerance. Anglo-
Jewry did little to explore the interplay between these conflicting
currents, let alone make use of it by showing more frequently how
anti-semitism was a threat to Britain and democracy – a plausible
task in a country fighting an anti-Nazi war. The community's
leadership preferred to avoid such issues.

The fear of domestic anti-semitism was, then, a major constraint
on Anglo-Jewish response to the tragedy of European Jewry. It was
a fear shared by all those in positions of communal authority. It
occupied a prominent position on the communal agenda and
effectively prevented any vociferous or autonomous action by the
community on any issue involving the Gentile world. The British
Jewish community attempted to appease anti-semitic sentiment by
trying to modify its own behaviour, which effectively meant pandering to the extreme and violent Jew-haters. British Jews failed to
recognise, or more probably were too afraid to acknowledge, that
most of their Gentile neighbours were ambivalent towards the Jews,
capable of both anti-semitism and philosemitism. Anglo-Jewry was
unwilling to test this hypothesis; to do so would have entailed more
risk than it was prepared to tolerate, this despite the fact that the

potential return for such a risk, such as the easing of immigration restrictions and more direct government attention to the plight of European Jewry, could have been significant. Indeed the downside risk was severely minimised – any sign of a violent anti-semitic backlash during wartime would certainly have been snuffed out by the government.[69]

British Jewry had failed to differentiate between different forms of Jew-hatred. It thus convinced itself of an exaggerated danger of domestic anti-semitism. Such a preoccupying conviction was a result of the socio-political ideologies which so dominated the Anglo-Jewish community, and which so severely restricted its behaviour.

CHAPTER 2

The institutional response to the Holocaust

It was not the destruction of European Jewry that was at the top of the Anglo-Jewish institutional agenda during the Second World War. There were, as we have seen, other dominant Jewish concerns; some of these were indirectly connected with the Holocaust, but in none was it central. The standard histories of the Jewish communal life of this period, such as those written by Cohen, Shimoni and Wasserstein,[1] agree that the outstanding communal preoccupation of these years – indeed the major organisational contest in all of Anglo-Jewish history – was the successful battle waged by the Zionists for hegemony at the Board of Deputies. At the same time, of course, the organised community did respond to the disaster in various ways, perhaps most visibly through delegations to government officials and through extensive philanthropic efforts. Nonetheless, these were dwarfed by the conflict between Zionists and non-Zionists and were severely circumscribed by the political strategies employed by the Anglo-Jewish leadership.

The conflict over Zionism centred, ostensibly at least, on the question of whether or not the Jews constituted a nation. The Zionists saw the establishment of a Jewish national entity in Palestine as the only answer to Jewry's problems. The possibility that the conquest of the Anglo-Jewish community by the Zionist Caucus might, in some instances, be in potential conflict with the need to address the plight of European Jewry under Nazism never occurred to the leaders of the Caucus.[2] They saw the events of the Second World War as confirmation of the correctness of their analysis and of the Zionist cause. As a result, they considered the establishment of a Jewish homeland in Palestine as the only way to save Jews from the Nazis. A Jewish homeland was, for them, clearly the answer to the Jewish plight; they did not contemplate any other solution, however temporary. Many other British Jews, including those outside the Zionist Caucus, shared comparable assumptions. Indeed, by 1942 the bulk of the Anglo-Jewish community had come to accept the need for a Jewish National Home in Palestine, if only because it seemed to promise the most plausible solution to the problem of Jewish refugeeism.

The Zionist Caucus was the political anchor of those descendants of the 1881 Eastern European immigration who sought to influence communal government, and during the years of the Second World War it remained fixated by a policy of institutional infiltration and eventual control. It was carried by its own momentum toward the conquest of the Board of Deputies regardless of the need to address new problems. Its non-Zionist opponents were equally fixated and were certainly not inclined to give up the struggle for power without a bitter fight. The resultant dissolution of the Joint Foreign Committee, which had until that time presented a unified communal response to matters affecting Jewry abroad, dissipated energy and produced considerable overlapping and confusion.

The destruction of European Jewry was hardly mentioned during the debates over Zionism. On some rare occasions the events in Europe were referred to, but only to reinforce rhetorical points. For instance, the Zionist Lavy Bakstansky, in a speech at the 1944 Zionist Conference in Manchester, charged his opponents:

Jewish history will never forgive you. Your fathers in 1917 did not succeed in killing the Balfour Declaration, but they may have helped in whittling down its original terms and it is not unreasonable to argue that, had the original Declaration been allowed to prevail, many hundreds of thousands of Jews who have since perished at the hand of Hitler, would have been citizens of a Jewish Commonwealth in Palestine.[3]

For non-Zionists, such as Claude G. Montefiore, Hitler was proof of their prophecies, a gruesome by-product of Zionism. He wrote in 1937: 'Weizmann is abler than all the other Jews in the world put together. He is a Jewish Parnell but even abler and alas respectably married ... It is appalling beyond words. But Hitlerism, is, at least partially, Weizmann's creation.'[4]

Selig Brodetsky did at one point proclaim on the manner in which the conflict over Zionism had preoccupied the community at a time when the Jews of Europe were being slaughtered. The *Jewish Chronicle* reported his final statement at the end of the Board of Deputies' meeting of 12 September 1943:

The work of the Board and of the Community as a whole had in the last couple of months been pushed to a very low level by considerations, which were based upon all sorts of interests, most of which had nothing to do with the interest of the community. As far as they were concerned in the offices of the Board, it was impossible to get on with any job. Their time was taken up with irrelevant matters which had nothing to do with the interest of Jewry in this country or outside ... This was how the energy of the community was being used up at the present moment at a time when they were told on the evidence of Washington, that something like 4,000,000 Jews had been exterminated in Europe.[5]

This statement came at the end of the third monthly meeting devoted to the Zionist dispute, after twelve and a half hours of debate on that issue alone. His statement seems more polemical than central and had little impact, even on his own behaviour as leader of the Zionist Caucus.

The conflict over Zionism was, as we have seen, by no means the only communal battle during this period. Dr Israel Feldman, one of the few non-Caucus members on the Board of Deputies' Executive Committee, in a letter to the *Jewish Chronicle* published on 30 July 1943 spoke of 'a succession of domestic controversies, both confusing and dangerous' presenting 'a situation, which has in most of us, aroused a sense of frustration'.[6] As we have seen in the previous chapter, none of these communal battles, including that over Zionism, had real ideological content. As Feldman said in a 1943 speech, 'The tragedy of it all is that in fact there is no major clash of ideologies which is dissipating the energies both of leaders and lay. Most of the controversies seem to revolve around persons or the machines or organisations old and new.'[7]

During the period of the Second World War power struggles and conflicts between egos were the dominant themes in communal life. The continual arguments between communal organisations and leading personalities damaged their effectiveness in lobbying government, the general public and the grass-roots Jewish community. They inspired neither confidence nor trust in their ability to manage affairs. The effective loss to the Board of many of the older established families deprived it of its most traditional form of diplomacy – personal intercessions with ministers and civil servants. Those who replaced them, like Brodetsky, had few contacts in Whitehall and any continuing intercession by the older families now lacked some formal institutional backing. As A. M. Hyamson commented, in his article on 'British Jewry in Wartime' written for the *Contemporary Jewish Record* in February 1943, 'the new leaders, with very few exceptions, have not acquired ... the influence of their predecessors. To this extent Anglo-Jewry is growing weaker.'[8] The *Jewish Chronicle* on 21 January 1944 went further, denying the Board its much-vaunted representative status: 'not even the most fatuous of supporters of this movement can preserve a scintilla of belief that the Board of Deputies is now, or will be so long as Caucus rule persists, anything resembling the voice of British Jewry'.[9]

The constitutions of each of the three leading communal organisations (the Board, the Anglo-Jewish Association and the World Jewish Congress British Section) declared the amelioration of the condition of Jewries abroad as an object. But with no co-ordinated action they were destined to overlap and conflict on matters relating to Jewish victims in Nazi-occupied Europe. Moreover, as Shimoni describes, 'various other representations, at times overlapping and at times complementary, reached the Foreign Office from the ultra-Orthodox Agudas Yisrael and from the Emergency Council of the Chief Rabbi'.[10] Norman Bentwich recalled that the Jewish bodies were 'presenting the Jewish case to the public in unhelpful competition'.[11]

A number of attempts were made to co-ordinate response and action but none were successful. In a speech at Maidenhead in March 1943, nearly a year after the first reports of the Nazi extermination programme reached Britain, Israel Feldman, then Vice-President of the Board of Deputies, commented:

In connection with the present tragedy of European Jewry a Consultative Committee was set up by the Joint Foreign Committee of the Board. I myself – I have to say this in all sincerity and with deep regret – am still looking for the evidence of that mutual unqualified reciprocal confidence amongst the four bodies there represented [the Board, the Association, the Congress and the Agudah] which must constitute the basis of any fruitful results ensuing.[12]

Norman Bentwich states in his autobiography: 'consultative committees and joint deputations were initiated. But they served to accentuate differences rather than unify action ... For six months I took part in ... meetings; but they had a monotony of unreality. We got nowhere, we wasted hours protesting, and composing and criticising memoranda which had no hope of serious attention by the Governments'.[13]

The *Jewish Chronicle* editorialised on, and A. M. Hyamson, the London correspondent of the *Contemporary Jewish Record*, lamented, the 'growing lack of leadership and leaders in Anglo-Jewry',[14] who, in any case, were primarily reduced to crisis management. The columns of the *Chronicle* are filled with complaints on this score. D. L. Sandelson, the President of the United Hebrew Congregation in Leeds, gave an address in January 1944 which was the lead story in the paper, headlined 'Power-Politics – The Communal Chaos'.[15] On a previous occasion he had commented on the excessive number of institutions with exactly the same remit, and had referred to the 'promiscuous organisations' within the community.[16] The *Chronicle* referred to the 'Jewish community with its variegated chaos euphemistically called communal organisation'.[17] In the two weeks following Anglo-Jewry's Week of Mourning and the Allied Declaration in December 1942, *Chronicle* editorials were devoted to 'Chaos in Anglo-Jewry'.[18] The paper asked in August 1944 whether Anglo-Jewry was 'Community or Jungle?'[19] and characterised it as 'sterile', marked by 'conceited egotism, materialism, sordid self-seeking and squalid pettiness'.[20] The community's leaders, the newspaper declared, were 'fifth-rate nobodies and communal windbags'.[21] The language might be florid but the sentiments were certainly sincere. The paper lamented the Anglo-Jewish community's response to the news from Europe in an editorial of 3 September 1943:

How have the Jews reacted to their misfortunes? It is not a misreading of the attitude to say that, in the main, they have stood bewildered, stunned, unable to grasp the situation as events have unfolded themselves. And not merely bewildered but divided! ... Jewish feelings tend to find an emotional outlet in domestic faction and quarrels which can only still further confuse their minds and confound their counsels ... The story of impotence may well drive them, not the first people to be so affected, along the path leading to moral deterioration.[22]

In addition to the predominance of communal conflict, other organisational impediments further consigned the situation of European Jewry to a rather low point on Anglo-Jewry's agenda. The community wished, at all costs, to avoid any implication of a Jewish vote. It did not want even the appearance of a Jewish political interest, let alone an organised Jewish parliamentary lobby. Another of the factors that militated against a more organised political response by British Jews to events in Europe, and one frequently noted in the *Jewish Chronicle*, was the poor status which salaried communal workers held in the community (in contrast to lay office holders, who were typically well-off and commanded high status). Most of the major institutions with no direct charitable goal, such as the Board, were funded by dues that might or might not be collected from constituent synagogues; hence they were starved financially. Whatever funds the Board had at its disposal were spent primarily by its Defence Committee to combat domestic anti-semitism. For these reasons, as Neville Laski told the Board of Deputies in March 1943, 'the apparatus for this most important Jewish civil service was hopelessly undersized'.[23] He might easily have added that it was underpaid, unprofessionalised and over-worked. The career did not attract much talent; the *Chronicle* often referred to the 'problem of recruiting fresh blood for the communal service, those "best brains" in Jewry'.[24] Board employees were, according to most reports, hard-working and committed, but they were rarely, if ever, consulted on policy issues and executive matters, which the lay leaders considered to be their exclusive preserve. They were asked to implement but not to formulate policy. Even when money was available lack of professionalism meant that inefficiency abounded. As Sir John Lawrence, one of the few non-Jews who worked with the German Jewish Aid Committee, wrote to the *Sunday Times* on 23 February 1986, 'The many needless delays which I know of were the result of a tragic mistake on the part of English Jewry. Their generosity was great but their efficiency was uneven.[25]

Moreover, the community did not at this time conduct any in-depth analytical research into any aspects of Nazism or the Jewish question. Indeed such books on Jewish themes as were being published by members of the community were overwhelmingly apologetic in content and designed to combat domestic anti-semitism. Nor was there much detailed investigation or open dis-cussion of political strategy alternatives – such as to persuade the Allies to threaten Hitler's satellite leaders or German officials, or to call very much more frequently for the peoples of Europe to extend help to the Jews or for more widespread broadcasting of information on the extermination, or, from 1944, to bomb the railway lines leading to the extermination centres and the centres themselves – much of which could have been done without deflecting major resources from the general war effort.[26]

It is significant that given this communal confusion many of those in Anglo-Jewry who were most vociferous in their efforts for Europe's Jews felt forced to operate almost entirely from outside the formal communal structures. As one of them, Rabbi Dr Solomon

Schonfeld, wrote in a letter published in the *Chronicle* on 6 August 1943 under the heading 'Partisan Plague', 'Many valuable forces whom we can ill afford to dispense with are being driven away. Agreement even on minor matters is impossible.'[27] Brodetsky himself wrote in his memoirs of this period that 'in British Jewry there is a great deal of indiscipline'.[28] After detailing the conflicts and overlappings at this time he commented resignedly that while Anglo-Jewry was engaged in internal petty squabbling, 'All the time the Jewish mass-extermination in Europe continued.'[29] Others perceived the futility of communal conflict. A demoralised *Jewish Chronicle* correspondent, Mrs Julius Jacob, wrote a letter published on 18 February 1944 surveying the communal scene.

Against the bloodstained back-cloth of persecution and agony there does not appear ... the least efforts even towards Jewish unity. What then, does the stage reveal? Faction and discord wherever one looks. The Board of Deputies, embittered by the political wire-pulling of the last election is divided against itself and at war with the Anglo-Jewish Association. The Zionist Organisation, while refusing representation to the Revisionist New Zionist Organisation on its Executive, and on the Jewish Agency as far as possible, is also divided in itself. Meanwhile ... the World Jewish Congress throws into this welter of opposed and opposing interests the challenging claim to be the authoritative Jewish spokesman ... Jewish war-aims remained undefined, and no steps are being taken to tackle fundamentals. To those who scan the horizon of the future of the Jews, what could be more depressing? Meanwhile, in a small field, a battle rages between the Orthodox and the less Orthodox over the handling of refugee children by the Jewish workers of the Refugee Children's Movement. On all sides civil war has been let loose in Jewry. How petty all these disputes look against the background of world affairs.[30]

The *Chronicle*'s own 'Sermon for the Week' on 11 February 1944, speaking for grass-roots community members, despaired that

only in the Jewish community are we faced with the distressing picture of a complete lack of awareness of the truth ... on every side we see disorganisation instead of organisation, disintegration in place of integration, strife where harmony should reign. There is a wastage of power in these quarrels and disputations which exhausts not only the participants but the anxious and bewildered people who hopefully await results.[31]

Alex Easterman, in an address to the Council of Continental Zionists in August 1942, lamented that

despite the present incredible catastrophe to Jews in Europe there was never a time when there was more disintegration in Jewry than there is now in a hundred different ways. In this so-called Anglo-Jewish Community there was disruption, disunity and dissatisfaction. There were groups of people all playing their own little role of unifying, not together, but individually, separately, all maintaining a geographical entity. Zionists had always denounced disruption but here they were, in the midst of the greatest onslaught in Jewry, maintaining disruption within disruption. I see unity groups set up which only created disunity.[32]

H. L. Selby resigned from his position as Chairman of the Editorial and Publicity Committee of the Trades Advisory Council (his only communal post) in protest against the general communal scene. To him the leaders of Anglo-Jewry were 'dancing a minuet on the edge of disaster and having arguments as to who shall, or who shall not, speak for Jewry.[33]

Some made agonised pleas for a unified and complementary response to events in Europe. Dayan Yehezkel Abramsky, the most important figure in the world of traditional Jewish scholarship in England and head of the London Beth Din, wrote to the *Chronicle* in April 1943:

How can we create among us unity – at least a united action in the rescue work for our tortured brethren ... This problem demands an immediate solution, more particularly because all have lost hope that our terrible tragedy is per se able to effect unity ... the cry of agony of those tortured in the many prisons has not stilled or softened the alarms of partisan obstinacy and squabble![34]

Another correspondent, A. Freedland, in a letter appearing under the heading 'Fiddling While Jewries Burn', published on 10 December 1943, urged that 'we Jews in this country should stop for a moment from our internal wranglings and contemplate the indescribable agony of our Jewish brethren and of humanity in general throughout Europe'. As the Agudist weekly *Di Vochenzaitung* put it, 'while Anglo-Jewry plays at parliaments Hitler is "solving" the Jewish problem'.[35]

Anglo-Jewry's continuing (and futile) internal conflict and the inefficiencies of the Anglo-Jewish organisations continued to be the major topics for communal discussion during the war. Mr Freeman Basi wrote to the *Chronicle* in July 1943, six months after the Allied Declaration and one year after news of the extermination programme had reached Britain:

While Jews in Europe are systematically slaughtered, and the remnant in Great Britain is all that remains of Jewry able to carry on the fight in

Europe, the Deputies take up their time on matters entirely irrelevant to the war effort ... This is a situation for which British Jews will have to answer; one day the question will surely be asked: What part did organised British Jewry play in the life and death struggle with Fascism?[36]

And Cecil Roth, the Jewish historian, wrote bitterly in September 1943 of the discord in Anglo-Jewry: 'It is an act of treachery to the suffering, dumb Jewish communities of all Europe, whose eyes are turned to us and to us almost alone ... Jewish history will not lightly pardon the leaders of the community.'[37]

Of course many of these letters were as much part of the communal conflict as criticisms of it. Cecil Roth himself was as bellicose as anyone in the community. Anglo-Jewry was beset by conflict and disunity arising from the inevitable clashes resulting from competing egos. The community was in this case, as in other cases, very much the victim of its own values and inclinations.

Aside from the community's fundamental propensity to conflict, the basic preoccupations of everyday life also diverted Anglo-Jewish attention from the European situation. Chief Rabbi Hertz referred to this problem consistently from the onset of Hitler's Reich Chancellorship. In the first Service of Prayer and Intercession on behalf of German Jewry on 9 July 1933 he implicitly refers to it on three occasions. The prayer he composed for the occasion (and which was repeated at future such services) included the line 'And in our own hearts, plant Thou brotherly compassion, so that there be an increase in deeds of benevolence on behalf of the oppressed [נטע אחוה ורחמנות בלבנו].'[38] In his sermon developing this theme, Gentile activity was to spur British Jews into action. 'We, Jews of Britain, are deeply grateful to these latter-day apostles of humanity for their large-mindedness. Their example should help us to large-mindedness, and save us from partial or superficial views in our approach to the unprecedented problems of relief now confronting us',[39] and further on he echoed the sentiments of his prayer: 'And in our own heart, plant Thou brotherly compassion, so that we hide not ourselves from our flesh and blood.'[40]

Hertz's fears were not groundless. The mundane business of running the home community with its own fears and preoccupations relegated the European situation to a relatively low position on the communal agenda. In April 1942 the *Jewish Chronicle* reported in a manner which now might appear indifferent:

The question of the non-attendance of Deputies at Board and Committee meetings, complaints received by the Board of inadequate arrangements for the distribution of Passover provisions, Sir Robert Waley Cohen's address to the Trade Press (under the auspices of the T.A.C.); and in foreign affairs, the terrible starvations in the ghettos of Poland – these were some of the matters dealt with at Tuesday's meeting at the Board of Deputies at Woburn House.[41]

During the war years, as we have seen, it was the Zionist conflict, not the extermination of Europe's Jews, which prompted the largest attendances at the Board of Deputies. At the Board meeting of 19 July 1942, when the first revelations of the Final Solution were still fresh, it was not the first item on the agenda. The *Chronicle* reported, 'The meeting last Sunday of the Board of Deputies presided over by the President, Selig Brodetsky (Leeds United) at Woburn House was noteworthy for one of the best attendances since the war began.' The first item, and one hotly debated, was a question 'put by Mr J. Shorn (Leytonstone and Wanstead) on the unpleasant publicity given about a Synagogue in the East End in recent court proceedings'.[42]

In August 1942 Captain Jeremiah Helpern, an American sent to Britain to organise the Committee for a Jewish Army, commented on English Jews, 'The majority of them are more interested in their own fate than in the fate of their people.'[43] Following the Day of Mourning and Fasting called by the Chief Rabbi for 13 December 1942, the *Jewish Chronicle* reported bitterly that 'Jewish shops in certain districts remained open and the stall-holders in the East End made only a pitiful show of complying with official entreaty, compromising with plain duty by observing only a five minute silence. After that, it was a case of on with the money game!' The paper went on to refer to such Jews as 'dross'.[44]

As 1943 arrived, periodic letters to the *Jewish Chronicle* returned to the same theme. Jan Schneider from Birmingham, whose letter appeared on 29 January, protested that 'while six million Jews are being brutally exterminated Jewish clubs in England are merrily organising dance evenings'.[45] In similar vein, Rabbi L. Honig of the Agudah lamented on 5 March that 'announcements of dances side with reports of the annihilation now going on in the Continent'.[46] Honig and Schneider clearly saw these dances as evidence of Anglo-Jewry's overwhelming self-interest, not as a form of escapism from wartime realities.

Much of the community, even its well-meaning members, seemed to lack imagination. They were unable to appreciate, even as late as

1943, the uniquely horrific epic they were living through. H. Feint-uck of Salford replied to Jan Schneider, with the centrality of the philanthropic approach firmly in his mind:

May I state that whilst I agree that it is heart breaking to read of the sufferings of the persecuted Jews in Europe, it certainly cannot benefit them at all if Jewish societies, etc. do not hold dances and concerts. In these days one does need a certain amount of diversion from war work etc. and does not Mr Schneider agree with me that it would be much more helpful to our brethren were we to show our sympathy in a practical way, such as by organising dances, etc., the proceeds to be given to help to get the children out of parts of Nazi Europe?[47]

Even the editor of *Jewish Chronicle*, Ivan Greenberg, in March 1944 commented on a letter from Marcus Shloimovitz concerning dances and celebrations at a time of weeping. In line with the general Anglo-Jewish spirit Greenberg depicted Jewry as thoroughly in keeping with the general mood of the country.

The people of these islands did not close the theatres, cinemas and dance halls when the Japanese massacres at Hong Kong were enacted. It may be argued that if we Jews were to abstain from all expression of happiness when some of Israel are in dire torment we should, after 2,000 years, have forgotten how to laugh. There was much sense and good psychology in the Prime Minister's advice, in these dark days, to be 'grim and gay'.[48]

There were other more considered responses. Joseph Leftwich, a man intimately aware of, and concerned with, the tragedy of Euro-pean Jewry, wrote in an article entitled 'Dancing While the War Goes On';

War or no war, life goes on and if we are to keep our sanity and our hope we must relax when we can. It is not indifference. It is the life instinct refusing to be suppressed. Else we would cease to live and bring forth life . . . It has a definite survival value. That is why we continue in war-time to marry and give in marriage, and between battles to dance and fiddle and rejoice. It is a true instinct.[49]

Some lone voices, who no doubt would have considered Leftwich unrealistically sanguine and overly charitable, continued to rage against what they saw as apathy and indifference. The sharpest letter of all was written by Rabbi M. Cohen of Northampton, appearing under the headline 'While our People Perish' on 3 December 1943. He ends it by challenging implicitly the widely held Anglo-Jewish assumptions of the effectiveness of the politics of liberalism as well as the philanthropic approach of low-profile political strategies:

Some three weeks ago there appeared in the *Jewish Chronicle* a report by Dr Schwarzbart that 'there were no more Jewish children left in Poland'. I have sought in your news columns in vain for some reaction to this most terrible tragedy in our history. Nearly twelve months ago, the Chief Rabbi called for a Day of Prayer and Intercession for the tortured millions in Europe (many of our coreligionists refused to heed this call) and nothing further has been done by our Community to save even a remnant of our people. Where is our 'Rachmanut', we who have prided ourselves as merciful, Children of the Merciful? Have we degenerated to the level of the nations who for seven years, stood silently by and saw our people being done to death? Where is the unity of Jewry, where is our Jewish conscience? Your columns contain reports of many happy functions for public welfare: of dances held for all conceivable objects. One body arranges a Guy Fawkes dance, other youth organisations 'proudly present' numerous dances in series. The sound of joyous music is heard in the land, to drown, maybe, the memory of the cries of our tortured children. Anglo-Jewry dances while the best and noblest of our people are being systematically destroyed ... Money alone cannot save us. Is it not time that we took stock of our position?[50]

Letters occasionally speculated on the reasons for this: in June 1943 a letter from David Hammond was published commenting on the Anglo-Jewish scene: 'to my mind, the greatest tragedy is Jewry's own indifference. We are so engrossed in our own petty selves and our daily existence that we have no time, thought, or care for Jewry as a whole. Time is passing. The sands are running out.'[51] The *Jewish Chronicle* editorialised in similar vein on 4 February 1944: 'the preoccupation of the average Jewish citizen with his personal interest prevented him from seeing through the hollowness and sham of a great deal of the community's activities'.[52] Pierre Gildesgame exprobated in a letter published in September 1944:

[T]he conscience of Anglo-Jewry ... seems to be sinking rapidly into a state of lethargy ... I have as yet to meet a young Jew or Jewess, born and bred in this country, who is aware of the scope of the Jewish tragedy and this, for a simple reason. They just cannot be bothered ... the majority of Jews in this country have failed to realise that the Jewish tragedy concerns *them*.[53]

Chief Rabbi Joseph Hertz also occasionally showed anger and impatience. At a prize distribution at the Finchley District Synagogue on 12 March 1944, he was reported as saying that 'while they were sitting in that hall, hundreds of their brethren were being murdered. One feature of that unparalleled tragedy was the general indifference. "Anglo-Jewry does not know what is going on, and the few who do, do not seem to care much!" '[54] And at the service to commemorate the Warsaw ghetto uprising at Bevis Marks Synagogue in May 1944, he charted a course from inaction to resignation.

What has Anglo-Jewry done to arouse world opinion in regard to a moral cataclysm that threatens to engulf half the Jewish race? ... Although the Nazi killing of thousands daily began early in 1941 it was the 29th October 1942 before the lay leaders of Anglo-Jewry arranged a public protest meeting. Some of these leaders were distressed even over the Day of Mourning and Prayer I proclaimed in the December following. I need not now comment on such Olympic calm, reticence and indifference. Suffice it to say that they were not calculated to stir the men at the helm of the political universe to speedy action in human salvage, so that dismay seized many a one at the procrastination and inertia of those who alone had the power to save.[55]

Yet at the same time, the community did make formal centralised responses to the events in Europe as well as considerable philanthropic efforts on behalf of Europe's Jews. Such actions, however, were typically unconnected and limited in character. They did not form part of a continuous organised campaign. Nevertheless they did follow certain set patterns, and the following pages will highlight the watersheds in formal communal action from 1942 to 1945.

On 12 January 1942 the Board of Deputies and Anglo-Jewish Association Joint Foreign Committee appealed both to the signatories of the Nine-Power Declaration on Nazi War Crimes, which was to be issued on the following day, and to the Foreign Office, to recognise the murder of Jews which had occurred in Europe under the Nazi occupation. They argued that the Declaration should contain some reference 'to the suffering of the Jews and to the part played by them in the common struggle'.[56] The World Jewish Congress British Section tried again on 18 February to draw the attention of the British Government and other allies to the particular sufferings of European Jews.[57] They forwarded to the Foreign Office a 160-page volume entitled 'Jews in Nazi Europe: February 1933 to November 1941', a documented account of the persecution.[58] A. G. Brotman, the Secretary of the Board of Deputies, met with P. Stanczyk, the Minister of Social Welfare in the

Polish government-in-exile, about publicity to make 'an organised endeavour to keep the conscience of the civilised world alive to the crimes and atrocities committed by the Nazis and their associates against all the rules of warfare'.[59]

On 29 October 1942 the Board of Deputies held a formal protest meeting at the Albert Hall. The resolution was moved by the Polish Prime Minister Sikorski. 'Also attending were Jan Masaryk of Czechoslovakia, Bishop Mathew (representing Cardinal Hinsley), the Moderator of the Free Church Council, Viscount Cecil and Walter Elliott'.[60] A month later, on 26 November, Sydney Silverman and Alex Easterman of the World Jewish Congress British Section called at the Foreign Office to hand over a document received from the Polish government the previous evening detailing the extent of the Nazi extermination of the Jews, amounting, it was estimated, to over one million Jewish deaths in Poland since September 1939.[61]

The beginning of December saw the intensification of representations. The Soviet Ambassador in London, Ivan Maisky, told Eden on 2 December 1942 that he had been approached by a Jewish deputation who had asked that the USSR associate itself with a declaration concerning the Nazi extermination of the Jews.[62] The following day the Joint Foreign Committee of the Board of Deputies and the Anglo-Jewish Association convened an emergency meeting 'to consider action to be taken to meet the situation described in the recent reports on the wholesale extermination of the Jewish population in the areas occupied by the Germans'. The meeting was attended by representatives of the Jewish Agency, the World Jewish Congress and the Agudah, as well as by the Chief Rabbi and the Jewish members of the Polish and Czechoslovak governments in London, and resolved to intensify pressure on the government to issue a declaration 'covering specifically the extermination and persecution of the Jews'.[63] The American Ambassador in London, J. G. Winant, cabled the State Department on 7 December stating that he had been approached two or three times by committees of British Jews asking for intercession.[64] On 11 December the *Jewish Chronicle* appeared with a black border, giving details of the Nazi massacres. The Chief Rabbi proclaimed a 'Week of Mourning and Prayer' beginning with a day of fasting for the victims of the Nazis on 13 December and a service in the Bevis Marks Synagogue.[65] A deputation of the Council of Christians and Jews, including the

Archbishop of Canterbury and the Moderator of the Free Churches, met Richard Law, Junior Minister at the Foreign Office, on 16 December.[66] The following day the Women's International Zionist Organisation held a mass meeting at the Wigmore Hall.[67] On 20 December the Board of Deputies held a public meeting with Brodetsky in the chair and Count Racynski of the Polish government-in-exile, Lord Nathan, Eleanor Rathbone MP, Professor A. V. Hill MP, Sydney Silverman MP and Berl Locker among the speakers, and the British Section of the World Jewish Congress held a meeting in the House of Commons.[68] Two days later a deputation of Jewish leaders, including Brodetsky, the Chief Rabbi, Lord Samuel, James de Rothschild MP, Sir Robert Waley Cohen, Sir Simon Marks and others met with the Foreign Secretary Anthony Eden and urged steps to save Jewish lives. At the meeting Samuel suggested that some alteration might be made to the arrangements for granting visas to Britain.[69] At an interview with Richard Law on 30 December, Brodetsky appealed for at least a token intake of refugees to Britain and to the Dominions, for warnings to be issued in leaflets and broadcasts to Europe, and for the establishment of United Nations refugee camps.[70] Eva Marchioness of Reading, President of the British Section of the World Jewish Congress, wrote to Churchill on 16 January 1943 pleading for refugees' lives to be saved.[71] In a speech delivered in the House of Lords on 23 March 1943 Lord Samuel appealed for a sense of urgency to be infused in government policy particularly with regard to the admission of Jewish refugees into Palestine where they could contribute to the war effort, though he added that he thought that it was unlikely that more than a small number of Jews would be able to escape from Nazi control.[72] Harold Laski wrote to the Prime Minister on 6 July 1943 suggesting the granting of visas for Jewish refugees by British Consular offices in neutral countries.[73]

There was a further increase of activity from March 1944. Silverman, Easterman and Nahum Goldmann of the World Jewish Congress pressed the Foreign Office on 14 March 1944 to issue 'fresh and emphatic warnings to the Germans' and also to speed up rescue of Jews 'by all possible means', mentioning a report from Lvow they had received the previous day.[74] The Board of Deputies' emergency meeting regarding the Hungarian situation was held a week later on 21 March, two days after the German occupation. Present were Chief Rabbi Hertz, Brodetsky, Dr Schmorak (a member of the

Jewish Agency's Board of Directors in Jerusalem), Blanche Dugdale (of the Jewish Agency in London), Noah Barou (of the World Jewish Congress), Eleanor Rathbone MP, and representatives of the Agudah and the Anglo-Jewish Association.[75] In the light of the news emanating from Hungary, Chief Rabbi Hertz wrote an appeal to Churchill in which he suggested that a declaration be published to the effect that 'all Jews in enemy territories are under British protection and as such must be offered facilities deriving from their status, including the provision of travel documents, facilities for exchange and places of refuge'. This idea in regard to safeguarding Jews against atrocities was 'conceived as quite aside from any steps that H.M.G. may undertake in connection with Palestine'.[76] In July 1944 the World Jewish Congress British Section petitioned the government to conduct air sallies against concentration camps.[77] Two months later they appealed for precision air strikes against the gas chambers and SS barracks,[78] and on 12 October 1944 A. G. Brotman, Secretary of the Board of Deputies, asked whether the Government had considered a joint bombing attack with the Soviets.[79]

In addition to these formalised events and delegations, there was another important way in which Anglo-Jewry responded to events in Europe – through financial donations. This constituted a vehicle of affiliation and action which both conformed to the traditional Jewish ethic of charity-giving and avoided the disadvantages, as British Jewry saw it, of more high-profile political intervention. Within weeks of Hilter's rise to power, Chief Rabbi Hertz in his First Day Passover sermon, 'A Moral Challenge to British Jewry', spoke of the 'immeasurable' importance of the 'sacred resolve to render the sufferers practical help; to organise the deep sympathy we all feel for them, so as to salvage the victims of this new tyranny, whether the victims remain under the Swastika, or emigrate to start life anew in the Holy Land or in other lands of freedom. Large funds are required if we are to save the refugees from hunger and want.'[80] It was philanthropy, not politics, that was of crucial help. 'It depends purely upon the measure of support to the Appeal Funds, how many tens of thousands are rescued from the supreme crucifixion of a concentration camp',[81] declared Hertz in 1938. During the war large sums were raised by Anglo-Jewish organisations (almost all headed by members of the older, established and wealthiest Anglo-Jewish families) to bring relief to Jewish refugees. There were various forms of relief – to help with housing and clothing via the Red Cross (though sometimes these were sent to places where it had been reliably reported that there were no longer any Jews alive); to support the Soviet Eastern Front War Effort; and to build Palestine. This effort – undoubtedly considerable – gave rise to some self-congratulation. One *Jewish Chronicle* correspondent even stated that Anglo-Jewry was the 'only Jewry which through ... their generosity showed that the cause of Hitler's victims was their own'.[82]

However, fear of domestic anti-semitism, a constant preoccupation of Anglo-Jewry, minimised the effectiveness of this philanthropic effort. A. J. Sherman, in his book on *Britain and Refugees from the Third Reich 1933–9* concludes disapprovingly that

the fateful pledge given by the Jewish community in 1933 that no Jewish refugee admitted to the United Kingdom would become a public charge operated in the last year before the war in an entirely unforeseen way to tie the hands of the Home Office in issuing visas, and thus to exclude those refugees for whom private guarantees of maintenance could not be found. The Home Office consistently took its lead on admissions policy from the private organisations, a logical consequence of their assumption of the ultimate financial responsibility for refugees admitted to Britain: a blank cheque issued at a time when no one foresaw the dimensions of the burden which had been freely undertaken. If therefore more refugees could not be admitted, as Colonel Wedgwood frequently pointed out, the fault lay perforce quite as much with the refugee organisations as with the Government.[83]

The implication of this policy for the Jews of Europe was obviously dangerous, but the Jews of Britain, so wedded to the philosophic underpinnings of the philanthropic approach, could not abandon it.

With the outbreak of the war it became clear that the Jewish refugee organisations were no longer able to honour the commitment given to the government in 1933. That undertaking had been given on the basis of an estimate that the number of Jewish refugees coming to Britain 'might be as many as 3,000 to 4,000'.[84] By 1939 some 55,000 had arrived (about 50,000 from the expanded Reich, 5,000 from elsewhere), at a cost to the Jewish community of more than £3,000,000.[85] Before the outbreak of the war the refugee organisations had decided it would be necessary to halt the influx because of their severe shortage of funds.[86] After September 1939 the number of refugees requiring financial assistance greatly increased; by December, 13,300 were maintained by the voluntary organisations.[87] It was now impossible for the voluntary organisations to continue, and they therefore turned to the government for help. The Home Office was at first reluctant to abandon the long-established principle of voluntary maintenance.[88] The government knew of the community's fears and priorities. The Cabinet Committee on Refugees was informed that 'the heads of the Jewish Organisation [*sic*] had been reminded of the appalling consequences which must follow if their Organisation collapsed and if some 13,000 Jewish refugees were left to be maintained out of public funds. It was inevitable that in such circumstances anti-semitic tendencies in the country would be strengthened.'[89]

Rather than allow the full cost of refugee maintenance to fall on public funds, the committee endorsed a proposal by the Home Secretary that the Government should henceforth pay half the cost of maintenance of destitute refugees, the remainder of the burden to be borne as before by the voluntary organisations.[90] On this understanding the Government granted £533,000 to the Central Council for Jewish Refugees in 1940.[91] A public appeal in the community in early 1940 contributed a further £380,000 for the Central British Fund for Jewish Relief and Rehabilitation.[92] During the war, refugee unemployment declined, subsequently lowering spending on refugee maintenance. However, the government's share was increased: in 1941 it contributed £264,000 towards the Central Council's total spending of £302,000. By 1945 the government paid £140,000 – the entire cost of maintenance.[93]

Furthermore, the philanthropic approach provided no strategy when the gates of Europe closed, as they did in 1939 and 1940. Nevertheless, throughout the war, the community continued to place emphasis on relief for refugees who escaped Nazi Europe, despite the fact that their number was small.

As the war went on the construction of the Jewish Home in Palestine, the ultimate haven for refugees, became increasingly important. Though few, if any, at the time thought that the homeland goal and the rescue goal might be in conflict, Palestine may well have diverted money and efforts away from Europe. In 1944 British Jewry contributed £238,000 to the Jewish Agency, which amounted to twelve and a half per cent of the Agency's budget. Altogether, including WIZO and Youth Aliya, the British community donated £740,640 to Palestine.[94] Out of this they earmarked ten per cent of their allocations for the purpose of *Hatzalah* (rescue from Europe).[95] The homeland goal and the rescue goal were almost synonymous in philanthropic terms.

Philanthropy was a well-established avenue to communal prestige and was well integrated into Anglo-Jewish culture. However, the act of giving had become, to some extent, ritualistic and the reasons behind the donation did not seem to penetrate deeply into the minds of the donors. Philanthropy obviated in some respect the need to confront issues directly; it depersonalised them. More direct and active sacrifice, it would appear, was far less forthcoming. When in late 1944 Norman Bentwich called for volunteers for Jewish Units of the Executive Committee for European Relief to take part in relief work in Europe with particular regard to the needs of the Jewish population as they were liberated, the response was 'disappointing'.[96] Dayan Dr I. Grunfeld reported to the *Jewish Chronicle* on the 10,000 Jewish children brought over to Britain as refugees: 'When the children were brought over in 1938 the Jewish community, which had shown such great generosity when it was a question of donating money for the refugee organisation, showed themselves very reluctant to take Jewish refugee children into their homes.'[97] Grunfeld described many of these children as 'lost souls' brought up by non-Jews. He cited many cases of conversions. Most of the children had lost their parents and had been entirely dependent on the Jewish Community for any form of Jewish education. The *Chronicle* also carried a number of letters regarding the failure of Jewish communities in Britain to meet Jews released from Nazi incarceration when they disembarked at English ports.[98] When calls were made to Rabbis to go as temporary chaplains to the liberated concentration camps there was also relatively little response. In a memorandum on 7 May 1945, the Secretary of the United Synagogue recorded a telephone conversation with the Treasurer of the Amersham and District Synagogue, Mr A. Winer, following the United Synagogue's direct and urgent appeal to the synagogue's minister Rev. Indech to go on a two-month attachment to Bergen-Belsen: 'Mr Winer shouted at me on the telephone for more than 10 minutes – we were discouraging the H.O.'s (Honorary Officers) – they had paid £500 for a house for the congregation. Mr Winer impressed upon me that it was more important for Mr Indech to remain with Amersham than it was for him to go to concentration camps.' On 9 May 1945 the Executive Officers of the Synagogue, Messrs. M. Levy, M. E. Moses and A. Winer, wrote to the United

Synagogue, 'While we realise to the full the importance of Welfare and Rehabilitation work amongst the survivors of our Continental brethren, the members of our committee whom we have consulted on this matter unanimously agree with us that the position of this Community renders the service to it of the Rev. J. Indech of greater importance.'[99]

The philanthropic ethos and strategy developed by the Anglo-Jewish community, in accordance with the limits they felt were permitted by the emancipation contract, had engendered an attitude of benevolent superiority toward the Jews of Eastern Europe. They were touched by their distress and ready to give them succour. But they had not looked at the Jewish problem in continental Europe as their own problem. 'Their attitude was ... *de haut en bas.*'[100]

Anglo-Jewry, in common with other Western Jewries, had developed philanthropic institutions to assist unfortunate co-religionists overseas. These organisations, such as the Alliance Israelite Universelle in France or the Anglo-Jewish Association, professed their loyalty to the countries in which they were based, and denigrated any suggestion of a supra-national Jewish body politic. Such a philanthropic tradition meant that unified action on the part of the Jews of America, Australasia and Britain was different to conceive and implement, and there was, as Morris Ginsberg wrote in February 1943, 'accordingly very little effective unitary action ... This lack of unity accounts in large measure for the helplessness of the Jews as a whole when confronted with a major crisis.'[101]

When faced with Hitlerian extermination British Jewry's philanthropic efforts to provide relief to the Jews of Europe, though financially considerable, were in the end inadequate. The strategy was flawed by its wholesale inappropriateness to the magnitude of the events in Europe. British Jewry had nowhere near the financial resources required even if these had been useful. The philanthropic strategy had been considered sufficient to deal with any problem, no matter what its size. Consequently it had prevented the development of other more direct political strategies. When it failed there was nothing to replace it, and the Anglo-Jewish philosophies which underpinned it remained intact.

PART III

The ideologies

Introduction: social and political philosophies

A community of some 385,000 people with such a polygenetic communal background as that of Anglo-Jewry cannot be said to have thought with one mind on any issue, even on those which directly and explicitly concerned Jewry. Indeed, most particularly, this period saw a certain liquefaction of the Anglo-Jewish political system caused by political and social circumstances. For these years coincided with a major demographic, economic and social shift in the community which was the culmination of a process dating back to the 1880s, and which now had a decisive impact on the leadership and priorities of the Jews of Britain. This shift had much to do with the changing distribution of power between the descendants of the different immigrations that constituted the community. For each wave of immigration, beginning with those from Central Europe and including the more recent East European migrants of the late nineteenth century and the influx of refugees from Nazism, brought its different perspectives to bear on the problems of the day, and within each group differences in social and religious development also shaped political philosophy.

Despite this a communal consensus on many issues did emerge, mainly because the ramifications of the nineteenth-century struggle for emancipation continued to dominate Anglo-Jewish political thought. Indeed, commonly-held ideologies regarding emancipation and the non-Jewish world confined the scope of ideological divergencies within the community to a very narrow range. The community saw the civic equality which resulted from emancipation as a gift, and the hospitality bestowed upon Jews by the British as one side of a contract demanding in return loyalty and gratitude. Beneath it all they still feared that they were aliens. British Jews feared the charge of dual loyalty and therefore vociferously proclaimed their patriotism. As a result public controversy with the government was assiduously avoided by all Jewish leaders – political invisibility was the goal. British Jews took civic loyalty to mean conformity. Consequent to this, virtually all self-identified Jews pursued a policy of what is today called 'acculturation' – of social integration and acceptance. This process was based on their belief that Jews might absorb without pain, coercion or compromise what they saw as the undoubtedly beneficial elements and characteristics of the culture and society in which they lived, in the hope that the resulting contact would prove beneficial to both parties. They hoped that the literature, language and mores of their birthplace would become imprinted on their characters, with only a difference in religious beliefs and rituals remaining. Jews sought respectability, a policy consciously pursued in the fields of education and charity, through the Jews' Free School and the Board of Guardians. This emancipation 'contract' negated political action; it prevented the community from asserting its influence on any issue involving the Gentile world. This resulted in a poverty of political doctrine as the contract forswore any form of Jewish factionalism.

In the light of Jewry's assessment of its medieval role as outcast, and its gratitude for the granting of religious tolerance, which stemmed from the liberal philosophies of the Enlightenment, Anglo-Jewry came to believe that the condition of Jews everywhere would improve with the universal diffusion of liberalism and emancipation. Liberalism, in its eyes, was the philosophy of the modern age; anti-semitism was an anachronism from an age that had passed. These optimistic assumptions, part and parcel of the Enlightenment, underpinned the political behaviour of Anglo-Jewry. Most Jews in Britain continued to maintain that the 'Jewish problem' would have to be solved everywhere as it had been in England, by measures of economic reform and political emancipation which stemmed from enlightened, 'educated', liberal thought. Progress, the byword of modernity, meant for them the eradication of anti-semitism. Their optimism in the face of anti-semitism elsewhere came from their experience of economic opportunity and of freedom from persecution and terror in Britain. The British solution was surely applicable everywhere.

Looking beyond the confines of the Anglo-Saxon world, British Jewry perceived, as Stuart Cohen writes, an ongoing battle between the forces of progress and reaction within the Gentile world. At this level the relationship between Jews and Gentiles had to be regarded as nothing less than the yardstick of the liberal progress of European civilisation. The ethical evolution of societies, in other words, could be evaluated by the extent of their tolerance towards the Jews. Persecution reflected a retarded, barbarian society; emancipation was the sign of an advanced, humane environment. Conceived in dialectical terms, anti-semitism constituted the thesis and liberalism the antithesis. The victory of the latter was dependent upon the eradication of the former. Decent, healthy – even stable – orders were inconceivable as long as the blight of the persecution of the Jews persisted.[1]

It was thus only under the cover of petitioning for the cause and practice of liberalism, which they assumed was a policy endorsed or even embodied by the British, that lobbying on Jewish conditions overseas was allowed; even then it was on a paternalistic basis, to help those Jews less fortunate than themselves. Fundamentally they believed that petitioning the British government or its allies on behalf of specifically Jewish causes would probably do more harm than good. Liberalism to Anglo-Jewry was universalism, and factional interests ran counter to it. It was important, they thought, not to give any grounds for the suspicion that the Jew was cosmopolitan and thought of his own affairs before those of the country to which he owed allegiance.

The fear of arousing anti-semitism, as a force in determining behaviour, has already been discussed. On an individual level, British Jews saw anti-semitism as caused by ignorance, the opposite of 'enlightenment', or by some unfortunate experience with bad Jews. These assumptions naturally derived from the liberal belief in the equality of man at birth and the subsequent beneficial (or detrimental) effects of education and environment. The cure to this 'personal' problem was, therefore, firstly the spread of education about Jews and Judaism (this educational objective was strenuously promoted by the community at this time), and secondly vigilance on the part of the Jews themselves, particularly in regard to trade practices.

On a national scale, matters became more complicated. British Jewry, as we have seen, saw emancipation in England as a contract such that the Gentile state and nation promised civic equality to the Jews, and the Jews promised to be solely a religious community marked only by a particular system of faith and worship, and to abandon all non-theological 'national' qualities. Consequently they assumed that if Jewry abrogated its side of the bargain, that is, if it 'returned' to adopting specific sectarian Jewish demands, the Gentile nation might also abrogate its side of the bargain and 'return' to its medieval solution, namely anti-semitism. Such is how the community saw the agitation surrounding the eighteenth-century Jew Bill and the turn-of-the-century anti-alienism. As a result any direct lobbying on Jewish issues (particularly on any of a non-religious, 'national' nature) had to maintain a low profile, that of traditional *shtadlanut,* and it was better still if one could persuade non-Jews to voice the demands, thus masking the issue as one of general liberal concern. This was not merely a matter relating to the community's actual power and authority, but one which had much more to do with its socio-political philosophy. In the light of this understanding of the emancipation contract, the accession to any sectarian demands, they feared, might lead to anti-semitism. British Jews, as we have seen, even had some element of Jewish anti-alienism, or, at least, of ambivalence, which was habitually displayed towards recent arrivals by the indigents. An influx of refugees, so they thought, might endanger their own position, standing and safety. The presence of conspicuously foreign-born Jewish 'aliens' obviously distinctive in more than faith and worship could upset the notion of the melting-pot. Even British Zionism had a tinge of this, for it diverted the tide of emigration away from these shores.[2] As a direct result of this belief in the avoidance of making national demands upon the state, any Jewish request for asylum for foreign Jewish refugees was submitted with a guarantee that the costs would be underwritten by the Jewish community so that they would not become a burden or demand on the public purse. This constituted a profound tension within a community so openly celebrating British liberalism, yet so obviously insecure about its strength.

On one issue the communal consensus was challenged – that of Zionism. To some the very concept of Jewish nationalism flew in the face of the principle of emancipation. The British Jewish battle over Zionism is an odd one, but a testimony to the basic Anglo-Jewish belief in emancipation as a contract. In practical and ideological terms the two camps which arose hardly differed – even non-Zionists and anti-Zionists eventually also campaigned for Palestine to serve as a refuge for Jews fleeing from persecution. The Zionists, for their part, in the vast majority of cases at any rate, did not see the establishment of a Jewish state as having direct implications for them. They did not seriously envisage going there. All were agreed that emancipation was the solution in Britain; all wished that emancipation would spread throughout Europe. Palestine, for the Zionists and, eventually, even for anti-Zionists, was a haven for the persecuted Jews in more 'backward', unemancipated countries. By few, if any, British Zionists was Zionism seen as a denial of the emancipatory struggle in the democracies. For British supporters, Zionism was refugeeism, and thus neither was it incompatible with their understanding of liberalism nor did it compromise their desire not to appear cosmopolitan. As for non-Zionists, they wished their refugeeism to be untainted by nationalistic connotations, though for them too, Palestine, because of its availability, was seen as the primary haven for Jewish refugees. The battle as such raged, remarkably for a community usually so unconcerned with theories, still less with inconsistencies, over the very principle of Jewish statehood itself. For those opposed to Zionism, nationalism and modern religion (the latter being their explanation of Jewishness) were incompatible and broke the emancipation contract. The battle also masked another less philosophic cause of conflict – that of the old-established families of Anglo-Jewry with the sons of the East European immigration of 1881–1914.

As the Second World War continued, Zionism became more and more popular. Emancipatory explanations, based on the inevitable triumph of progress, and, therefore, emancipatory solutions were seen as insufficient to deal with Nazism. Increasing numbers of British Jews turned to the only available alternative – Zionism. In the face of calamity a single, all-embracing solution for the elimination of anti-semitism was attractive. It at least provided a solution to anti-semitism where the hope of emancipation had been severely tarnished. Zionism was a panacea for all anti-semitic ills and was, therefore, more attractive than piecemeal, less all-embracing, or less radical solutions in the face of catastrophe. Such other solutions only accentuated Anglo-Jewry's feelings of powerlessness and frustration.

There were other minor strings to the community's political bow. One was a love of authority, of institutions and of leaders, which were seen as more trustworthy and less terrifying than the unbridled masses. The community was also never, as we have seen, short of personal 'rancour, minor feuds and wearisome trivial vendettas'. Communal strife, with the Zionist issue and its underlying concerns for the 'democratisation' of the community and inadequate provincial representation, over-rode many other considerations. As a result much available leadership talent may have been lost, as the community was seen by men of ability as beset by 'mediocrity and small-mindedness', 'materialism and superficiality'.[3] On many 'issues of communal concern ... its leaders ... did not immediately either grasp the implications or the potentialities of the questions with which they were dealing. Matters took on an unforseen course which belied many of the assumptions upon which the community's leaders had based their attitudes.'[4]

Naturally there were exceptions to the picture of communal consensus painted above – the theocratic Agudah and the Revisionist Zionists being the most obvious active political elements operating independently. However, on the whole, the Anglo-Jewish community operated within the very narrow confines of a political philosophy based on near-universal assumptions about its own place in British society. Thus the Anglo-Jewish community during the Second World War held two contradictory understandings of the emancipation. These, despite their opposition one to another, were advocated with equal force simultaneously by almost all British Jews. The first view saw emancipation as marking the fact that human society was on an indomitable road to progress and that consequently anti-semitism was on the wane. Furthermore, government represented the people arriving at policies after considered, rational debate rather than dictated by established interests. The second view saw emancipation as a contract between the state and the Jews. The Gentile state granted Jews civic equality and the Jews cast aside any notions of a corporate national identity. However, implicit in the contract theory was the assumption that if the Jews abrogated their side of the bargain the Gentiles would abrogate theirs, initiating a revival of anti-semitism – a direct contradiction of the first theory.

This fundamental inconsistency provided the basis for two different Anglo-Jewish strategies which will be characterised in this book as the 'politics of hope' and the 'politics of fear', to be discussed in the following chapters. Complete contradictions in regard to policies were often found within the same British Jew, and reflected the struggles to define identity in a modern British milieu.

CHAPTER 3

The politics of hope

Whilst the previous section dealt with the organisational structures of Anglo-Jewry and how they responded to events in Europe, this chapter and the following one will look at how Nazi persecution was viewed in the light of Anglo-Jewry's prevailing socio-political ideologies. For while Anglo-Jewry's institutional framework is important in our consideration of Anglo-Jewish response, we must remember that world Jewry, having no power of state, was, of course, not organised during this period as a belligerent. Like all Western Jewries, Anglo-Jewry was a voluntary association and organised itself on synagogal lines. Its organisational activities, thus limited, only tell part of the story. Prevailing attitudes are also important. The present chapter will therefore explore those political and religious communal philosophies which shaped British Jewry's opinions of wartime conditions. Various factors figured in the response. Heterogeneous as the community was, it is possible, as I shall argue, to delineate the ways in which it reacted to catastrophe. I shall further argue that aspects of Anglo-Jewish thinking, and even the inherent contradictions between them, might have militated against a clearer comprehension of events in Europe and to some extent suppressed a coherent response.

As we have seen, Anglo-Jewry understood Jewish emancipation as built upon two contradictory premises. They led to two separate political strategies, both of which influenced the community's response to the catastrophe in Europe. The first, which I have styled the 'politics of hope' and which is the subject of the present chapter, deals with religious and liberal perspectives which reinforced optimistic, even expansive, views of present and future. The second, the 'politics of fear', which is dealt with in the following chapter, examines those simultaneously-held ideologies that produced conflicting, pessimistic outlooks.

RELIGION

Religious perspectives played an outstanding role in influencing Anglo-Jewish attitudes, and the most influential religious perspective was Orthodoxy. Its most important spokesman was Chief Rabbi Hertz. Hertz, as well as many Anglo-Jewish leaders of the period, held simultaneously transcendent and immanent views of history. According to the former, it was man who played the central role; in the latter it was God. Little effort was expended by Hertz to explain the reasons for Jewry's contemporary persecutions, though when he advocated his transcendent view he effectively described them as products of assimilation and German religious reform. In a 1934 sermon on Hitler's Jewish policy he asked, 'Have all these dread happenings no message for Jews of other lands? Some Jews neither learn anything nor forget anything. They still place pathetic trust in absolute assimilation ... Will the assimilation rampant in the Western Jewries on both sides of the Atlantic ... not likewise rouse the demons of envy, jealousy and racial rishus?'[1] Hertz simultaneously held another view: in it he saw anti-Jewish activities as an intrinsic and unalterable part of the human patchwork, the wages of the Chosen People. God had decreed that persecution would be the lot of the Jews in exile, and such persecution formed part of a pattern dating back to Amalek. Hitler was, Hertz wrote, 'Amalek's latest spiritual descendant',[2] and Hertz's 1942 edition of the biblical collection produced for Jews in the military, *Readings from Holy Scriptures*, contained the following lament: 'Alas, that Haman's words 3:8 (Book of Esther) have found an echo in all succeeding ages, and his fiendish plan is in our day being carried into effect to a greater extent than ever before.'[3] Brodetsky, too, followed much the same line in the Lucien Wolf Memorial Lecture of 1942: 'Hitlers are not natives of Germany alone, it was a Persian Prime Minister who said to his King twenty-five centuries ago: "The Jews are a different people and therefore have to be persecuted"'.[4] Hertz's *Book of Jewish Thoughts* in its section on anti-semitism cites the Passover Hagadah: 'Not one man alone has risen up against us, but in every generation there have risen up against us those who sought to destroy us but the Holy One, Blessed be He, delivers us from their hands.'

Victory then would eventually be Israel's, and this victory would be the triumph of righteousness. In response to the King's order for an August 1942 National Day of Prayer, Hertz issued a statement, citing the biblical passage 'Come and let us return unto the Lord – for He hath torn and He will heal us: He hath smitten and He will bind us up.'[5] Correspondents to the *Jewish Chronicle* frequently quoted the passage from the Book of Psalms: 'Some trust in chariots and some in horses, but we will call on the name of the Lord our God.'[6]

In particular, Hertz conjured up the centrality of God's relationship with Israel. He proclaimed in 1937, 'That helpless minority . . . places its trust in the God of Righteousness who in His own way will rescue His people from the grasp of destruction.'[7] He saw the divine hand in history as synonymous with the liberal ideal so cherished by Anglo-Jewry. In his New Year Message for 5696 (1935–6), which reflected many of the most important themes of Anglo-Jewish thinking, Hertz explained that

Nazi leaders have repealed the emancipation of the Jew, and in doing so have repealed many things besides, things fundamental to civilised human living. Therein lies our hope. The attack is directed not merely against the Jew, but even more implacably against the ideals symbolised by the Jew – human freedom, the inalienable right to justice, the holiness of the Peace ideal. These Divine ideals are indestructible and, moreover, destroy all those who would destroy them, even as the Rosh Hashanah Reading proclaims: 'The wicked shall be put to silence in darkness, For by Strength shall no man prevail. They that strive with the Lord shall be broken to pieces.' The liturgy of the Solemn Season gives supreme expression to Israel's burning faith that justice alone is mighty and will prevail, that every dominion of arrogance is cast down and humbled, and that all iniquity passes away like so much smoke from under the heavens of the Lord.[8]

Hertz was by no means alone in the use of these expressions of ultimate Jewish victory. Neville Laski, when President of the Board of Deputies, quoted Psalm 130:7–8 in his July 1938 lecture, 'The Jews of Greater Germany': 'With the Lord there is loving kindness, and with Him is plenteous deliverance. And He shall deliver Israel from all his iniquities. In that hope we cannot, and will not, despair.'[9] In a community which restricted itself, on the whole, to a religious self-definition, it was such views which were frequently cited even by those whose religiosity was barely visible. The *Jewish Chronicle*, by no means an Orthodox newspaper, accompanied the first reports of the planned extermination of Jewry with an editorial that stated,

'No weapon that is formed against Thee shall prosper and every tongue that shall rise against Thee in judgment Thou shalt condemn. This is the heritage of the servants of the Lord, and their righteousness is of me, saith the Lord.' Thousands of years have vindicated that Divine promise. Countless Hitlers have raged in vain. The Jewish people cannot be killed. Even to-day the prophet's lament has lost some of its poignancy. The city that was 'full of people' does not now sit so 'solitary' . . . Every Jew knows in his heart that the moral law must needs at last reign. Every Jew deep in his consciousness repeats the words of Job: 'I know my redeemer liveth.'[10]

Nazism was frequently referred to as the 'dominion of arrogance', the מלכות זדון of the weekday Amidah where God is called upon to 'uproot and crush, cast down and humble it speedily in our days'. In his *Book of Jewish Thoughts* Hertz recalls a statement of his own:

As for the House of Israel, we were the first victims of Hitler's callous godlessness, and to-day his declared aim is the disappearance of the Jew from Europe. Our trust is the God of righteousness and truth. 'He disappointeth the devices of the crafty, so that their hands cannot perform their enterprise. And the loftiness of man shall be bowed down, and the haughtiness of men shall be made low: and the Lord alone shall be exalted in that day. And the idols shall utterly pass away.' (Job 5:12, Isaiah 2:17–18).[11]

The force of such a philosophy was implicitly escapist, and led to a degree of resignation as news of catastrophe spread. Even those who spoke of the unprecedented nature of the Holocaust relied on familiar motifs. In his peroration to the second edition (1943) of his *Short History of the Jewish People* Cecil Roth declared that this was

a war which was ultimately . . . to see the revival of the Ghetto and the Jewish badge over vast areas, to result in massacres on a scale and of a ferocity which former history could not parallel, and in deportations which made the great Expulsions of the Middle Ages pale into insignificance. Never, since the dawn of their history, had the menace to the Jewish people been greater. Never could there have been more comfort in the prophetic teaching, which is the essential teaching of Judaism – that, however dark the future may seem and however long tribulation may endure, in the end unrighteousness cannot prevail.[12]

There were even some who saw some spiritual benefit, some cathartic effect, in the enactment of tragedy. Such thinking drew on longstanding traditional Jewish thought. Hertz cited with favour the 1933 statement of the Orthodox Rabbinate of Germany: 'These sufferings bear within them the seeds of future good. Our courage must not fail. They that sow in tears shall reap in joy.'[13] Hertz himself in his Shavuot (Pentecost) sermon of 1938, 'The Tragedy of Vienna', declared, 'Tragedy ... purifies. It displays the elemental force of Religion in human life, fills us with admiration of what the human soul can endure; fortifies us by the example of heroic men and women.'[14] Cecil Roth also returned to this theme with frequency, and he was of the opinion that 'our people is inured to suffering';[15] 'the sufferings of the Jews had only tended to increase the speaker's belief that it was necessary for the instrument to be put through the fire before it could be tempered into the finest steel'.[16]

The *Jewish Chronicle* Sermon of the Week of 9 April 1943 took as its subject 'Jewish Martyrdom' and declared, 'the life and death and agony of these our brethren is the soil out of which we are confident that a new era will arise for the Jewish people and for the world. Otherwise there can be no justice and certainly no purpose in their unrelieved tragedy; and this no Jew can possibly believe.'[17] In October 1943 Rabbi Dr I. L. Mattuck of the Liberal Jewish Synagogue took up this theme in his New Year Message. Jewish martyrdom has a divine purpose for good, he stated. 'We mourn for the Jewish dead, victims of evil power. But their death will not have been in vain if it adds fire to the zeal to create a world wherein such terrible things shall never happen again.'[18]

Hertz did recognise by 1938 how dated such platitudes appeared. In the Preface to his three-volume work *Sermons, Addresses and Studies*, he admits that 'a number of these sermons date in a more unfortunate sense; later events have belied or, at any rate, considerably dimmed the hopes'.[19] Despite this rider Hertz's views, as far as his perception of Nazism are concerned, remained unchanged until his death. Anglo-Jewry's religious leaders continued to hold to an ultimately optimistic view of the course of history. In a 1942 editorial to mark Shabbat Nahamu (the Sabbath following the solemn Fast Day of the Ninth of Av), the Manchester *Jewish Gazette* crystallised Anglo-Jewry's religious and liberal outlook. 'The Jews, the most suffering and persecuted of peoples, are also the most optimistic. Our belief in a God of Justice, in the moral order of the universe and in the fundamental decency of human nature, leads us to the assurance that the forces of cruelty and bestiality will be defeated, and justice and humanity will prevail in the end.'[20] These views remained immensely powerful in a community so tied to its religious definition.

LIBERALISM

The 'politics of hope' saw the emancipation as a signal that man was unalterably set on the path of progress that led from savagery to civilisation. Liberal democracy was proof of a civilised political and economic system, and elected governments and leaders were inevitably responsive and accountable to the electorate rather than to vested interests. Policies in such advanced societies were arrived at after considered, rational debate. British government policies thus represented the will of the British people, who based their decisions on moral criteria rather than political, economic or national self-interest. Most British Jews, especially those prominent in British society (whose very position seemed to verify the hypothesis), believed in this liberal philosophy. In this they were by no means alone, for there were many non-Jewish liberals who believed like-wise. For such Jews and non-Jews, emancipation marked an advanced stage of human development; morality (some called this the 'Judeo-Christian ethic') was its guiding force. It was funda-mentally an optimistic view of human history, and the politics it engendered can indeed be described as the politics of hope.

Anglo-Jewry saw itself and its liberal optimism as thoroughly in keeping with the modern British *Zeitgeist*. The Anglo-Jewish Associ-ation General Meeting of 17 February 1944 declared that

[Our]aims, and the ideals which inspire them, are in harmony with the principles which the people of this country are resolved to follow in building a new world – a world in which freedom from fear and equality of rights and opportunity will be guaranteed to all men without distinction of creed or race.[21]

The election of Adolf Hitler by the people of Germany, a people once considered as enlightened as the British, obviously strained such beliefs about a liberal, tolerant world. Jewish leaders went to considerable lengths to reconcile the apparent contradiction. Anglo-Jewish liberal faith in the perpetual advancement of man resulted in pronouncements which seem, in retrospect, almost comical. Vis-count Samuel remarked in 1937, 'I regarded Hitler as a man with a conscience – a conscience that sometimes led him to do things that were very bad; but he was not a man who would do what he knew to be a crime as Napoleon would have. The danger was that, being a mystic and impetuous, he might easily be swept away at some moment of crisis.'[22] Samuel's attitude to Germany and his support of appeasement (a support he never regretted) were, as Wasserstein has pointed out, 'based more than anything else, on strong support for the League of Nations and for League principles'.[23] The League was the very apotheosis of the liberal ideology which struck such a resonant chord in Anglo-Jewry. This view held that international problems could be resolved by discussion between nations and that the moral force of diplomacy could bring about the needed results. Samuel, like most English Jews (at least until 1941), could not reconcile his view of Germany as a civilised, democratic power with its election of a dictator for whom anti-semitism was axiomatic.

Indeed liberalism had taught Jewry to regard anti-semitism as an anachronistic relic of medieval barbarism. Thus Nazism was, according to Cecil Roth, 'a relapse into medievalism'.[24] In the second edition of his *Short History of the Jewish People*, published in 1943, he wrote of Germany that 'scenes reminiscent of the Middle Ages were enacted throughout the country, and the frontiers of barbarism were thrust forward at a stroke from the Vistula to the Rhine'.[25] Sometimes 'we cannot go back for parallels to the Middle Ages but have to try and find them in the Dark Ages'.[26] As the persecutions of the European Jews worsened, Anglo-Jewry intensified its rhetoric along these lines, looking back even further in human development. 'Brown Bolshevism', said Hertz, 'reduces the countrymen of Lessing or Schiller, Kant and Goethe to the level of gorillas.'[27]

Nazism was retarded not only temporally but also mentally. According to Hertz it was 'an eclipse of reason'.[28] For Neville Laski it was 'a debased mentality',[29] indeed 'inhuman', for humanity was civilised and 'none will gainsay that in more than one country the sun of humanity has, alas, suffered total eclipse'.[30] Nazism had occurred, as Hertz put it, in the 'storm and stress of social upheaval and political convulsion. At such times the masses are possessed by hallucinations of suspicion and hatred.'[31] The German people had been deviously indoctrinated and poisoned with false and twisted history and ideas.[32] However the phenomenon, though very disturbing, was temporary. Progress would soon be resumed.

In the meantime, however, doubts did creep in. On receiving the first reports of German poison gas experiments in April 1942, the *Jewish Chronicle* commented that 'one is tempted to ask whether the perpetrators of this ghastly infamy can be regarded as other than dehumanised monsters whose existence at this advanced stage in history throws doubt upon all our boasted progress'.[33] It was, however, a temptation that was nearly always resisted.

British Jewry understood society as developing through three stages, those of savagery, barbarism and, finally, civilisation. In the light of this philosophy, the war was a war between the forces of civilisation and barbarism, and Hitler's attack constituted an attack on civilisation as a whole, not an explicit war against the Jews. Such a distinction, predicated upon the community's need to believe in the ultimate progress of mankind, moulded responses to the European catastrophe. For horrific as Nazism was, it could be reversed by those same processes of education, rationality and morality that had first brought about Enlightenment.

It is against this background that English Jewry's first attempts to respond must be evaluated. Shortly after Hitler became Reich Chancellor, Chief Rabbi Hertz wrote to the *Times* on 6 April 1933, entitling his letter 'Civic Right and Human Dignity'. In it he spoke of German Jewry as an integral, loyal, honourable and emancipated part of their 'Fatherland', and restated his faith in the inherent tolerance of the German people. The German-Jewish community was bearing the indignities imposed by Hitler

with courage and dignity firmly trusting that the countrymen of Goethe and Kant will accord it complete rehabilitation of civic equality and religious freedom. At any rate the struggle, by every legitimate spiritual weapon, for such complete rehabilitation cannot be shirked by a population that has lived for over 1,500 years on German soil, and has added renown to the German name in every field of human endeavour, by a community whose spokesmen during the fight for Jewish emancipation 100 years ago, declared 'We are resolved to be part and parcel of our Fatherland, and we shall be, whatever betide, part and parcel of our Fatherland. Our Fatherland can and may and should demand of us what it has a right to demand of its citizens; gladly shall we sacrifice all things for it – except our faith and our honour. And we will not sacrifice our faith and our honour, because Germany's heroes and Germany's sages have not taught us that by sacrificing these things one becomes a German.' All good men and true will wish speedy fulfilment to the hopes of German Jewry. It will mean the triumph of the forces of Justice and Liberty in the Germany of to-day, and to-morrow.[34]

A few days later, on the first day of Passover, Hertz continued his theme that the forces of morality could effect change in Germany.

May the moral indignation of the civilised peoples lead to at least a partial resurrection of the forces of justice and liberty in Germany. Otherwise the

outlook is dark for our brethren, and darker still for their persecutors ...
One need be neither Rabbi nor even religionist to see that the world is built
somehow on moral foundations, and that no nation which chooses anti-
semitism, i.e. the will to hate, as the basis of its national life, can have a
future ... It is the fervent prayer of all good men and true that, both for the
sake of Jewry and Germany, the eyes of its blind rulers be opened, racial
hysteria and oppression vanish like so much smoke from that land, and
righteousness and peace and freedom again become mighty on earth.[35]

Hertz was convinced not only that the modern world was built on
moral foundations, but also that this was the belief of everyone in the
civilised world, religious or secular. Anti-semitism was irrational
and therefore unrighteous. Nazism was hysteria and could be eradicated if the eyes of Germany were turned once again towards the
values of the Enlightenment.

Throughout the 1930s these beliefs in the morality and ultimate
triumph of enlightened civilisation continued to inform Anglo-
Jewish attitudes. The Board of Deputies 'gathered in solemn
assembly' on 17 July 1938 to 'place on record their deep indignation
at the persecutions and defamation to which their defenceless co-
religionists ... were being subjected'. The President, Neville Laski,
ended his speech by summing up Anglo-Jewish faith in the ability of
the civilised nations to persuade Germany of its wrong:

We appeal to all those who are striving for peace and appeasement in the
world to declare their reprobation of this persecution, and not to rest until
the status of complete equality with their fellow-citizens, to which they are
entitled by every law of God and man, has been restored to our brethren in
faith, and their fellow-sufferers in the lands of persecution.[36]

Emancipated civilisation, then, was the ultimate coalescence of the
'law of God and man' – liberalism was *ex cathedra* to Anglo-Jewry.

Even as late as 1944 the belief that even Hitler could be re-
educated and persuaded to reject his Jew-hatred was not unknown
in the Jewish community. In a *Jewish Chronicle* review of Paul
Emden's *Jews of Britain*, a rather apologetic work which recounted
the biographies of forty noteworthy British Jews, Henry Baerlein
wrote 'If Hitler survives this war he should be made to learn by
heart the contents of Mr Emden's most interesting book. He will be
filled with many vain regrets and not the least will be his treatment
of a people always prepared to place their outstanding talents at the
service of a nation which treats them decently.'[37]

Though British Jewish prayers, inspired by the situation in

Germany and composed on the whole by the Chief Rabbi, did
include some short biblical phrases, they primarily reflected the
basic tenets of Anglo-Jewish liberalism rather than traditional litur-
gical compositions written at times of Jewish tragedy. Thus the first,
composed for the Service of Prayer and Intercession on behalf of
German Jewry on 9 July 1933, sets the pattern:

> May it be the will of our Heavenly Father ... that the eyes of Germany's
> rulers be opened to the enormity of their assault on the inalienable rights of
> man! ... that the hysteria and hatred which now enslave them give place to
> the realisation that righteousness alone exalteth a nation. Then will these
> rulers no longer justify their counter-revolution by deeds of terror, but by
> deeds of magnanimity, and there will be an end to the apostasy of a great
> people from the ideals of civilisation and humanity. Amen.

The prayer concludes with a refrain repeatedly included in liturgi-
cal composition through the war:

> A spirit of perverseness has come over the rulers of that renowned nation,
> and they have set their face to destroy the House of Israel ... Almighty
> God, banish envy and causeless hatred from the hearts of the peoples.
> Renew within them the spirit of justice and humanity, and Thy children
> shall dwell safe from uncharitableness and persecution.[38]

The solution designed to end the German people's 'apostasy' was,
significantly, to renew the spirit of civilisation, justice and humanity
(interestingly in Hebrew, חדש רוח נכון, literally 'renew the correct
spirit' – presumably the 'correct spirit' of enlightened liberalism).
This theme was reflected in many prayers composed during the Nazi
period. The Nazis were מורדי אור[39] – those who rebelled against the
light, presumably the Enlightenment. Within all such prayers lay the
'conviction that God ... will restore the heart of flesh, the human
heart, to all the blinded followers of the Nazi and Fascist idola-
tries'.[40] Civilisation and humanity (significantly taken in the liberal
sense of the terms rather than the more general meanings) were
synonymous. 'Open the eyes of the enemy peoples, and cause them
to see the criminality of the hallucinations of the hatred that possessed them.'[41] The assumption remained that if only the Germans
would finally confront what they were doing they would realise the
error of their ways and return to civilisation. Now they were blinded
and prevented from rationally assessing their actions.

This theme reappeared in discussions on the collective guilt or
responsibility of the German nation. The thought that such a

civilised people could support Hitlerism was hard for Anglo-Jewry (and others) to understand. Hertz wrote, 'Men and women who speak the language of Edmund Burke do not indict a whole nation.'[42] After the war, said Hertz, 'punishment must be confined to the blood-stained leaders who conceived and the dehumanised agents who carried out these devilish crimes'.[43] Elsewhere he states, 'It is for the victors so to frame the post-war re-education of the enemy peoples that the extraordinary discipline, astounding industry, and deadly efficiency which these people have so often put to Satanic uses shall be transformed to finer issues and be lifted to the highest plane for the good of all mankind.'[44] Education was the answer to Nazism.

Liberal faith in the inherent civility of the Germans led Anglo-Jewry to go to considerable lengths. Harold Laski, who was by 1942 devoting much of his attention to the Jewish question, wrote that the Germans, once taken out of the 'storm and stress of social upheaval and political convulsion', would show their true character. 'It is worth noting', Laski wrote, 'that where the German settles down into an environment of freedom his civic virtues are very great ... America has been enriched by men like Louis Brandeis.'[45] The irony that Brandeis himself was Jewish was apparently lost on Laski.

In short, this philosophy of Anglo-Jewish liberalism said of the German people, as Sidney Silverman formulated it, 'Forgive them, as we ask forgiveness ourselves, for indeed they know not what they do.'[46]

The politics of hope also led British Jews to over-emphasise the decent actions of the citizens of German-occupied Europe, in order to retain faith in liberal ideology. Sir Robert Waley Cohen, presenting the Joint Foreign Committee Report at the Board of Deputies of 21 June 1942, said

the report was a very distressing tale of cruelty, persecution, oppression and every possible humiliation to which the Jewish population in Nazi-dominated countries were subjected. Against this there was the consolation of the very warm, brotherly sympathy shown by those sections of the population who realised the meaning of the Nazi philosophy to civilisation and who showed every possible consideration for their Jewish fellow-citizens often at great danger to themselves.[47]

The theme continued at the following meeting with Brodetsky commenting that 'the only important fact which gave them a certain consolation was the remarkable way in which considerable numbers of non-Jews in various countries did whatever they could even in public and even in the observation of the Nazi authorities to show their sympathy with Jews who were being humiliated'.[48]

This Anglo-Jewish identification with emancipation and liberalism remained substantially unchanged by the events around them, which ensured that optimism would prevail in the face of unceasing gloom. The annual Lucien Wolf Memorial Lectures, the premier lectures of Anglo-Jewry's academic society, the Jewish Historical Society of England, delivered during the war reflected this commitment to liberalism: 'Humanity and the Refugees', 'Jews in the Post-War Settlement', 'Minorities and the Democratic State', the 'Hebrew University and its Place in the Modern World' were the subjects chosen. Throughout this period Anglo-Jewry continued to pray for a 'world restored to peace, in which justice again prevails and racial freedom is again triumphant'.[49] In short, a return to a tolerant, humane Europe – that imagined idyll of liberal, emancipatory politics.

Even when it seemed that the Nazi era and the complicity of many of the dominated countries had shaken some British Jews out of such beliefs they nevertheless drew back. Professor Norman Bentwich writes in his autobiography *Wanderer Between Two Worlds*, published in February 1941, that 'Jewry everywhere was roused to consciousness. It realised that the foundations of Jewish emancipation as well as of European liberalism were being undermined ... Europe, following the sorry surrender at Munich, was rushing to its doom, and we had come to the penultimate act of the tragedy. But the spirit of humanity was again ascendant.'[50] It is not uncommon to find Jewish spokesmen stunned by Nazism and yet affirming their belief in human progress. Brodetsky, for instance, in his 1942 essay 'The Balfour Declaration: Its Political Significance', seemed on the brink of rejecting such optimism and yet pulled away:

The world has changed over and over again during the last 2,000 years, has there been any progress in regard to the Jewish people? It is true that between the middle of the nineteenth century and our own time we had a short period of comparative freedom from anti-semitism, but looking down the centuries of Jewish history can we say that Jews in the twentieth century are better treated than in the nineteenth or in the eighteenth century, or in the darkest ages of early and later medievalism? Is not Jewry to-day in a far worse position than it has ever been in its history? We believe that humanity is going forward to greater and to finer ideals.[51]

The incongruity of this last sentence in the context of the immediately preceding lines would not have been noticed by most British Jews.

Liberalism, along with other ideologies, religious and Zionist (we shall explore the latter later), sometimes informed an almost lyrical, utopian optimism. Bentwich writes, 'the forcible teachings of the War may, it is hoped, dispel the old fears and feuds, so that each people will be willing to let the other dwell under his own vine and fig-tree, "and none shall make him afraid".'[52]

Much of British Jews' faith in liberalism derived from their belief that tolerance prevailed in Britain. To them Britain was the embodiment of the liberal ideal, and the British people could be relied upon to fulfil its moral duty to the Jews of Europe; according to some Jews this was why Britain went to war. The *Jewish Chronicle* reported Brodetsky's proclamation in January 1942:

It was important that the British people and particularly the more educated sections of the public should be given the facts and stimulated to think about the Jewish situation. He felt sure that they would then soon realise that what the Jewish people required was a guarantee of citizen equality in the various countries in which they lived and national equality in the sense that the Jewish people, like other nations, should have their own state in Palestine.[53]

In September 1942, in his New Year Message, Hertz wrote that 'the powerful sanity of British men and women cannot but condemn such exhibitions of injustice and racial hatred, which corrode a people's will and disintegrate its public life'.[54] Indeed the rhetoric became increasingly florid, and Blake was invoked at the Day of Fast and Mourning for the Victims of Mass Massacres of Jews on 13 December 1942. Hertz exclaimed, 'Therefore, we turn to our beloved England, that has for so many centuries been the conscience of Europe, that has been the leader in so many humanitarian crusades, and we agonisingly exclaim in the words of the poet:

> England, awake! awake! awake!
> Jerusalem thy sister calls
> Why wilt thou sleep the sleep of death
> And close her from thy ancient walls?'[55]

In his letter to the *Times* of 28 January 1943 entitled 'Rescue European Jewry' Hertz wrote, 'We do not underrate the difficulties, although few of them are of such a nature that the might, practical wisdom, and humanity of Britain could not overcome them.'[56]

British Jewish confidence in the inherent liberalism of British society and its identity with the Jewish cause, or at least their need to believe in it, led to some striking observations. A. M. Hyamson, writing as London Correspondent of the *Contemporary Jewish Record*, reported that

another evidence of the British attitude toward Jews is the horror, indignation and sympathy – spontaneous not manufactured – aroused throughout the country by each new wave of Nazi cruelty against Jews on the Continent. So widespread and so sincere is this feeling, so well are the reports publicised that the Anglo-Jewish propaganda organisation might do worse than bring its activities to an end, leaving the British press as its heir.[57]

Anglo-Jewry's assumption that humanitarianism was the cornerstone of Britain's political tradition led them to rely greatly on petition and appeal. Dr Israel Feldman, a Vice-President of the Board of Deputies, presenting the report of the Joint Foreign Committee on 17 April 1942, noted that 'those who had the privilege of coming into contact with British Government authorities on subjects of this nature involving humanitarian action had met on all sides with practical sympathy and a desire to help'.[58] The same day that the United Nations declaration was broadcast to all countries in Nazi-occupied Europe, Brodetsky wrote to Eden that Jews would see it as 'a further high example of the traditional British attitude in all that concerns humanity and civilisation'.[59] Britain had taken on Jewry's struggle: 'All Jews', wrote Hertz, 'are with our beloved country in her struggle to blot out the memory of Amalek from under the heavens of the Lord.'[60] In his Lucien Wolf Memorial Lecture, Brodetsky recalled that Lord Palmerston had declared that this country was interested in 'the welfare of the Jews in general'. He went on to appeal to the 'great principle' that 'the attitude towards the Jews is the real test of loyalty to human liberty'.[61] Such appeals were based solely on humanitarian grounds, a strategy unlikely to bear fruit at a time when Britain's own survival was not fully assured until mid-1943.

A renewed stress on morality, as an outstanding feature of both Christianity and Judaism, could, it was felt, bring about change. This was one of the reasons for the foundation of the Council of Christians and Jews in 1942, and the Archbishop of Canterbury and the Cardinal Archbishop of Westminster were among the most vocal protesters on behalf of European Jewry. Nonetheless the *Jewish*

Chronicle noted in June 1943 that the efforts of the Churches for European Jewry were having little effect and saw this fact as 'evidence of the decline of their authority and power'.[62] Anglo-Jewish faith in religion as a formative influence in British society, however, remained more or less unshaken.

Of course, after the initial Government declarations of December 1942, little positive action followed and British Jews had to explain this apparent lack of concern in both government and public circles. In this search for explanatory factors, Anglo-Jewry did have an established scapegoat which had been well entrenched as such in its political outlook since the early 1930s, namely the Civil Service, which had been singled out for criticism for its Middle East policies. As we shall see, Anglo-Jewry did not, remarkably, focus on the established stereotype as an explanation of British inactivity. This was surprising given the ferocity of the earlier criticisms levelled at that quarter. For Anglo-Jewry had long before the 1940s understood the Civil Service as prompted by overtly political rather than moral considerations. It was not subject to the same electoral restraints as were party politicians, and it was one of the few remaining vested interests which Anglo-Jewry thought of as corrupting the liberal state. For Sir Lewis Namier in the 1930s, 'the villains were not so much the conservative leaders ... "but the Arab-loving pen-pushers of the Foreign Office" and "the hypocritical idiots at the Colonial Office"'.[63] Hertz commented, at the meeting to mark the twenty-fifth anniversary of the Balfour Declaration, on the separation of civil servants from party politicians: 'The statesmen of Whitehall, with certain exceptions, were men of vision and of wisdom ... civil servants not only failed to try, but tried to fail.'[64] In January 1944 Hyamson went as far as to state that in Anglo-Jewry's eyes the British Civil Servant was 'invariably ... in effect described as the spiritual descendant of Satan or at least Torquemada or Hitler.'[65] The forced resignation of the Jewish Secretary of State for War, Leslie Hore-Belisha, in January 1940 was widely interpreted by Anglo-Jewry, as the *Jewish Chronicle* testified on 12 January 1940, as an instance of the Conservative party's unwillingness to resist anti-semitism both in the Foreign Office and among the army generals.[66]

Despite this well-established tradition, on the question of European Jewry the community directed less criticism at the Civil Service and much more at the British press.[67] Hertz maintained that the fault for the general public's lack of concern for the fate of

European Jewry lay largely with newspaper journalists, editors and proprietors. At the Albert Hall protest meeting in October 1942 he declared that

[I]t was difficult to understand their reticence. The plain man rarely saw, down in black and white, any attention-compelling information on these massacres. Such indifference encouraged the gorillas of Berlin to go on perfecting their technique of extermination. The British public could not show its inborn undying hatred of all bestiality, if so much of that bestiality was carelessly screened from public knowledge.[68]

At the other end of the spectrum, as far as Anglo-Jewry was concerned, was Winston Churchill. As Hertz proclaimed at the Intercession Service for German Jewry on 23 March 1941: 'we have much for which to thank God in the course of this War ... At the height of our calamity, the leadership of a wise, bold, magnetic personality has been vouchsafed unto us.'[69] The *Jewish Chronicle* wrote in its review of the Anglo-Jewish writer Philip Guedalla's oft-reprinted *Mr Churchill*: 'Already it is safe to assert that he is the greatest Prime Minister this land has ever had.'[70] In November 1944 the newspaper editorialised that

Jewish people throughout the world are aware of all that humanity owes to him for his dauntless and unflagging devotion to liberty, and his fearless hostility to tyranny and injustice. As such, Jews everywhere revere and honour him, as well as – it is not too much to say – love him. As such, it is also not too much to say, Jews always will.[71]

So resounding and unanimous was Anglo-Jewish admiration for Churchill that Hertz allowed himself an uncharacteristic statement with political overtones in December 1944: 'But for your wisdom and courage there would have been a Vichy England lying prostrate before an all-powerful Satanism that spelt slavery to the Western peoples, death to Israel, and night to the sacred heritage of man. May Heaven grant you many more years of brilliant leadership in the rebuilding of a ruined world.'[72] Anglo-Jewry placed absolute faith in his ability and willingness to pursue policies regarding the Jews of Europe based on morality and humanity, a confidence that marked the apotheosis of the Anglo-Jewish faith in British liberal democracy.

As a consequence Anglo-Jewry accepted the government argument that the only way to save Jews was to win the war; 'the most deadly argument of all', as far as Allied policy was concerned, writes

Yehuda Bauer. 'Nothing could be done to interfere with that objective – including, ironically, the rescue of the Jews.'[73] That Britain might pursue some other course to save Jews, or, for that matter, that it might be largely indifferent to the fate of foreign Jews, was barely considered. As Captain Edmund de Rothschild claimed in September 1943, 'the best help that can be given to those in the hell of Europe is to win the war as quickly as possible by the utmost co-operation'.[74] This view was not unique to British Jews. In America too, the mainstream Zionist and American Jewish politicians thought similarly. Any form of negotiation with the Germans, such as the Brand Mission plan to exchange trucks for Jews, was anathema to almost all leading British Jews, as it was to Allied leaders. Not all rescue efforts, however, required treating with the enemy, but the thinking was so deeply ingrained that it was rarely challenged. The *Jewish Chronicle* throughout these years notes only one example of a more lateral approach to the problem, when Daniel Frankel, the Jewish MP for Mile End and a man with only minimal links to Jewish communal affairs, asked in the Commons, 'would not saving the lives of many thousands of Jews also help win the war?'[75] Indeed only one Anglo-Jewish organisation, in this instance with an explicitly international character – the World Jewish Congress British Section – advocated such views. The organisation's report of July 1943 states that no-one can

be unaware of the fact that the ultimate salvation of Hitler's victims depends upon the final overthrow of those who deliberately force human beings to become refugees. It does not follow, however, that more should not be done, in the meantime, to save those in peril of murder. It can be left to Hitler to secure that if the war continues for a sufficient length of time, there will be no Jewish rescue problem left for the Allies to solve, at least so far as the occupied and Axis-dominated countries are concerned. Hitler will have solved it for them. If, on the other hand, the problem of saving Jewish refugees from Hitler is seen as what it really is; the problem of saving the lives of human beings in imminent danger of being murdered – then reliance on a speedy victory is for them a prospect of despair and hopelessness.

Some leading political figures agreed. The World Jewish Congress report quotes Harold Nicolson MP:

If we wait only for victory there will be but few to save ... The duty of rescuing the Jews from Hitler's Europe ... is that of saving people specifically condemned to murder at the hands of the Nazis who have decreed their annihilation for no reason other than their Jewish race and faith. If nothing is done now, the Jews will no longer be alive to be rescued by the defeat of Hitler.[76]

These, however, were very much minority views.

The prevailing politics of hope had led British Jewry to a policy of moral suasion initially directed at the German government and subsequently at the British government and public opinion. According to these beliefs, Jewry's fate and that of civilisation were inextricably linked, and Britain was civilisation's vanguard. This reliance on petition and appeal and the politics of hope led to statements that often expressed horror but reiterated faith in ultimate human goodness. It even relegated the destruction of European Jewry to a point rather low down on Anglo-Jewry's priorities. It was frequently the very last item on the Board of Deputies' plenary session agenda, and sometimes it did not appear at all.

The rhetoric of hope entailed a fundamental belief in the power of moral indignation to sway events. In November 1942 the *Jewish Chronicle* editorialised:

the great protest meeting at the Albert Hall last week against Nazi persecution of Jews can be soberly described from all angles as a commendable success ... the attendance was as distinguished and representative as has ever been seen at a meeting in this country ... there was throughout the proceedings a dignity, almost a solemnity, begotten of profound awareness of the momentousness of the cause ... splendid handling of the occasion by the B.B.C. ... warmest thanks must be given to the Deputies who organised the demonstration.[77]

Eventually the *Jewish Chronicle* sensed a lack of effectiveness in Anglo-Jewry's faith in moral denunciation. In its report of the Board of Deputies meeting in October 1943, the writer permits himself a muted, even ironic, comment.

The Foreign Affairs Committee report was put. There was a long debate, the main burden of which can be summed up in the pious conviction that something must be done with regard to saving the Jewish refugees from the Continent and to persuade the United Nations to this effect, but no actual proposal was put forward, except the contention that the Jews should have an active part in the work of the Inter-Governmental Committee on Refugees. The reports of the Foreign Affairs Committee were adopted.[78]

Some British Jews sensed likewise, and had less faith in relying on British moral instincts to lead the Government to a more active policy regarding European Jewry. Victor Gollancz, the publisher and author, in his spirited plea *Let My People Go* written on Christmas Day 1942, suggested mobilising the population to lobby Governments, certainly more than any formal Jewish organisation was willing to do.

Now the one thing you cannot think is 'That is a matter for the Government.' We are a democracy: I had almost said 'We are still a democracy.' For this is certain, that we shall not remain a democracy unless we act like one. And in a democracy no Government can act in flat defiance of the public wish, provided that is sufficiently widespread, vocal and determined. So what you have to do is, in Miss Rathbone's words, to ask yourself, 'what can I do to influence the Government, the Press, my M.P., my Political Party, Church, Trade Union or other organisation to make it plain that the Democracy, much as it cares for its own social security, cares even more immediately for the immediate problem of how many of these innocent men, women and children can be rescued from torture and death?'

How can you do it? By writing letters to your M.P. (House of Commons, S.W.1), to the Home Secretary, the Foreign Secretary (Whitehall, S.W.1), and your local paper, by organising meetings, passing resolutions – all the usual methods of democracy – urging particularly that our own regulations for the admission of refugees should be relaxed and boldest possible measures of rescue adopted. In this way you will put to shame any doubts, if doubts there can really be, about your humanity.[79]

Later, in April 1945, he was to write bitterly, though of course not aiming his comment specifically at British Jewry, 'You are the citizens of a democracy, you are supposed to control your Government. In the final analysis, no democratic Government dare fly in the face of public opinion, if it is sufficiently strong and sufficiently vocal. But you 'preferred' to allow your Government, year after year, to pursue a policy which actively consolidated Hitler's power.'[80]

It wasn't merely that British Jewry wished to avoid the impression that it constituted a lobby. The community was also deeply committed to the assumption that it was the government's role to prevent suffering and protect life. Not only Gollancz but also others were frustrated by this stance. Lewis Namier wrote in 1940, 'The Jews of England were victims of pathetic illusions – ostriches with their heads in some very inferior sands – foolish, ridiculous creatures not worth saving.'[81] However, for most British Jews liberalism remained unshaken. For instance, British Jews did not see Zionism as a post-emancipatory solution to the Jewish problem or as an implicit acknowledgement of the ineradicability of anti-semitism. Nor did the horrific news from Europe shake this faith.

The politics of the emancipation had led the Jews in England and elsewhere in the West to a perception of liberalism triumphant. With this world view, Nazism seemed incomprehensible. This vision of the 'civilised world' was pronounced in the imagination of Anglo-Jewry, though none the less real to them for that. The Chief Rabbi was in this sense right in his depiction of Anglo-Jewry as אסירי תקוה, Prisoners of Hope.[82] But did Jews truly feel so secure? Though few British Jews questioned these liberal assumptions – to do so would have required Anglo-Jewry to emphasise the tenuousness of its own position – the fragility of this optimistic ideology is evidenced by a second co-existent philosophy which also originated in a perception of the emancipation. It suggests that Anglo-Jewry was, at heart, less sanguine than the rhetoric of the 'politics of hope' might suggest. This philosophy, which I have styled 'the politics of fear', is discussed in the following chapter.

CHAPTER 4

The politics of fear

The second dimension of Anglo-Jewry's socio-political identity derived from a perception contradictory to the optimistic liberal philosophy outlined above. Anglo-Jewry, through the prism of this more pessimistic philosophy, saw emancipation as a contract between the Gentile state and the Jews. The state promised civic equality to the Jews and in return Jews promised to abandon all claims to nationality, existing solely as a religious community. Such thinking played a substantial role in Anglo-Jewish politics throughout the war and was adhered to by all sections of the community, Orthodox and non-Orthodox, Zionist and non-Zionist. The politics it engendered can be described as the 'politics of fear', for implicit in this contract was the hidden and fearsome agenda of what could happen to Jews if they abrogated their side of the bargain. This fear of a retributive anti-semitism led British Jewry to dread appearing cosmopolitan or supra-national and to avoid any semblance of dual loyalty.

Brodetsky consistently alluded to these concerns. In his Lucien Wolf Memorial Lecture, he reiterated that 'unlike most other minorities, the Jews always aim at closer and closer identification with the life of the state in which they live, and in accordance with a passage in Jeremiah, desire nothing better than complete endowment with all the citizen's functions and duties'.[1] The *Jewish Chronicle* reported on a 31 July 1942 luncheon in the Civic Hall, Leeds, at which Mr E. B. Laycock, Chairman of the Leeds Chamber of Commerce, spoke. 'He was afraid that the general feeling was that "you put the Jews first and the country second"'. He was 'Very grateful to Professor Brodetsky for stating that you put the country first and the Jewish community second. The more you can put this idea across, the better for the Jewish community as a whole.'[2] This was advice that the Anglo-Jewish leadership followed carefully.

Historians, amongst them Cohen and Shimoni, have argued that on this issue the Zionists contrasted markedly with the non-Zionists. In fact, in ideological terms there was little on this score to separate the two groups. Brodetsky, the standard-bearer for English Zionism, for instance, was unambiguous in his attempts to avoid the accusation of dual loyalty. He records in his memoirs an exchange of letters he had with Lord Ironside in 1944.

> I wrote to him to explain that I did not mean that a Jew who lives in a state would also owe allegiance to another state of Palestine. This certainly was not Jewish doctrine. I quoted Jeremiah: 'And seek the peace of the city whither I have caused you to be carried away captives, and pray unto the Lord for it, and the Law of the land must prevail.' I had asked for civic equality in any land for a Jew who lives there, and also for a free national life in Palestine for the Jew who lives there.[3]

This ideology, which had been common to all Western Jewish communities since Napoleon's Sanhedrin, led British Jewry to picture the Jewish world as a number of separate Jewish communities, religiously self-defined. These communities were, like their own in England, fiercely loyal to the countries in which they lived. It was even contended that this was no less so in wartime Poland than for France or England. The *Jewish Year Book* of 1940 in its review of the year writes that

> as the year 5699 drew itself out from month to month, the shadow of the impending war lengthened and became ever more threatening. To the Jew, as to the non-Jew, the threat was fraught with misery, unhappiness, fear and foreboding.
>
> English Jew and French Jew in common with their non-Jewish fellow-citizens, as integral parts of Britain and of France, were touched to the quick, and with the firing of the first shot, or even its anticipation, lost their identity in the greater call of their country.
>
> Their fellow-Jews in Poland, also, in the great crisis found themselves Poles first and at every time, but in the great catastrophe that has overtaken their country they are suffering first as Poles and again as Jews, for the greater part of the three and a quarter million Jews of Poland have passed under the Nazi dominion with its record of diabolic cruelties.[4]

Throughout the war, British Jewry's overwhelming desire was to appear loyal and in keeping with the national spirit, to demonstrate devoted loyalty to Britain and its institutions. These feelings were at the heart of the Anglo-Jewish communal perception. The Jewish community, many of whom had memories of the Pale of Settlement, essentially perceived Jewish history as martyrology. As a result they saw their existence in England, with its economic liberty and civic equality, as distinctly privileged. For this they felt grateful to the country which had taken them in and allowed them to prosper unfettered. Loyalty to Britain constituted loyalty to the democratic will of the British people embodied in the majority government. The concept of the loyal opposition had not fully permeated the Anglo-Jewish mind, and open criticisms of government policy were almost never considered. Naturally this was particularly so at a time when Britain was fighting such an implacable foe of Jewry. Indeed this merely served to make Anglo-Jewish feelings of gratitude and loyalty all the more pronounced. In an article published in 1946, the Senior Jewish Chaplain to HM Forces, Israel Brodie, who was soon, significantly, to be made Chief Rabbi on Hertz's death in 1947, wrote that:

the story of the participation of British Jews in World War II provides a record of proud sharing in the total national effort of the peoples of the British Isles to resist to the last the menace of invasion, to defeat the enemy on land, on the sea and in the air, to strike a triumphant blow for freedom and justice. In factory and on the field of battle, in the grim hours of blitz, flying bombs and rockets, in the willing acceptance of restrictions and sacrifice, the Jews of Britain stood side by side with their fellow citizens. They displayed the same high patriotism, the virtues of mutual help and selflessness, as well as the charcteristic humour and the 'we-can-take-it' attitude, which reflected the spirit of Britain and were justly admired by the world when Britain stood alone ... British Jews did their full duty as loyal citizens and stood side by side with other subjects of the King in the hour of crisis. As lovers of freedom and democracy, they upheld the cause of England against her enemies in a spirit of loyalty and self-sacrifice, and bore their full share in the war in every quarter of the globe in the operations on sea, on land, and in the air.[5]

Anglo-Jewry consistently stressed this loyalty to Britain throughout the war, and was particularly sensitive to any implication that Jews might be shirking their duty. British Jewry's patriotism could be 'confirmed by the fact that, according to the records ... approximately 1,150 British Jews paid the supreme sacrifice'.[6] The *Jewish Chronicle* published its Rolls of Honour detailing Jewish casualites and honours weekly, partly to counteract accusations of disloyalty. These lists were of paramount importance. Many wrote to the *Jewish Chronicle* to say that they posted their Rolls in their front windows every week and it was often suggested that they should be published and distributed more widely. The putative accusation that Jews were shirking, an accusation which stressed their alien status and lack of patriotism, was keenly felt by the community with the result that it internalised the charge, frequently making it a factor in Anglo-Jewish policy-making.

Prayers composed during this period also underline English Jewry's patriotism. Jews prayed 'for all who have bravely laid down their lives for their King and Country.'[7] Interestingly, in some prayers the first personal plural was now used for Britain, rather than its normal use in Jewish liturgy for the community of Israel, and loyalty became a theological concept. The specially composed 'Prayer for Victory' read: 'Gird our hosts with strength and courage, and grant victory on land, on the sea and in the air ... save us for Thy name's sake, so that loyalty and faithfulness be indeed the stability of our times' (והיה צדק ומישרים אמונת עתיינו).[8] Sometimes even more significant theological concepts were adapted for the purpose. 'Verily, in a cause of righteousness and loyalty have we gone out to war. It is to keep our covenant in faithfulness that Britain's sons are imperilling their lives unto death; to silence the vengeance of the enemy, and to rescue guiltless nations from the fury of the oppressor' (אכן למען שמור ברית חרפו בני בריטניה נפשם למות).[9] The covenant, a concept central to Israel, was transferred to embrace the emancipation contract, as it had frequently been in many Western Jewries since the late eighteenth century. Jewry's desire to assert its own loyalty and avoid placing Jewish interests above those of Britain led to the use of strange comparisons in Anglo-Jewish forums. After the first news of Nazi exterminations reached England the Board of Deputies produced a booklet which collapsed the distinction between Jews who were under Nazi occupation and those who were not. Both, it claimed, were neglected. The preface noted:

this is the first attempt to give an account of what the Jews are suffering and of what they are doing in the war ... this account should serve to enlighten public opinion, which unfortunately knows very little of the martyrdom the Jews are enduring under the barbarous Nazi regime on the Continent, and still less of the contributions – military, economic and technical – that the Jews of the Allied Democracies are making to the overthrow of Hitlerism.[10]

The booklet contained four chapters ('The Jewish Issue', 'Hitler's First War', 'The Destruction of European Jewry' and 'The Jewish Contribution') along with two appendices ('Decorations awarded to

British Jews in the Navy, Army and Air Force' and 'Honours awarded to British Jews in Civil Defence'). No doubt, as I shall show in chapter 5, some of the impulse for such writing derived from the desire to project an image of the fighting Jew.[11] However, much was due to Anglo-Jewry's belief that it must stress loyalty to Britain prior to any requests for sympathy or practical help for the Jews of Europe. This theme occurred consistently in Anglo-Jewish representations, and affected the prioritising of the European catastrophe in the concerns of Anglo-Jewry.

British Jewry was quick to defend Britain's record when outsiders, including foreign Jews, criticised it. Following Roosevelt's creation of the War Refugee Board in 1944, American leaders began accusing Britain of inactivity on this issue, prompting the *Jewish Chronicle* to editorialise:

> the more credulous observers of the scene cannot be altogether blamed for entertaining doubts when they are told categorically from supporters of this or that organisation or movement that there definitely are possibilities of rescuing Euorpean Jewry even at this critical stage, and hear them outlining a comprehensive relief scheme and appealing to British Jews to take a share in the rescue plan which must be carried out before it is too late, etc., etc. . . . This is the very last moment at which suspicions of British sincerity or humanitarian energy should be permitted to spread and foster abroad.

The paper went on to say that it wanted to see 'positive rescue achievement' before supporting rescue work, and finished with an uncharacteristic lack of a sense of proportion: 'Is the view that only German overthrow can help the Jews still the guiding and justified principle of British action? If so, the false hopes engendered by Mr Roosevelt or by private assurances are painfully unfair to the menaced Jews and their anxious relatives elsewhere.'[12]

Feelings of loyalty meant that, with the exception of the Agudah, Jewish communal institutions did not on the whole consider a strategy of direct approaches to neutral governments. Such an approach would have seemed to them contrary to their status as British citizens. This, they considered, was the proper work of the British government.

The desire to be in keeping with the national spirit and to affirm their integration into British society led British Jews not only to frequent expressions of loyalty, but also to take what in retrospect appears to be an almost detached view of European Jewish life under Hitler. At the first Board of Deputies' meeting following receipt of the news of wholesale murder in Europe, held on 21 June 1942, Brodetsky was unable to chair the meeting because of university examination duties. Elsewhere in his memoirs, published in 1955, the tercentenary of Newton's birth on 25 December 1942 seems almost as important as the fate of Jews in Europe. He wrote,

Owing to the War there was no celebration in December 1942. There was only a special issue of *Nature* containing four articles on Newton, by Lord Rayleigh, Sir James Jeans, Professor Andrade and myself. But my main concern at that time was to do something to save Jews from the Nazi hell. The Board of Deputies wrote to the Prime Minister asking him to receive a deputation from the Jewish community of this country. But Churchill was understandably too busy to deal with it himself, and he asked Eden to receive us.[13]

A similar lack of emotional engagement seems evident when Lord Nathan's biographer cites a correspondence with a former articled clerk, Herbert Garfield, who wrote from Berlin on 11 August 1945, 'I am enclosing a "Commentary of the Nuremberg Laws" which I extracted from amongst the rubble of what was once Hitler's private study in the Reich Chancellory . . . I am assured by Russian experts that this was the Fuehrer's personal copy and that he must have made the annotations himself.' Nathan (a respected and prominent member of the community and of the Board of Deputies) accepted the gift gladly, and assured Garfield that it would be placed among his 'trophies' as one of the most interesting and valued of them. He added, 'It is, as a matter of fact, the only one I have had so far from Berlin and I think it most unselfish of you to have parted with it.'[14] Thus a document acutely symbolic of the destruction of European Jewry seems to be treated as no more than a war curio.

Such statements point to Anglo-Jewry's tendency to submerge the specifically Jewish aspects of Nazi horror. The community attempted to transfer specifically Jewish concerns into more general concerns lest it compromise its standing in the larger society. After the British fascist leader Oswald Mosley's release from prison in 1943 the *Jewish Chronicle* felt the need to comment on the demonstration in Trafalgar Square. 'This anti-Mosley demonstration was clearly no "Jewish" or "Red" affair. It was a spontaneous demonstration of the British hatred of fascism and the recognition that Mosley stands for the same bestiality as Hitler.'[15]

In particular, parliamentary activity by Jewish MPs and Peers was constrained by the need to avoid presenting a specifically Jewish interest. The thought that there might be a Jewish vote, or even Jewish interests in politics, worried Anglo-Jewish leaders and they strenuously denied any such implications. British Jewry wished to avoid coming into open collision with prevailing opinion. The *Jewish Chronicle* reported that during the debate in the Commons following the Bermuda Conference on Refugees in 1943, Daniel Lipson addressed the House, declaring that

> representations which had been made to him by many constituents were all from non-Jews urging him to press on the Government the need for action. No Jew asked for special treatment for Jews. They knew the Jews had been singled out for particularly vindictive treatment, but they did not say: "Take the Jew and leave the others." He appealed to the Government to do everything they could without interfering with the war effort.[16]

Jewish leaders were even anxious that the efforts of non-Jews on their behalf, unfettered by the restraints felt by Anglo-Jewry, might compromise the community's position as loyal British citizens. Lord Wedgwood, a non-Jewish public figure consistently and fervently sympathetic to Jews and their concerns, made a passionate speech in favour of the establishment of a Jewish army (supported, in addition, by another non-Jewish Peer active on this and other Jewish questions, Lord Strabolgi) in a broadcast he made on the BBC in June 1942. His frustration with what he saw as British government prevarication on the issue of the Jews in Europe was clear. However, the question of a Jewish army was awkward for Anglo-Jewry because of the possibility of armed conflict between the Jews of Palestine, particularly the Revisionists, and the British Mandatory Authorities. Lord Moyne, the Colonial Secretary, accused Wedgwood of inciting the Jews to seize the land of Palestine. Addressing the Lords, he stated that

> Lord Melchett had a motion down for discussion ... on the necessity of arming the Jews of Palestine, but as soon as Lord Wedgwood made his broadcast Lord Melchett and the responsible leaders of the Jews in this country generally sought to be saved from Lord Wedgwood in his attempt to make political capital of the natural desire of the Jews to do their utmost to defend the cause of freedom against Nazi tyrany.[17]

Lord Wedgwood was later frequently to complain, as he did when speaking on the Second Reading of the Allied Powers (War Service) Bill, that 'it is idle for me to conceal the fact that most of these people I am speaking of are Jews. I wish I did not always have to speak for the Jews; I wish the Jewish Members of this House would do it instead.'[18] On another occasion, a non-Jewish MP, Tom Driberg (Independent, Maldon), addressed the Commons in April 1944 on the issue of anti-semitism in the Polish army, and the subsequent desertion of Jewish servicemen who then offered themselves for alternate service in British regiments. He notes in his memoirs:

> the odd thing was that we had pursued this matter in the House against the advice, the almost lachrymose pleading – of the official spokesman of the Jewish community in Britain. They felt that any publicity about this might lead to more anti-semitism, perhaps directed against their own flock ... I felt afterwards that, if I had listened to them, those Jewish soldiers would still have been suffering bullying in Scotland or been killed by Polish bullets in Normandy.[19]

During the Board of Deputies' meeting following Driberg's interventions, Mr J. M. Rubens read a letter he had received from the MP who

> had been told that a peer who was originally going to raise the question in the Lords [Lord Strabolgi] had been persuaded by an eminent Jewish peer not to do so ... Throughout this campaign I am bound to say that the attitude of some of what I may call the official Jewish spokesmen has not been altogether helpful. They have seemed over-anxious to appease and willing to be put off with vague assurances.[20]

This theme was present throughout the war and underlay all British Jewish political activity. In a letter to the *Jewish Chronicle* on 24 December 1943, Chimen Abramsky, then active in left-wing circles, accused the community heads of 'appeasement'. He added, 'one gets the impression that our worthy leaders are what the great Jewish writer Mendele so aptly described "afraid of annoying Malchus"'.[21] In another issue, correspondent Basil Feldman notes that 'Jewish MPs are silent ... on any point concerning Jews'[22] – certainly an exaggeration but nonetheless indicative. The paper itself was to comment on Daniel Lipson's speech in the House of Commons on a motion discussing the establishment of a Jewish army that he was 'the only Jew to speak in this discussion about Jews, as the non-Jews present must have noticed – with astonishment or perhaps something worse'.[23] Later in the war it noted that 'Jewish MP's ... have hitherto stood markedly aloof when subjects of Jewish concern were discussed.'[24] They, like most English Jews, did not want to be seen as trail-blazers or vanguards of movements which stressed the uniquely Jewish nature of a problem.

Some Jewish parliamentarians, such as Silverman and Samuel, did make several speeches and interventions on Jewish matters. In a speech delivered in the House of Lords on 23 March 1943, Samuel complained of government inaction:

The declaration of the United Nations was made on December 17th. Today is March 23rd, and, so far as is publicly known, nothing has happened except discussions, conferences and exchanges of notes. We are glad to learn that measures are afoot for securing close co-operation between this country and the United States. But there seems to be a great danger that action is liable to be lost in the sands of diplomatic negotiations ... While Governments prepare memoranda and exchange notes and hold conferences, week after week, month after month the Nazis go on killing men, women and children.

Samuel, however, continued to say that it was now improbable that any more than a small number would escape Nazi control. He laid stress on Palestine, with its shortage of labour, as a haven of refuge, and continued:

So small is the number that it seems monstrous to refer to difficulties of food supply, in this country of forty-seven million people, or to difficulties of employment, when we know that here also is a shortage of labour ... There is still in this country, however, a rigid refusal to grant visas to any persons who are still in enemy occupied territory.[25]

This speech was, as Wasserstein affirms, 'uncharacteristically bitter',[26] and like almost all of Samuel's declarations it concentrated almost entirely on the refugee issue.

Reluctant to draw attention to 'sectarian' issues, British Jewry tended to refer to wider Nazi racism rather than to specify the anti-Jewish nature of Nazi actions. This strategy was similar to that of the politics of liberalism, which promoted the defence of civilisation in order to defend the Jews. In the philosophy of the emancipation contract matters were inverted and the defence of the Jews was enjoined in order to defend civilisation. Chief Rabbi Hertz in his *Book of Jewish Thoughts*, considered an outstanding compendium of Jewish thought, cites Arnold Zweig: 'Civic equality, spiritual and economic progress, the rights of man, these great achievements are at one with the cause of the German Jews; and those who are defending the German Jews are defending civilisation.'[27] Thus the book includes a section on the 'War to Save Human Freedom'. Many of the prayers composed by the Chief Rabbi relating to the war made no reference or specific mention of its Jewish aspects, in either content or title.[28] There were prayers composed for the Jews of Europe, but these were often separated in theme from those relating to the war in general. British Jewish leaders were content to contextualise the uniquely Jewish aspects of the war. Bentwich wrote in 1944 that 'as Freud pointed out, the root of anti-semitism in Germany is a hatred of Christianity inherited from the pagan Teutons'. Thus 'the attack of the Nazis on the moral basis of our civilisation and on the principles of Christianity has been directed primarily against the Jews and Judaism'.[29] Hertz followed similar lines. In his Passover broadcast of April 1942 on the BBC African Service he commented, 'we cannot in justice condone, and we shall not condone, the studied inhumanities of the Nazis, and even less so the devilish ritual of unspeakable cruelties performed by the Japanese'.[30] In a later broadcast on the European Service on 28 June 1942, he remarked that 'the systematic mass murder now in full swing against the Jews is not intended to end with them. There is little doubt that many other people will similarly be doomed to extermination by these dehumanized criminals.'[31]

There was, of course, an element of strategy in such statements, but underlying the strategy was the fear that specifying the Jewish nature of Nazi action would diminish the cause. In his Pastoral Letter for the New Year 5704 (September 1943), Hertz wrote, 'the ghouls of Berlin do not confine their policy of extermination to only one branch of the human family, and attempts to bring home its full significance to the general public will no longer be decried as "atrocity-mongering"'.[32] This phenomenon was taken to extreme length by E. F. Q. Henriques in an article entitled 'Aryanisation' published in the *Anglo-Jewish Association Review* in September 1944. The article relates to non-Jews affected by Nazi Aryanisation measures, such as those involved in part-owned Jewish businesses as well as other forms of confiscation affecting non-Jews aside from Aryanisation. He writes:

the feelings of the population at large who have suffered depredations under the guise of Aryanisation may well be imagined. On the liberation of the occupied countries Jewish interests may therefore find that they have much in common with a considerable section of the general population.

He continues:

Further, it may not be generally realised that, side by side with confiscation under the Aryanisation measures, there has been going on a parallel system of robbery in which the ostensible pretext is, not to purge the country's economy of Jewish influence, but to eliminate from the ownership of property 'persons suspected of activities detrimental to the Reich'.

He concludes by suggesting that

common cause should be made between all classes of the population who have incurred the hatred of the Nazis and suffered on parallel lines from Nazi greed, and that the better course would be so to frame any remedial measures which may be practicable that they apply equally to Jews and to other classes of persons who have been persecuted on account of their race, religion or political opinions.[33]

Even the idea of specific Jewish suffering offended Henriques's interpretation of the contract.

The desire to avoid any stress on the specifically anti-Jewish nature of Nazi policy prevented Anglo-Jewry from accepting anti-semitism for what it was, a process already made difficult by the Anglo-Jewish liberal perception of history. The fear that Jewry might be accused of being interested only in its own fate prompted the community to present the murder of the Jews as being only one of a range of wartime persecutions and to minimise the uniquely anti-Jewish elements of Nazism, laying more stress on Aryan despising of all other 'races'.

The need to avoid the accusation of sectional interest also promoted the belief and policy that it was desirable to let non-Jewish personalities voice concerns regarding Jewry overseas. This would again disguise the Jewish concern as one of general humanitarian interest. The tone had been set at the first service of Prayer and Intercession on behalf of German Jewry held in the Albert Hall on 9 July 1933. Hertz declared:

The Jew is a symbol and, by his mere presence in any society, a living reminder of the liberty of conscience and freedom of the mind that the modern State accords to all its citizens. Rejection of the Jew, therefore, carries with it rejection of these ideals of freedom ... Thus, in raising their voice on behalf of the Jew, the leaders of enlightened public opinion have at the same time championed the highest ideals of mankind ... When the noonday of our German brethren was turned into the darkness of some deep well they ... beheld their firmament studded with stars. I refer to the חסידי אומות העולם [Righteous Gentiles] the men of light and leading who in Parliament, in the Press, and on the Platform have given expression to the world's indignation at the attempt to humiliate and degrade a whole section of the human family ... We Jews, of Britain, are deeply grateful to these latter-day apostles of humanity for their largemindedness.

This need for third-party endorsement was absolutely fundamental to Jewish response to anti-semitism in general, and to the extermination of Jews in particular.[34] The frontispiece of Hertz's *Book of Jewish Thoughts* states that 'it contains the testimony of illustrous non-Jews to the ideals and achievement of Israel, as well as their solemn protests against the defamation and persecution of the Jew'. The book had two chapters on 'The German Tragedy', one containing Jewish and the other non-Jewish opinions. This attitude turned into policy, and it was a Christian prelate not a Jewish authority who could bestow a *hechsher* (literally, religious validation) on a protest meeting.

It is to be hoped the forthcoming demonstration in the Albert Hall on Thursday week 29 October 1942 against Nazi atrocities will attract the large attendance that the occasion most assuredly warrants. That, indeed, is demanded, if for no other reasons, by the fact that the Archbishop of Canterbury will preside over the meeting and will be supported by other distinguished and representative speakers.[35]

At the demonstration itself, Hertz declared,

Obviously, the words of passionate loathing at such diabolic policy and practice came most appropriately and effectively, from non-Jewish lips. If nevertheless, I am now addressing you, and shall be followed by another Jewish speaker, it is because of our plain duty to thank the chairman, His Grace and Primate of All England, the eminent spokesmen of the Catholic and Free Churches, as well as the illustrious statesmen, British and Allied, for their fervent testimony to the unity of the Human Cause.[36]

Anglo-Jewish belief in this philosophy was ritualistic and the incantation was automatic. In March, 1944, at a meeting of the National Committee for Rescue from Nazi Terror, an organisation presided over by the Independent MP Eleanor Rathbone, the *Jewish Chronicle* reported:

The Chief Rabbi said they would have noted only one of the speakers that night was a Jew. And rightly so. The protest against the deliberately pursued annihilation of the entire Jewish population in Nazi-controlled lands came most effectively and appropriately from non-Jewish lips. Equally appropriate was it for the one Jewish speaker to assure the

Archbishop and other speakers how grateful Jews were for the noble testimony that this meeting bore to the unity of the human cause, how deeply appreciative they were of the solemn protest it voiced.[37]

The paper had reported a similar comment by the same author on 1 October 1942.

This dependence on non-Jews obviously threatened to limit the scope of the internal response. Constantly wondering what others might think, say or do in the wake of any action by the Anglo-Jewish community severely restricted action. Harold Brotz, in a 1959 survey of 'The Position of the Jews in English Society', referred to 'an obsessional concern with the approval of the non-Jewish world; with all the emptiness of life in a glass house'.[38] The situation of Anglo-Jewry during the war years of 1942–5 was even more acute.

The self-imposed dependence on third-party endorsement by non-Jewish figures combined with Anglo-Jewry's feelings of gratitude and loyalty to Britain. As a result, Anglo-Jewish leaders greeted any favourable statement by a non-Jewish national figure on a specifically Jewish issue with ritualistic expressions of gratitude. This gratitude was so deeply ingrained that even when non-Jewish leaders failed to do or say something, the community thanked them for having at least given of their time to consider the matter. Leonard Stein, in reply to a letter from the Prime Minister's Office on 12 October, 1942, after Churchill had refused requests to send a message of support or even a Minister to represent the government at the Board of Deputies' Albert Hall Meeting on the Nazi extermination of the Jews, wrote,

Though I am sorry to have to convey to the Board an adverse reply on both points, I fully appreciate (and so, I am sure, will those for whom I was speaking) the reasons for Mr Churchill's decision. As you point out, Mr Churchill has already made clear his views on a number of occasions, and the statements to which you refer have – I need hardly say – been noted by the Anglo-Jewish community with profound satisfaction and genuine gratitude. I have to thank you for the consideration which has been given to the matter and I hope you will forgive me for having troubled you.[39]

The expression of gratitude may even, as Tumin and Fein have suggested, have become cultic, entailing formalised homage to non-Jewish England.[40] When the House of Commons responded by standing up in silence after Anthony Eden's condemnation of the extermination of two million Jews in December 1942, Sydney

Silverman 'was the first to thank him'. James De Rothschild spoke of 'the great emotion and really grateful feeling that would permeate the Jews in this country and the Empire at the eloquent and just denunciation which had just been made'. Daniel Lipson associated himself with everything said by the previous two speakers. Jewish MPs followed each other in making what by now were ritualistic incantations. In the Lords, where Eden's statement was repeated, Viscount Samuel wished to 'express on behalf of the Jews of this country and throughout the world, gratitude to His Majesty's Government and the United Nations for the action that they are taking'.[41] The Board of Deputies issued a statement 'expressing Anglo-Jewry's gratitude for the Allied declaration ... The Anglo-Jewish Community, in common with Jews all over the world are deeply moved and profoundly grateful for the Declaration.'[42] Jewish leaders rushed to utter suitably obsequious statements. Indeed, just in case Anglo-Jewry's message had not been heard by the Gentile world, a deputation representing British Jewry, and led by Professor Brodetsky, conveyed to Eden at the Foreign Office 'the thanks of the Jewish Community for the recent Allied declaration denouncing the Nazi extermination policy'.[43] However, statements of gratitude were rarely accompanied by suggestions for further action. The *Jewish Chronicle* noted its disappointment with Eden's failure to avail himself of the opportunity for a 'splendid offer of sanctuary – something without civil service qualifications', but it did so 'without wishing to appear ungracious'.[44]

The policy of cultic gratitude continued throughout the war. The *Jewish Chronicle* in March 1944 declared that 'the stern warning uttered on behalf of Great Britain by Mr Eden in the House of Commons ... will be widely and gratefully welcomed ... by Jews everywhere'.[45] Even constructive appeals by British Jewish leaders were constrained by the gratitude they felt bound to express. In July 1944 in the House of Commons, Sidney Silverman 'while appreciating to the full Mr Eden's sympathy and constructive activity in this matter, asked if he realised that the Jewish community in Hungary was now the last remaining organised Jewish community in Europe. Could any further appeal be made, not to the butcher gang now running German affairs but to the Hungarian Government who had in the past not resorted to this kind of activity, except under German pressure?'[46] The gratitude strategy had severe limitations. It did nothing to increase Government action and added to

Anglo-Jewry's basic acceptance that nothing, save denunciations and the ultimate Allied victory, could be done to rescue the Jews of Europe.

Brodetsky, addressing the Board of Deputies on 'Government Action', revealed the weakness in the tactic. 'He need hardly say that they were very grateful for anything that was done in order to help save Jews. But in expressing this gratitude they could not help expressing also a certain amount of dissatisfaction with the smallness of what had been done so far (hear, hear).'[47] Leonard Stein, President of the Anglo-Jewish Association, followed similar lines at the organisation's AGM in June. 'They were grateful to the Churches and the British public and to Parliament for their sympathy and protests, but the results of the Bermuda Conference, so far as they had been made known, were distressingly meagre. Yet they could not be blind to the practical difficulties.'[48]

In this context there was one crucial line of argument in respect of the war. That was the Government's stated view that the best way to arrest the extermination was the destruction of Hitler. This, as has already been pointed out, is in Bauer's opinion the fatal argument as regards the fate of European Jewry. Some British Jews as well as non-Jews did question it. However, in the main, Anglo-Jewry's understanding of what loyalty to Britain entailed led it to feel that it could not suggest any form of action which might potentially run counter to the British war effort. British Jews wished to give the impression that they were as concerned with the British predicament as the Jewish one, or indeed more so. The more sophisticated argument that a direct attack on the extermination programme might be in itself an integral part of the war effort was too risky for the Anglo-Jewish community to promote. The community's acceptance of the government position that there was nothing to be done until the war was over helps explain both Anglo-Jewry's resignation in the light of the news of deportations and exterminations and their concentration on post-war planning.

The apportioning of honour and prestige within the community, which played such a significant role in the recruitment and maintenance of leadership, occasionally went hand in hand with the gratitude strategy. From the vantage-point of hindsight the combination often seems to border on the grotesque. At the Board of Deputies in July 1944 Brodetsky announced the visit of a special deputation, organised by the National Committee for Rescue from Nazi Terror, to Eden on the question of the Jews of Hungary.

The impression he carried away from the deputation ... was that they believed that steps were possible which might lead to very important results for the very large numbers of Jews. He wished to express his very sincere thanks to everybody who had co-operated in dealing with this problem. He offered his thanks to the other Jewish bodies, including the World Jewish Congress, the Aguda, and the Anglo-Jewish Association, which had co-operated with the Board in many of these matters (applause). With regard to non-Jewish authorities, he need hardly say that the gratitude of Jews everywhere was bound to be expressed to that wonderful woman who had been the leader in this work for such a long time – Miss Eleanor Rathbone (applause).[49]

The gratitude strategy failed. As Richard Law, a diplomat at the Foreign Office, noted on a deputation of the Council of Christians and Jews on 16 December 1942, 'In spite of the fact that the deputation expressed great appreciation of my alleged sympathetic attitude, I don't think I gave anything away.'[50]

Some within the community did see the pathos of the situation. In a letter published in the *Jewish Chronicle* of 14 May 1943, correspondent Jacob Sarna railed that 'there is manifest in Anglo-Jewry a most objectionable tendency to express obsequious gratitude and joy whenever a non-Jew utters a few flattering and truthful words about us. Is this really necessary? Must we be the only people in the world from whom gratitude is expected when a few true words are said about them?'[51]

Even those whose political thinking was in some ways at variance with Anglo-Jewish social philosophy were keenly aware of the need felt by Anglo-Jewry to express gratitude. Victor Gollancz in his plea *Let My People Go* noted,

I already hear one or two people saying, 'Your ancestors were freely admitted to this country; they, and you, have lived here with no disabilities and with little, if any, discrimination. It would become you to show gratitude. Leave any attack or agitation, necessary or otherwise, to others; as a Jew, be silent. Let me make the position clear on behalf, not only of myself, but of all self-respecting Jewry. There can be no one in this island who loves it more than I do; it is my country and I know no other. But before I am either an Englishman or a Jew I am a man, with the rights and dignity of a man.[52]

In his first article after hearing news of the fate of the Jews of Europe, Sidney Silverman wrote, 'My socialist friends who will applaud my efforts for socialism must agree it means nothing if it does not mean the relief of the persecuted and the oppressed, and the fact that I too am a Jew does not, I hope, disqualify my efforts when the Jews are the immediate victims.'[53] Harold Laski commented, 'if he speaks as a Jew, the climate of opinion he is certain, sooner or later, to encounter will emphasise to him that those to whom he appeals have, at bottom, the half conscious sense that he is, after all, an alien amongst them pleading for aliens whose claims are in no aspect rights'.[54]

No doubt British society did impose some restrictions on Jewish identity, but not to the extent that British Jews felt. Tumin, in a perceptive argument, suggests that the British Jew, instead of asking that Britain 'accept him as he is and treat him as an equal in his full self-proclaimed identity ... is, in effect, asking that his separateness shall be forgotten and ignored'.[55] The emancipation contract theory led British Jewry publicly to de-emphasise its distinctiveness in English society.

Though the comparison with events in Europe should not be pushed too far, it is instructive to note the difference in rhetoric in the denunciation by prominent British Jews of the perpetrators of the murder of Lord Moyne, the Colonial Secretary, by members of the Irgun Zvei Leumi in Cairo in 1944. This murder deeply worried Anglo-Jewish leaders as it directly touched on the dual loyalty issue. Brodetsky, displaying the extreme sensitivity of British Jews on this question in a statement which in retrospect seems to lack all sense of proportion, proclaimed that '[a]mong the great disasters that befell the Jews in the past, this [murder] is one of the greatest'. Viscount Samuel declared in the House of Lords that if the 'murders have come from the Jewish Palestinian population then that population, I feel certain, will see that it is vital to exterminate from their midst this hateful group of criminals',[56] and Lipson declared in the Commons that 'every Jew worthy of the name ... will pray that the efforts to eradicate speedily and completely this murderous gang and their associates will be successful'.[57] The Irgun was not to be educated out of its misguided ideas, but to be exterminated. Anglo-Jewish leaders did their utmost to display the supremacy of British and not Jewish interests in the formation of their politics. Such vehemence was rarely heard in connection with the Jews of Europe.

Thus the politics of fear formed a consistent constraint on Anglo-Jewish action. It derived from a fundamental understanding of emancipation as a contract, a view held by the community in near unanimity. It prescribed the boundaries of permissible action and statement, at times severely restricting and constraining them. Jews felt they must behave as a purely religious community without national connotations. Faced with an enemy who persecuted the Jews simply because of their nationality, such sentiments might now appear irrelevant. Yet throughout the years of the Second World War, Anglo-Jewry did little to explore, let alone reject, this philosophy.

CHAPTER 5

The Jewish fighting model

During the course of the war a positive self-image of the Jew emerged. This paradigm depicted Jews both as they were and as they could potentially become in the future. The spiritual resistance of Jews to Nazism, the Warsaw Ghetto uprising, the bravery of English Jews fighting in Allied forces, even the dignified demeanour of Anglo-Jewry's leaders, all suggested in the minds of many British Jews an alternative image to a European Jewry killed passively and without resistance. Quite inevitably this image came to be linked with that of Zionism.

The previous two chapters examined the philosophies that lay behind Anglo-Jewry's political strategies of petition and appeal. This chapter investigates one by-product of over-riding significance that derived, yet was radically different, from all traditional forms of political philosophy. Previously dominant strategies frequently pictured the Jew as a supplicant, a picture reinforced by the internalisation of a persistent anti-semitic accusation. 'Spineless supplicants' is how even the *Jewish Chronicle* characterised Jews, or as 'the world's most persistent and unfortunate beggars'.[1] This chapter examines how Anglo-Jewry sought to eradicate such images at a time when Hitler's war highlighted Jewish powerlessness. The counter-image was that of the Jewish fighter. Andrew Sharf writes of perceptions of European Jewry prevalent in contemporary British society that while 'the majority did go ignorant or unprotesting ... the picture of the Jewish fighter ... was not understood in its full significance'. The struggle to understand and create this picture played an increasingly dominant role on the Anglo-Jewish agenda.

The need for a counter-image was paramount because, as Victor Gollancz suggested,

The Jewish suffering was so utterly meaningless. For the most part they couldn't fight, though when at last a desperate opportunity came at

Warsaw and Bialystok and even Treblinka they showed a gallantry of which no people need to be ashamed. They couldn't, by their death, contribute, as British and Russian and American soldiers could contribute, to the victory over Hitler: they couldn't feel, as bombarded London could feel, that frightened though they might be, there was still some happiness and glory about sharing in the common peril. Loaded into cattle trucks, gassed, burnt, and machine-gunned, killed wholesale by the most modern and scientific methods – they met a fate of which the sheer sordid futility surpassed even the horror.[2]

Thus Gollancz summarised in 1945 the feelings of despondency and senselessness which the extermination of the Jews of Europe engendered. The impotence of British Jewry compounded such emotions, resulting in the demoralisation of many British Jews. Hence the search for a model of a Jewish fighter who resisted Nazism; this would assuage their sense of powerlessness. This was done in various ways. There were few models of direct armed combat available, and so those which most readily emerged frequently related to an image of the Jew as proud, erect and dignified in the face of adversity, as contrasted with the prevalent notion of the submissive Jew. This was part and parcel of a search for Jewish honour at a time of collective dishonour. New alternative images were fashioned in various forms, all designed to combat the pathos surrounding the Jews. Some drew on traditional emancipatory paradigms – for instance that of the Jew as spiritual innovator. At the Board of Deputies' meeting in March 1943 Professor Brodetsky suggested that 'Much more should be done to make clear to the Jew that he was not only a victim of extermination and of anti-semitism, but that he was, in fact, the pioneer of civilisation today as much as he had been for thousands of years'.[3] Two months later Brodetsky declared that the Jews 'were not just a group of refugees waiting for Evian and Bermuda. They were not simply a group of beggars spending all their energies in begging people to save them. They were a people with a great ideal and with a great Law'.[4]

The Anglo-Jewish community's prevalent political and social philosophy stressed the traditional liberal view of graded stages of human progress. In such a philosophy the civilised and humanitarian, even if physically damaged, was at least spiritually victorious. Gollancz illustrated this same theme in 1942 with a story:

On a Day of Atonement before the War the SS men took a Jewish Rabbi in one of the concentration camps and whipped him; then they led him into the yard, where they had built up a pile of human excrement, and forced him knee-deep into it, and they put his praying shawl on him, and soiled the fringes of it, which are its most sacred part, with the dung, and that for him was an outrage even worse than the pain and shame of the whipping. Then they said to him, 'Now, Jew preach to us on this Day of Atonement about the Jewish religion' ... he said 'Meine Freunde' – my friends, to the SS men who had tormented him – 'My friends, the fundamental principle of the Jewish religion, as of all the other great religions of the world, is: Love thy neighbour as thyself'.[5]

To Gollancz, nobility was synonymous with humanity, and the refusal to hate one's enemy constituted the highest form of resistance.

On the home front the model was that of the English gentleman, a man who retained his dignity and honour even in times of great adversity and humiliation. Such dignity not only reflected on the victim, whose self-esteem remained intact, but also on the persecutors, whose own dignity, such as it was, was debased and shown for all its obscenity. Here the roles of victim and victor were interchanged and the vanquished, not the conqueror, was triumphant. Hence the *Jewish Chronicle*'s description of the synagogue ceremony at Bevis Marks on 13 December 1942, the Day of Fasting and Prayer called by Chief Rabbi Hertz. The Lord Mayor of London, a Jew, Sir Samuel Joseph,

took part in the Service, opening the Ark for the most poignant part of the service – the recital of the El Mole Rochamin ... It was an unforgettable moment ... [His] face was set, as he stood with head held high and gazed up into the holy ark. His erect, majestic bearing symbolised the undying spirit of his people. It was as a Jew that one saw him at that moment, one looked at his tallit rather than at his chain of office. 'I will outlive Hitler' seemed to be the expression of this Jew whose office proclaimed to the world that he was still recognised in this country as a man equal with his fellowman, even though others of evil mind conspired to consign him to oblivion.[6]

The mere fact of a man standing straight and staring ahead unblinking was thought in this way to undermine, even defeat, the enemy. The spirit remained unbroken, and it was this, not the body, that the Nazis wished above all to destroy. The very posture of the Jewish Lord Mayor of London challenged Hitler.

The role of the Jewish soldier fighting for the Allies was also of central importance in this same search for a model of resistance to

Nazism. The gentleman-soldier was depicted in such circumstances where Jewish Allied soldiers and commanders came into direct contact with Germans in British POW camps and military hospitals. Here again Jewish honour was demonstrated by restraint: no vengeance was wreaked upon even his bitterest foe. This symbolised the civilised man in contrast to the barbarian. Such acts of nobility contrasted with Nazi savagery. In a two-page lead story entitled 'Chivalry – As Befits a Kingdom of Priests' published in the *Jewish Chronicle* in April 1942, Captain (Rabbi) Louis Rabinowitz declared, 'the remarkable, the astonishing, the admirable fact is that on the basis of widespread experience, I can unhesitatingly aver that, with the Jews in this war opportunity has come, time and again, but the desire for revenge has been utterly stilled and killed and made of no effect by an unconscious application of the ethical teachings of Judaism'.[7] This model derived much from the liberal ideal of the civilised and humane and is seen once again in Rabinowitz's description of a Jewish commander of a POW camp:

He had formerly been in charge of Italian prisoners, and he expatiated on the better behaviour, greater cleanliness, and smarter discipline of his German prisoners. This attitude of unreserved appreciation of such praiseworthy qualities as the Germans revealed, struck me even more forcibly than the Jewish officer's kindness. A South African Jewish Captain escaped from the Germans told an attentive audience in the mess that the Germans treated their captured wounded with more consideration than did the Italians; a British Jewish medical officer spoke in terms of praise of their fortitude under pain, a Palestinian officer spoke of their readiness to help. Not a trace of an attempt to score even a verbal advantage over their enemies. The only temptation, which some Jewish men found themselves unable to resist, was to make it clear to their prisoners that they were Jews ... But, be it noted, in no single case so far recorded has Jewish aid been spurned by these Germans ... The simple set of facts which I have related are to me a brilliant example of Jewish ethical teachings put to the most difficult of tests, and finding a triumphant vindication. 'When thine enemy falleth, rejoice not'.[8]

This model of 'a warm sympathetic, helpful and even friendly attitude towards the foes that hated them'[9] gave the Jews back the dignity of which they had been robbed by the Nazis.

As Gollancz's story of the Rabbi on the Day of Atonement shows, this model was also applied to Jews living under Nazi rule. Dr Redcliffe N. Salaman, drawing on the politics of hope at the Lucien Wolf Memorial Lecture on 'Humanity and the Refugees' in February 1938, had stated: 'This 1,000 year old pain, nay 2,000 years of pain, may still not satisfy the lust of our persecutors, yet am I confident that Jewish courage and Jewish faith will triumph over cruelty and ignorance.'[10] It was this theme of courage and faith which was repeated in Israel Cohen's booklet 'The Jews in the War', produced by the Board of Deputies in June 1942. Of the Jews of Europe he stated: 'But great as is their agony, they bear it with unfaltering fortitude and indomitable faith, confident that the day must and will come when ... they will once again live in peace and liberty in a liberated Europe.'[11]

Even descriptions of the liberation of the death camps tried to depict the decrepit survivors as defiant and unyielding. The *Jewish Chronicle* reported on Louis Rabinowitz's depiction of entering Breendonck concentration camp in November 1944: 'Wherever he went, he said, he always found that despite the fact that all the mighty and ponderous machinery of German organisation had been pitted against the Jews, and despite the fact that they had lived miserable lives, their spirit was absolutely unbroken.'[12]

Some Jews, as described above, tried to turn evil into good by suggesting the cathartic and fortifying impact of adversity – a view which had its roots both in traditional Jewish thinking and in Anglo-Jewry's optimistic liberal philosophy. These desperate attempts to avoid conceding defeat even when defeated and to cling to hope became increasingly important as the war continued. But for the most part the need to find some model to replace the image of the passive European Jew spurred the creation of new paradigms. An assertion of Jewry's unbroken spirit was not sufficient. Increasingly a substantial part of the community sought a model of physical rather than spiritual strength as an antidote to charges of Jewish passivity. Stories of heroism and gallantry performed by Jewish soldiers frequently dominated the front page of the *Jewish Chronicle*. Of the nine front-page stories on 27 August 1943, for instance, five related to this model: 'Fearless Air-Gunner's DFM – Attacks on the Ruhr Valley', 'Valiant Soldiers, Red Army's Jewish Heroes', 'DFC for Deputy Flight Commander, Aircraft Captain in Famous Raids', '2 MMs for Middle East Gallantry', and 'Jewish Guerillas' Daring Rescue'.[13] This model was buttressed by the desire of British Jews to prove themselves loyal servants of the crown and to combat the accusation of shirking, but above all, it was badly needed for psychological reasons.

A stark distinction between the passivity of the Jews of Europe and the model of the fighting Jew is made in Louis Rabinowitz's report on the death, in July 1943, of three Jews who had escaped from Germany to England and subsequently volunteered. The need for those Jews under Hitlerite domination to provide a model of resistance is clear. The earlier model in which ethical superiority alone bestowed victory was now superseded.

> Three more Jews killed by Hitler, to be added to the millions of other Jews barbarously put to death by the Nazis. But what a difference between the death of these gallant soldiers and the fate which has overtaken their kindred! ... They had been killed by the Germans as perhaps their parents and brothers and sisters have been killed. But they died fighting, gallantly, wreaking the 'vengeance of the Lord' against his and their enemy. They died 'with their boots on' as men, with colours flying and honour high.[14]

When Jews died and fell in battle their deaths were contrasted with the horrible, even embarrassing, fate of their European brethren.

It was to this heroic fighting model that the community increasingly turned. As the *Jewish Chronicle* editorialised on 7 August 1942, 'If a people is confronted by a ruthless and implacable enemy intent on its complete destruction, do not honour and humanity cry, or rather shriek, that it be allowed the opportunity, as a people, to defend itself?'[15] In its black border issue of 11 December 1942 it stated, 'The Jew wishes to confront them [the Nazis] as Jew, sword in hand. That would at least be balm to his wounded spirit.'[16] John D. Mack MP declared, 'Jews of all categories are straining at the leash in order to participate in the real fight ... for they are implacable foes of Hitler and all his regime stands for.'[17]

This model sought to escape 'The Curse of Anonymity', as Rabinowitz described it in an article of that title in the *Jewish Chronicle* of 22 September 1944.[18] It was a model of the Jew to combat the one which had in many ways resulted from Anglo-Jewry's low-profile politics. For here it was assertion, not suppression, of national identity which would counter anti-semitism and bolster Jewish pride.

This Jewish assertiveness was not merely to be literary in form. Anglo-Jewish efforts to translate the model of a Jewish fighter into a concrete reality began early in the war and only increased after the first news of extermination. They drew initially on the exploits of the First World War Jewish Legion of Palestinian soldiers in the British Army,[19] and developed into a campaign for a separate Jewish fighting force within Allied ranks. Two organisations championed the cause, the Jewish Agency and the Anglo-American Committee for a Jewish Army. The Agency, which was the representative body of the Jews of Palestine and of mainstream General Zionist sympathisers in the Diaspora, had pressed for a force from as early as 1940. The campaign was enjoined in Britain by the Zionist Federation of Great Britain and Ireland (the British Jewish Community's main Zionist organisation and affiliated to the Agency) and by those working in the Agency office in London, particularly Berl Locker, Lewis Namier and Selig Brodetsky. Their campaign for a Jewish fighting force intensified when news of the extermination reached Britain, and between 23 August and 1 September 1942 the Zionist Federation of Great Britain and Ireland held eight mass meetings to call for the conversion of Jewish Battalions in a Palestine Regiment into a Jewish fighting force in the British army.[20]

This issue, however, was but one of many on the Federation's agenda, though it remained a policy aim throughout the war. The fourth annual conference meeting between 29 and 31 January 1944 'demanded the establishment of a Jewish fighting force to participate in the battle of Europe to help in the liberation of Jews and other enslaved peoples'.[21] The Federation's motives reflected in large measure the desire to play an active resisting role against Hitler. However the campaign had other political aims. An army was the symbol of the nation-state, and a Jewish army would thereby hasten the establishment of a Jewish national entity in Palestine.

The Agency's campaign for a Jewish army did not, however, have the flair, drama or imagination of that of the Anglo-American Committee. It would be incorrect to give the impression that the Committee commanded unequivocal support within British Jewry. Most of its Jewish leaders were situated on the periphery of the formal Jewish communal institutions and included such men as the Yiddishist and journalist Joseph Leftwich, the novelist Louis Golding and the Labour MP John D. Mack, a man who is universally ignored in the historiography of Anglo-Jewry, and yet was constantly engaged in attempts to relieve the Jewish plight in Europe. However, many of the Community's leading figures did at various stages lend their names to the Committee's activities. The campaign was also actively supported, as we have seen, by many non-Jewish politicians and statesmen, notably Lord Strabolgi and Field-

Marshal Sir Philip Chetwode, unfettered as were most British Jews, by the fear of asserting Jewish national identity.

The Committee was consistently supported by the *Jewish Chronicle*, which saw in the creation of a Jewish army a source of pride. In its editorial 'Massacre', in the 3 July 1942 issue, the first issue to publish details of planned extermination, the *Chronicle* urged the formation of 'a Jewish Army that could show by its valour that Jews are not the feeble, ready-made prey of assassins and adventurers, but a people that can and assuredly will strike back'.[22] Continuing this theme a month later, the paper declared, 'The question of a Jewish Army is a question of Jewish honour, of Jewish self-respect'; were Jews 'to rely upon the old schnorrerie whose pitiful course has been marked through the centuries by retrogression on the heels of progress, by derision, by contumely and futility?'[23] It was this rhetorical question that the Committee sought to answer. Its slogan declared, 'We shall no longer witness with pity alone', and its call to arms was badly needed by Anglo-Jewry in the face of the European Jewish plight.

The campaign's Executive Director, United States Captain Jeremiah Helpern, was sent to Britain to organise on behalf of the American parent body. This body was supported primarily by Revisionist Zionists of whom Hillel Kook was the most prominent. The Committee nonetheless attracted many non-Zionists to its ranks and satisfied a widespread need amongst Western Jews for a model of a Jewish fighter. Helpern declared, 'the main aim of my Committee remains to work for the creation of the Jewish Army of Stateless and Palestinian Jews and of volunteers, to fight on all required battle-fields, under the Jewish flag, so that Jews will at last be recognised as a fighting ally'.[24] The Committee's first manifesto was issued in January 1943 in the wake of the Allied Declaration of December 1942. Its front cover bore Arthur Szyk's cartoon logo: 'inspired by the ghastly massacre of Jewish people demanding the elementary right to fight AS JEWS against the ruthless murderers of our people'.[25] The Committee declared that 'about a million Jews are serving with the Allied forces ... They are the brothers and sisters of the millions tortured and massacred by Hitler and his satellites. They demand the right to fight for their fellow Jews on the battlefield and to be recognised as a fighting Ally'.[26] The manifesto proclaimed

That we shall no longer witness with pity alone, and with passive sympathy, the calculated extermination of the Jewish people ... Every footstep of the Jew in Europe is stained with his own blood ... They are caught between

the blows of Hitler's hammer and the anvil of our own passive sympathy ...
To commiserate is not enough. Our pity will not stay the doom of millions
more. To pride ourselves on tolerance and good-will and to make pre-
dictions and promises that after the war everybody and everything will
naturally slip back into place, is an evasion of the harrowing reality. We
will be guilty if we do not change our present aloof attitude to a positive,
bold course of moral action. An end will be put to the scandal of history, of
a great and ancient people compelled to haunt the corridors of time as
ghosts and beggars and waifs of every storm that rages. Thus our war-torn
world will witness the Army of the Fighting Jew.[27]

Such assertions ran counter to much of the deeply-held philosophy
of Anglo-Jewry, which sought to de-emphasise Jewry's national
identity and stressed a low profile and philanthropy. Whilst the
Committee was partly a rebellion against such ideas, it attracted
much interest and support even from central figures on the communal stage. Its Jewish supporters emphasised openly that its message
was contrary to mainstream Anglo-Jewish thinking. Joseph Leftwich, a leading advocate, speaking at Conway Hall on 12 April 1943
declared,

I would prefer the Jewish Army in this war to fight ... in Europe – to get to
grips there with Hitler's Nazi armies ... I hate Jewish anonymity. I want to
give expression to Jewish identity. And I will gladly risk other things to
secure Jewish identity. I cannot understand why any Jew objects to it. We
are Jews. We must show ourselves as Jews ... what else can we do than fight
as Jews, against those who vilify Judaism, who destroy our Synagogues and
burn our Scrolls? ... Should not Jews take part as a Jewish entity in the
fighting to bring about their overthrow? I advocate a Jewish Army because
I want to put an end to the cursed Jewish anonymity, because I want the
Jews to stand out in this war against Hitlerism as an entity. Nothing can
cure anti-Semitism except the disappearance of the Jews ... I demand a
Jewish Army, because I am not chasing after cures for anti-Semitism, but
because I want Jews to have a chance to stand up for themselves as Jews, to
hit back at their enemy as Jews, to demonstrate in this war in which we are
being attacked and exterminated as Jews that we can also defend ourselves
as Jews, that we can fight back as Jews, that we are a Jewish entity.[28]

At another meeting, held on 18 November 1943 in the Conway Hall,
John Mack betrayed his assumptions regarding the passivity of
European Jews. 'The Jews who had fought against Haman, against
Titus, the Jews who had fought with the Maccabeans, and had stood
out against the Inquisition, had not been cringing, grovelling
Jews.'[29] The Jewish army, declared Mack at a parliamentary

support meeting in June 1944, was 'to fight in [Allied Forces'] ranks for the vindication of their honour.'[30] It was, according to Dr Redcliffe Salaman (the Medical Officer of the Jewish Legion in the First World War), 'the Jews' natural and logical answer to the forces of evil'.[31]

The need for a new model Jew was so great that almost all in the community were prepared to challenge traditional low-profile political strategies. Selig Brodetsky himself, in a message to the Committee, indicated how desperately such new images were needed. The Committee's fourth publication printed Brodetsky's message of July 1944 under the headline 'Recognition of Jews Fighting in War not given in any Sense Corresponding to Greatness of Disaster that has overtaken Jewry and Heroism shown by Jews writes Professor Brodetsky'. The publication went on to explain this ambiguous statement. Brodetsky declared that 'It is true that the recognition ... of the hundreds of thousands of Jews who are fighting in every army of the United Nations is not given them in any sense corresponding to the greatness of the disaster that has overtaken Jewry, and of the heroism shown by Jews in every form of warfare.'[32] The language is confusing but the sense is clear: Brodetsky wished to de-emphasise the prevalent image of European Jews, and to do this required placing stress on the Jewish fighting model.

The old taboos died hard, and a few British Jews publicly opposed a Jewish fighting entity, so profound was its contradiction of their view of the emancipation contract. In a House of Commons debate on the formation of a Jewish army, held on 6 August 1942, the Independent MP Daniel Lipson was reported by the *Jewish Chronicle*:

Mr Lipson, who said he was a Jew, expressed gratitude to members for the sympathy shown for the Jews, and reminded the House that Jews were serving in the British Army. Mr Lipson proceeded to expound the 'dual nationality' argument against Jewish nationalism. The anti-semites argue that the Jews are a separate people, and that it is how they justify the discrimination which is exercised against them in various parts of the world. The argument is also supported by the views put forward by Jewish Nationalists, who also talk about a Jewish people. You could not have the best of both worlds. You could not claim all the advantages of a member of the Jewish people and also say I am British or French or American with equal rights with other citizens. He believed that if Jews fought together with non-Jews they would get to understand each other better. 'This was not the time when one wants to emphasise the differences between Jew and non-Jew.' It was for this reason that he could not support the proposal.[33]

To some Jews, in fact, this issue proved so embarrassing that they refused even to acknowledge its existence on the public agenda. Leonard Stein replied to allegations in July 1943 that the Joint Foreign Committee had opposed the Jewish army by declaring that 'the question of the Jewish Army had never come before the Joint Foreign Committee in any shape or form. They had never discussed it'[34] – a most revealing omission since Parliament itself had debated the issue. When a Jewish Brigade of Palestinian Jews was finally formed by the British government in September 1944, Sir Jack Brunel Cohen and Basil Henriques wrote to the *Times* opposing the move.[35]

The Warsaw Ghetto uprising of April 1943 was used to support a similar model of the Jewish fighter. Some British Jews saw the Warsaw Revolt as a negation of the widespread image of the Jew passively assaulted by Nazism. The revolt was contrasted with alternative, less attractive images. Joseph Leftwich declared, 'these were Jews who refused to die like sheep. They sold their lives bravely. There was gratification that Jews had shown themselves as brave as any other peoples fighting against Hitlerite domination.'[36] The uprising restored pride. This heroic episode provided the spur for a strengthened model of the Jewish fighter inspired by biblical progenitors, the Maccabees, who were now increasingly invoked as portraits of the strong Jew. Harold Laski wrote in 1944 of 'those half-armed Jews who, in the ghetto of Warsaw, made their Nazi task masters, with tanks and aeroplanes and heavy guns, give life for life before they died, make one realise that the tradition of Judas Maccabeas still proudly lives'.[37] The Chief Rabbi, J. H. Hertz, echoed this sentiment and added another image in a radio broadcast of August 1943: 'For staggering courage, this Battle of Warsaw is unsurpassed in the whole history of heroism. It is an epic struggle that recalls the glories of the Maccabees and the sublime self-slaughter of the defenders of Masada.'[38]

Such statements were signs of an attempt within the community to maintain hope and sustain morale. A model of a Jewish fighter was badly needed to contrast with British Jewry's own low self-esteem and with its beliefs concerning Jewish passivity in Europe. The Maccabees and the heroes of Masada were bands of national zealots who in Jewish tradition represented the Jewish fighting spirit, and their motif was a valuable prop in the formulation of a paradigm of physical resistance – a paradigm that was increasingly

applied to the Jews of Palestine. These were contrasted sharply with
the Jews of Europe. As Brodetsky mused in his memoirs on the
possibility of a German advance to Palestine, he asked, 'What would
be the fate of the Jews in Palestine if the Germans got there? We
know how they were massacring the Jews of Europe.' He answers
himself in the next sentence. 'The Jews of Palestine had no doubt
what was in store for them and they prepared to fight and sell their
lives dear, like the Maccabeans of old.'[39] Lewis Namier, in a letter to
Lord Moyne as early as 22 April 1941, had spelt out the two Jewish
models explicitly. 'There are ways of dying: defenceless Jews have
perished in pogroms in the Dispersion, or had to fly for life; the Jews
will not evacuate Palestine (even were this possible), nor will they let
themselves be slaughtered like sheep in a shambles. Their manner of
meeting their doom would count for all future in Jewish history.'[40]
The Jews of Palestine, unlike their European brethren, were not
afflicted with the curse of anonymity. Elsewhere he declared, 'The
Jews of Palestine ... have the privilege to be the only Jews in the
world who as Jews are fighting on behalf of civilisation against the
attack of the Nazis.'[41]

The search for a model of a Jewish fighting spirit, for Jewish
creativity in a landscape of destruction, for hope in despair, led to an
increasing emphasis on Zionism and the construction of the Land of
Israel. Zionism became the most radical Anglo-Jewish response to
the Nazi extermination of the Jews in Europe, and, as such, will
constitute the final section of this book.

ZIONISM

Zionism, the political ideology advocating the recreation of a Jewish
homeland in the Land of Israel, was not of course new to Britain. It
had existed at least since Herzl visited London in 1895. But during
the years of the Second World War it came to dominate the Jewish
institutional scene. Its philosophy drew on messianic impulses which
had been a feature of Jewish thought throughout history. But there
was more to it than millennarian expectations. Substantial numbers
of Jews were already in Palestine building up an infrastructure at a
rapid pace. Governments, including the British through the Balfour
Declaration, had, however equivocally, given the enterprise their
blessing. Zionism's promise of a radical transformation in Jewish life
and a Jewish return to Palestine naturally excited British Jews as it
did Jews everywhere, particularly at a time when Hitler had so

radically exposed the inadequacies of liberal conceptions of the world. More than that, Hitler had exploited the stereotype of the Jew as non-creative and many British Jews badly needed to negate this image; Zionism provided a means of so doing.

At its root, as John Mack told the Barcai Zionist Society in December 1944, Zionism taught that the Jews 'were a second-class nation because they held no land adequately of their own'.[42] The landless Jew was the suppliant Jew and Zionism could eradicate this image. As the *Jewish Chronicle* editorialised on 5 June 1942:

By removing the stigma of homelessness and the brand of the 'tolerated' stranger from the brow of the Jew, Zionism gave fair promise to raise his status in the eyes of the world, and make his grotesque classification by dictator brutes as 'second-class' or 'subhuman' more than ever absurd. By giving him a normal place in the family of nations this shameful moral crucifixion will be made a political impossibility. And the fact that the Jew will thus naturally enjoy the same rights and status as other peoples, will give him as Jew, a true spiritual freedom and that self-respect – the sole key to the respect of others – which must in due course impress itself upon his whole demeanour, his outlook on life, his faith in himself and his future.[43]

Zionism thus constituted a reaction to the classical emancipatory view of Jewish life in modern Western society, for according to Zionism it was the assertion and not the denial of Jewish identity that was the most effective antidote to anti-semitism. The same *Jewish Chronicle* leader continued: 'Against such a spiritually reborn Jewry, anti-semitism, the foe of all mankind, must, in the end, seek to poison the minds of men with dwindling chances of success.' Indeed the newspaper went on to declare even more emphatically that Zionism 'is the one movement which holds hope of banishing anti-semitism, this foul aberration'.[44]

In the face of calamity, Zionism suggested a comprehensive solution to the Jewish problem, and as a result became an irresistible attraction. On 6 March 1942, as the first reports from Europe arrived, a three-quarter-page advertisement in the *Jewish Chronicle* for the Second Palestine War Appeal signed by Chief Rabbi Hertz, Eva Marchioness of Reading, Simon Marks, Selig Brodetsky, Berl Locker and Barnet Janner, as well as Chaim Weizmann, declared:

We must build for our people and our people's spirit a hope which can resist the storms of time and the malice of our enemies. That home can only be a Jewish Palestine. The part which Palestine must play in the life of our people has been made immeasurably greater by all the harrowing of the war. It is the hope and life of our people, not only of the hunted millions but of each and every one of us. It is for that Palestine, that Jewish future, that the Keren Hayesod appeals to you.[45]

Hitler had exposed Jewish impotence which the Jews increasingly now conceived as having been bred out of homelessness. Zionism called for the restoration of a Jewish home and its advocates now constantly used the Nazi extermination as proof of their thesis. As Namier wrote to the *Times* on 5 December 1942, 'The Jews claim the right to establish a free Jewish Commonwealth in Palestine. The blood of a million Jews murdered by the Nazis cries to heaven, the world-wide Jewish problem calls for a solution. It has its roots in Jewish homelessness; in Palestine, and through Palestine alone, can a solution be found.'[46] In an address to the 23rd Annual Conference of the Inter-University Jewish Federation in Manchester in January 1942, Namier declared that

the stigma of inferiority which Hitler had cast upon the whole of the Jewish people could only be wiped away if the Jews secured recognition of their nationhood ... The four or more million Jews in Central and Eastern Europe must, after the war, be given the chance of a new life in the Jewish state of Palestine, and the establishment of this state must become from now on the most important endeavour of all Jewish endeavours throughout the world.[47]

Of course, even according to Namier, the rise of Zionism did not signal the end of Jewish liberalism in Britain. Zionism was viewed, as it had always been viewed by Anglo-Jewry, mainly as refugeeism. Few British Jews saw Zionism necessitating the abandonment of Diaspora. But it increasingly came to be seen as an answer to the Jewish problem in those countries under Nazi domination where liberalism, democracy and emancipation now seemed so remote. Moreover, few at the time could conceive of the goal of attaining a homeland and that of saving the Jews in Europe as conflicting; rather they saw them as identical. As Brodetsky wrote in an essay on the Balfour Declaration in 1942, an essay characterised by a force-fulness and stridency uncommon for an Anglo-Jewish leader, 'the urgent task to-day is to rescue Jews from immediate destruction, and Palestine is the obvious cure for these broken lives.'[48] Palestine became synonymous, not only for lifelong Zionists like Brodetsky but for most of British Jewry, with the Jewish future. As Brodetsky explained: 'Jews shall be free to go to Palestine, for without Jewish escape from the tragedy of Europe we cannot have Jewish life.'[49]

The Zionist idea and its goal came to dominate the thinking and planning of Anglo-Jewry – a small ray of light which distracted attention from so much darkness. The existence of the Zionist dream as an alternative to the catastrophic reality of continental Europe enabled English Jews to be resigned, despite their knowledge of what was occurring in Europe, and yet still hopeful. Zionism, like Anglo-Jewry's philanthropic relief work, allowed Jewish leaders to discuss plans for post-war European Jewish resettlement, at a time when most of Europe's Jews were being killed. The concentration on refugee relief was connected, it was felt, with the role refugees would play in the future building of Israel. From early in the war Anglo-Jewry, Zionists and non-Zionists alike, became preoccupied with long-range political goals placing considerable stress on post-war solutions to the Jewish problem and concentrating primarily on Palestine. Concentration on post-war planning had after all received the highest form of third-party endorsement: Churchill, in his oft-quoted message on the Centenary of the *Jewish Chronicle* in 1941, had stressed this point. 'The Jews bore the brunt of the first onslaught upon the citadels of freedom and human dignity. Assuredly in the day of victory, the Jew's suffering and his part in the struggle will not be forgotten.'[50]

Of course, post-war planning was not wholly devoted to Palestine, as too much emphasis on this subject would have placed question-marks over Anglo-Jewry's own future and loyalties. When the Board of Deputies first discussed post-war European Jewry in December 1941, it addressed 'the question of political equality for Jewish citizens in all States'.[51] Post-war planning often dominated present-day concerns. At the next meeting, the deputy for Vine Court Synagogue, Mr D. Brotmacher, said, 'they did not merely want sympathy – they wanted equality ... Therefore, their attention should be directed to the post-war problem and not so much to the collection of records of atrocities.'[52] Brodetsky agreed. In his speech of July 1942 entitled 'The Jewish People at the Coming Peace Conference' he made no mention of Nazi atrocities but rather spoke of worldwide anti-semitism, Soviet Jewry, and Jewish emigration to Palestine.[53] Throughout the years in question, post-war planning and Palestine were the pre-eminent topics of discussion of the Board of Deputies' Foreign Committee. It held two separate two-day conferences on post-war Jewry – unusually organised activities for the Jewish community. The first was held on 3 and 4 August 1942 and discussed 'aspects of the Jewish question under the main heads of relief and reconstruction; regularisation of the status of Jews in post-war Europe; Palestine; means of co-operation with Governments and Jewish organisations'.[54] The second, on 'Planning Post-War Relief' addressed similar topics in January 1943.[55] In 1944 the Contemporary Jewish Record, in line with such thinking, noted that 'the vital need for immediate rescue measures, however, did not eclipse the significance of long-range problems which would accompany the cessation of hostilities'.[56] In November 1944 the Board issued its 'Statement on Post-War Policy', a report calling for the establishment of a Jewish State in Palestine and for the reinstatement of Jewish rights in continental Europe.

The Board was by no means the only Jewish organisation so to concentrate on post-war planning. The same was true of the Anglo-Jewish Association as well as the Zionist Federation. In January 1944, at the annual conference of the Inter-University Jewish Federation, Britain's largest Jewish student body, the Jewish Chronicle reported that 'the prospect of victory over Nazism during the coming year gave the agenda a post-war bias, and for three days ... there was a discussion on various aspects of Jewish life in the post-war world'.[57]

The themes of post-war planning and Palestine ultimately merged into one. Of course, these issues were pushed into the forefront by Britain's Mandate over Palestine and the considerable debate and anxiety over Jewish nationhood. As a result Zionism, or at least the building of a Jewish entity in Palestine, now captured the imaginations of the Anglo-Jewish community and dominated discussions of foreign affairs. Brodetsky notes in his memoirs, 'In May 1942 I delivered the seventh Lucien Wolf Memorial Lecture ... My subject was "The Place of the Jews in the Post-War Settlement". I concentrated, of course, on Palestine as a land for the Jews.'[58] As we have seen, for Brodetsky, as for most other Anglo-Jewish leaders, the homeland goal and the rescue goal were synonymous. Later that same month Brodetsky said that the Board of Deputies' Executive should seek the abrogation of the 1939 White Paper on immigration into Palestine, in order to 'deal with the whole problem of what was to happen to Jewish refugees who wished to escape from Nazi persecution'.[59] The Zionist Federation of Great Britain and Ireland, having given their 'complete support for the Biltmore Policy' (the World Zionist Organisation's programme of May 1942 advocating that all of Palestine should become a Jewish state) at their 42nd annual conference in January 1943,[60] never wavered in their support for it until the end of the war, although the millions for whom it was intended had, as was widely known, already perished.[61] As we have noted, on the philanthropic front most of the funds contributed to Palestine earmarked ten per cent of their allocations for the purpose of rescue from Europe.[62] In a statement issued by the Conference on Palestine and Post-War Problems held under the auspices of the Council of Manchester and Salford Jews on 25 June 1944 and 'representative of all sections of the Jewish Community of Manchester, Salford and South East Lancashire', an appeal was made to 'H.M.G. to hasten all efforts for the rescue of the Jews in Nazi-occupied Europe and urges that Palestine, being the only country capable of giving sanctuary and refuge, be opened freely to those helpless victims of Nazi persecution'.[63]

Palestine would restore power to the hopeless and impotent. Zionist thinking interpreted the Nazi extermination in terms of a continuum in which creation would quite naturally follow destruction. The destruction of European jewry was juxtaposed with achievements in Palestine. Such parallelism affected perceptions of reality and hence the ordering of priorities.

The *Jewish Chronicle* reported a speech by Noah Barou of the Jewish Agency in London in honour of the King of Denmark in March 1944:

They were living in a time in which the main problems of the Jewish people, grim and great though they were, were problems that would arise when the war came to its victorious close than in the agony of these war years themselves. It behoved them ... to erect a monument to their dead [i.e. Palestine], worthy in every sense of the word of the sacrifice that they had made.[64]

The theme of imminent victory, which justified the concentration on post-war planning, was constant from 1942. Even when Brodetsky addressed the South East London Zionist Society on 27 June 1943 and referred to 'the fallacy of "waiting for victory" before saving measures could be undertaken', the saving measure he wished for, 'the only solution' and one which inevitably would have to wait until the end of the War, was a 'Jewish State in the Land of Israel'.[65]

Such an emphasis diverted attention from events in Europe. Thus the front page of the *Jewish Chronicle* of 6 November 1942 carried a report on the meeting for the 25th Anniversary of the Balfour Declaration (also the sole subject of that issue's editorial); included on the same page were three reports of Jews decorated in British forces and a list of medals awarded to South African Jews. The report of the Albert Hall protest demonstration, the first organised communal event following the news of exterminations, appeared on page 5.

The Zionist leadership did much to encourage combining homeland-related and rescue goals. The Palestinian Jew, the fighting model, was the saviour of those caught in the grip of the Nazis. On 1 June 1944 Chaim Weizmann addressed, for the first time, a Board of Deputies' plenary session. He disclosed his involvement in rescue operations (it was the abortive Brand mission he referred to), censured world Jewry for not doing enough, and lauded the extensive rescue efforts being made by the Jewish community of Palestine. 'They have even helped in the fight of the Warsaw ghetto.'[66] Help to get refugees to Palestine, though the number of these was very small, precluded alternative strategies such as pressure on Axis satellite countries. Such tactics were simply not considered.

Zionist rhetoric was strident and combative; in contrast the rhetoric of rescue was that of the petitioner. Thus the *Contemporary Jewish Record* of 1944 states that 'In addition to voicing Zionist demands, the Federation of Women Zionists of Great Britain and Ireland in annual conference November 8–9 protested against the arms trials (in Palestine) and appealed for the rescue of the Jews of Europe.'[67]

Viewing the past from the vantage-point of the Holocaust, Zionists hurled recriminations against their erstwhile opponents. In an address to the Anglo-Palestinian Club in December 1944, Brodetsky said:

The solution of the Jewish problem did not consist of getting Jews to settle down again to their old lives before disaster came to them ... If after the last war they had spent less of their money in helping Jews in Poland and other countries, and used more money for the purposes of encouraging these Jews to settle in Palestine then their disasters in the last few years would have been very much smaller.[68]

Namier, in a two-page article 'The Jewish Problem Re-argued: A Palestine State the Only Solution?' published in the *Manchester Guardian* on 16 November 1943, pointed the finger at the British Government:

[W]ith the McDonald White Paper substituted for the Royal Commission 1937 Report hundreds of thousands perished in agony who might have been saved. The existence of a Jewish State, even in a partitioned Palestine, would have enabled the Jews to play their part in this war as a nation and the name and flag of the Jews, Hitler's foremost victims and enemies, would have appeared among the United Nations, which has never been allowed to happen.[69]

In his essay on the political significance of the Balfour Declaration published in 1943, Brodetsky saw Zionism as redeeming the bond of Hitlerism.

The Balfour Declaration of 2nd November 1917, the first Declaration concerning the Jews, which promised release and freedom to Jewry, was followed by a second international Declaration concerning the Jews twenty-five years later, on 17th December 1942, declaring the agony of Jewry. The second Declaration promises retribution to the criminals, but says nothing of the salvation of Jewry – and our task today is to bring the world back to the idealism of the first Declaration ... the time will soon come when the realisation of the Declaration of 1917 will have wiped out the memory of the Declaration of 1942.[70]

Brodetsky continued:

If for a generation we have been divorced from the real aim of Zionism as intended by the Balfour Declaration, both the glory of achievement in Palestine and the extermination policy of Nazi Europe, force us to come back to it now, so as to establish our future on sound principles. A clear statement of the principles upon which the future of Jewry is to be based is indispensable now and the civilised world expects this in the face of our European tragedy.[71]

Zionism constituted the prospect of Jewish creation in a landscape of destruction, a concrete model of activism. John D. Mack told the *Jewish Chronicle* in July 1944, 'for centuries the Jews had helped others to build their lands and in many respects their contribution had not been credited to them. Only in their own land of Palestine could they build up something fine for themselves.'[72]

For some, Hitler's war was the prophesied Armageddon, the war of Gog and Magog, from which Israel would emerge triumphant. Such mythology was sorely needed, particularly now with the destruction of the Jewish heartland in Europe. Generally, of course, all wars are seen as redemptive, and the Second World War was no exception. The same is true of Zionism. It muted feelings of despair and constituted, it seemed, the most powerful form of resistance.

Zionism was the phoenix rising from the ashes of the crematoria. As Brodetsky declared at the Albert Hall Protest Meeting in October 1942, 'above all, the healing effect of Palestine must bring happiness to Jewry, and once again bring light to the world'.[73] The preface of Paul Goodman's *The Jewish National Home*, a collection of British Jewish essays on the 25th Anniversary of the Balfour Declaration published in 1943, declared itself 'a commemorative volume record-ing this greatest and most far-reaching event in modern Jewish history'.[74] The Nazi extermination of the Jews was offset by the Zionist ideal: 'An unimaginable tragedy has now overtaken Israel, but the night would have been even darker but for the New Judaea which is, to a large extent, the creation of the Balfour Declaration.'[75] A fund-raising appeal for the Jewish Agency which appeared on 13 October 1944 declared, 'My Yeshiva has been destroyed by the Huns. All over Eastern Europe the fountains of Jewish wisdom and learning are in ruins. But Palestine is filling the gap torn by savage destruction. Eretz Yisrael is again becoming the centre of Jewish learning "For out of Zion shall go forth the Law".'[76]

The lawyer and academic Norman Bentwich was perhaps the most eloquent advocate of Zionism as the antithesis of Hitlerism. Drawing on much in the politics of hope and on traditional religious understandings, he prefaced his *Wanderer between Two Worlds* (published in February 1941) in optimistic vein.

The book has been written in hours of darkness, while the freedom of Europe is crushed, and untold masses are physically and intellectually homeless. Yet I deem myself happy in my lot and my generation, and know that the Jews have something within that survives disaster, and that we are living now not only at our greatest hour, but at one of the turning points of humanity.[77]

Zionism was the cause of his optimism, for Jews 'entered the new era a stronger and more united people than they had been twenty-five years before, and conscious of a revival of their creative powers'.[78] This spiritual revival was bred directly from the European persecu-tion, for it 'may be detected in Palestine and in the young generation which has been thrown out of Germany'. There were two worlds of Jewry: 'one dead, one struggling to be born'.[79] In his memoirs Bentwich recalled November 1942, when he attended

two large Jewish gatherings which were sharply contrasted occasions of sorrow and tribute to achievement. One was a mass meeting at Albert Hall to voice the indignation of the heads of the religious communities, the

Allied Nations, and the political leaders, at the last infamy of the Nazis against the Jews of Europe. The other was a mass meeting to celebrate the twenty-fifth anniversary of the giving of the Balfour Declaration and to hear the testimony of leaders of English opinion to what Jews had done in the National Home. We had reached a supreme crisis in the history of the most historical of peoples; destruction and extermination were in one side of the balance and regeneration and fresh hope were in the other.[80]

As the war went on, Bentwich's rhetoric became more revivalist as the news from Europe further depressed him. It reached its apogee in his 1944 work significantly entitled *Judaea Lives Again*. His introduction spells out his almost messianic chronology. 'Hitler's savage persecution, with its frenzied and diabolical execution in Europe of the policy "Perish Judah", has provoked the response of "Judaea Revived".'[81] Zionism was for him most clearly an escape from Hitlerism.

During the last years of unparalleled ruin and suffering of the Jews in Europe, and unparalleled attack and stirring of hatred against the Jews everywhere, Jews inevitably have fallen back on mutual aid and encouragement, which is the lowest common denominator of solidarity against the foe. Their negative solidarity makes it more urgent for them to discover a bond of union other and higher than defence against anti-semitism. Nothing is more unwholesome and more destructive of spiritual integrity than the morbid interest in the manifestations of Jew-hatred. The Jewish revival affords a prospect of redemption from the slough of despond.

This revival in Israel would, he suggested,

lead on to the constructive achievement and transformation of Jewish life outside the land, which will mitigate the hostility against the Jews. They give at this period of crisis, when masses have been uprooted and events threaten to crush all vision and hope, a sense of a present creative power which constitutes the highest common denominator amongst the Jews throughout the world, and is an incontestable witness to the power of the spirit.

Emancipatory politics had not withstood the test of Nazism. Only the higher form of creation could assuage the depression of spirit – it alone could restore Jewish pride. 'The land of Israel is called in the Bible the Land of the Stag; and it is in that land that the Jew regenerated holds his head high as a stag.'[82]

This proud Jew offered the model that British Jewry required to balance with that of the homeless, vulnerable and abnormal Jew so widespread in the communal consciousness. Zionism came to be seen by many of them in these years as the single, all-embracing solution to anti-semitism, and therein lay its appeal. For though the subject of the Jewish settlement in Palestine did, of course, merit a prominent place on the communal agenda, it effectively dominated Anglo-Jewry to the exclusion of all else. Hitler's war posed the Jewish question in its starkest terms, and British Jewry sought and found one comprehensive answer to the sordid realities of the Holocaust.

British Jewish policy looked to the future rather than the present. As Eva Marchioness of Reading recorded of her work as President of the World Jewish Congress British Section, 'We were borne hopelessly on the tide of war, and our planning was for a future none of us could forsee. Nevertheless, Palestine remained in the centre of our thoughts, what it could do for our people, and what we could contribute to its well-being.'[83] In their records of this period, Anglo-Jewish leaders frequently recall their sharply alternating moods. Optimism was as much a reaction to depression as was gloom. For example, Lewis Namier's wife wrote that 'at times he would be consumed by an intense gloom, at others by an unshakeable optimism that the war, in spite of its horrors, would prove to be the catalyst for the creation of a Jewish sovereign state, the realisation of his most cherished dream'.[84]

Doubts were occasionally expressed, but far less frequently than one would otherwise imagine, even in literature produced long after the war. In a New Year Message to a South African Zionist newspaper in October 1943, Cecil Roth wrote:

I cannot repress the suspicion that our leaders (such as they are) are living in a fools' paradise, largely of their own construction. Zionists have as their mainstay the conviction that on the conclusion of the war the Jewish National Home in Palestine is at last going to be implemented. Non-Zionists, even more gullibly expect the Age of Emancipation, which we knew before 1933, to be renewed ... Both parties seem to me, however, to be blinding themselves, whether deliberately or not, to the facts ... We Jews are a broken remnant.[85]

Elsewhere Roth himself frequently championed both Zionism and liberalism, but such contradictions, as I have shown, were not uncommon in Anglo-Jewry. Even Bentwich, a British Zionist who placed great emphasis on messianism, wrote to the *Jewish Chronicle* in August 1944, pointing to the inadequacies of concentration on one goal. 'It is not just and not good Zionism to claim that all Jewish refugees turn to Palestine, and can hope to find a home only in Palestine.'[86]

But on the whole, Anglo-Jewry credited the Hitlerite extermination with the increase of support for Zionism. Elsewhere, in his May 1942 lecture on 'Jews in the Post-War Settlement', Brodetsky had even found some good arising from the horror of Nazi persecution. 'It will be a fine thing if the Nazi contribution will help to rebuild Palestine – what a contribution this will be to future historians!'[87] Chief Rabbi Hertz approvingly quoted Weizmann: מה שלא יעשה השכל יעשה היטלר (Hitler does things that Reason would never do).[88] Later he summarised Zionism's appeal: 'We feel that the miracle of Jewish Palestine ... has fully justified our dream and sacrifices of the past, and will yet prove the salvation of large portions of our hounded European brethren. We are the people of Hope.'[89]

Zionism was the hopeful image of the Jew resurgent, the fighting Jew. As such it was, moreover, the reassertion of identity and autonomy which had been denied Anglo-Jewry since the emancipation. This alone combated the frustrations of the powerlessness that resulted from the community's own socio-political philosophies. Zionism, then, was in many ways as much a refuge from Anglo-Jewish realities as it was from the realities of the European Holocaust.

Conclusion

This book has outlined the British Jewish community's socio-political philosophy and demonstrated how it shaped this Jewry's response to the fate of European Jews between 1942 and 1945. Indeed, Anglo-Jewry's response to the Holocaust exemplified its reactions to a wide range of matters in the external, Gentile world.

A narrative account of the statements, or even the actions, of Anglo-Jewish leaders concerning the Jews of Europe tells only part of the story. I have tried to show, in addition, why some things were said (or done) and others were not. In doing so, I have underlined the constraints on word and deed felt by British Jews. Such constraints were the product of Anglo-Jewry's perceptions of its history, of its place in contemporary British society and, at its most fundamental level, of its own Jewishness. These perceptions dictated the strategies which the community felt were feasible in a Gentile environment. Wartime conditions in Britain, and the destruction of the Jewries of Europe, brought these perceptions and their resultant constraints into clear focus. This most profound crisis, in effect, stretched Anglo-Jewry to its limit. A study of its reactions to the Holocaust thus illuminates Anglo-Jewry's attitudinal landscape.

In the course of the work several themes have emerged. During the years in question, for that matter as at most times, the community was beset by conflict. The bitter contention over Zionism which dominated the community stemmed from a struggle for power and prestige fought between two social strata. Much time and energy were devoted to this battle. Approaches to government on all issues were now made by a number of bodies claiming to represent Anglo-Jewry and deriving status from various sources. What effectiveness there had previously been in *shtadlanut* was diminished by this overlapping of communal representations and its resultant inefficiency. No dominant Anglo-Jewish leadership emerged; Jewish communal politics did not attract many talented British Jews; and there was little serious analysis of the political alternatives available to the community. British Jews were self-interested and distracted and were as preoccupied with their most immediate concerns as were others.

The emancipation of the Jews in England had given birth to two contradictory, yet simultaneously held, convictions. The first was a fundamental belief in the liberal view of the development of human society. Liberal democracy was the ultimate form of political achievement. The government existed to preserve life and prevent suffering, and its leaders, like Churchill or Roosevelt, embodied this mission. Right would always prevail and the condition of Jewry was the barometer of liberalism. This optimistic philosophy suggested a hopeful view of the Jew's position in British society. Anti-semitism was seen as a uniform phenomenon wherever it was encountered and it was, in any event, in its death throes. It was economic stress that had thrown Germany into temporary insanity, and appeals to human goodness would ultimately bring about an end to Nazi persecution of the Jews. When this strategy failed there was little else to replace it.

The other emancipatory philosophy stressed the contract between the Jew and the Gentile state, where religion was the only feature distinguishing Jew from non-Jew. Non-theological assertions by Jews on Jewish matters might imply dual loyalty, and this inclination resulted in what I have called the politics of fear. British Jewish political strategy stressed as a result the need to maintain a low profile and shunned any suggestion of Jewish nationality. Responses to atrocities committed on Jews were subsumed in general condemnation of Nazi brutality. Non-Jews were viewed as more effective advocates on Jewish matters than Jews. Gratitude and loyalty to Britain were unendingly proclaimed. Philanthropy was a preferred strategy to overt political lobbying, as it was self-contained, mostly unseen by the Gentile world, and therefore avoided accusations of Jewish clannish cosmopolitanism.

Fear of anti-semitism dogged the community and anti-semitic stereotypes were internalised. Much effort was expended on apologetics and disciplining Jewish behaviour, particularly in trade. Jewish refugees were seen as a potential cause of anti-semitic sentiment within Gentile society. Any policy which endangered the precarious *status quo* was anathema to the community. Appeals on behalf of the Jews of Europe had to be contained within this mould.

In line with both these philosophies, the British government's claim that the only way to save Europe's Jews was to pursue general war aims was persuasive. Hence, petition and appeal were viewed as the only acceptable Anglo-Jewish political strategies.

Traditional religious views regarding the fate of the Jews in Europe were also ambivalent, with both immanent and transcendent views widespread. These views were very influential in a community which, acculturated as it was to British norms, depicted itself primarily in religious terms. Nazi persecution was widely seen both as divine punishment for the sins of assimilation and as the harbinger of a future redemption. Both views led to resignation to the fate of European Jews. In the face of such powerlessness, and the psychological difficulties posed by the revelations from Europe and the reality of anti-semitism in Britain, the community sought refuge in a Jewish fighting model which would symbolise Jewish fortitude in body and spirit. This would stress Jewish honour and German dishonour at a time of Jewish collective shame at the hands of the Nazis. The community utilised this model both in its campaigns for a Jewish battalion in Allied ranks and, especially, in its campaign for Zionism as a counterpoint to the horrors of the Holocaust. The community never saw the two policies of Zionism and rescue from Europe as potentially conflicting; indeed it saw them as one and the same. Effectively, British Jewry linked the cause of European Jewry with Zionism, despite the community's unwillingness to see itself in national terms.

There were exceptions, however. Against this fairly homogeneous communal background there were also socialists, strictly orthodox Jews, academics and Revisionist Zionists, groups that did not conform to the general patterns outlined above. But these groups were all small, some tiny, and operated on the margins of the community, largely isolated and ignored by most of Britain's Jewish leadership. They had little in common, and there was considerable variation within the groups themselves. Many of their leaders were charismatic and idiosyncratic, and all of them were mistrusted by the mainstream of Anglo-Jewry, probably because they fitted so uneasily into a community dominated by leaders seeking peer group approbation. The groups had no common ground for agreement, let alone co-ordination.

The first group were socialists, by which I do not mean those many Jews who belonged to, let alone voted for, the British Labour Party. Most of these, and, indeed, even most of the Jews who played prominent roles in the Party hierarchy, seem to have derived their understanding of emancipation and anti-semitism from those same liberal criteria which informed the majority of the community. There were, however, some notable exceptions. Professor Harold Laski, scion of a well-known Manchester Jewish family, noted LSE academic and socialist theorist and member of the National Executive of the British Labour Party, addressed Jewish problems on a number of occasions. Unlike Anglo-Jewish liberals he saw anti-semitism as structural to Western society, part of the fundamental fabric of the class struggle, and ineradicable except by a radical change in that society. Anti-semitism, for him, was the tool of aristocratic privilege which could be destroyed only by revolution. Fear led to tyranny based on violence, and fear was the hallmark of the disinherited. 'Anti-semitism is the historic weapon of every ruler who needs an enemy to exploit and property to distribute.'[1] In his *Reflections on the Revolution of our Time*, published in 1943, he stated:

even if they [the disinherited, those rendered miserable by failure] only ... beat up an elderly Jew, they were defeating those whom they had been taught to regard as their enemies, the cause of the humiliation the nation had suffered, and thus to represent their defeat as a victory for the nation ... [As] the German Jews [were] still regarded as an alien element in the national life, Fascist violence was almost benevolently regarded as a contribution to a future order.[2]

This was not an anti-semitism that could be assuaged by liberal education or by appeals to the humanity of the persecutors. Indeed, these might even increase the tempo of destruction.[3]

Another idiosyncratic socialist, the publisher and author Victor Gollancz, though accepting, indeed championing, the liberal, humanistic understanding of anti-semitism, was less sanguine than the majority of the community in his faith in the moral intent of a nation-state. In direct opposition to the low-profile strategies of the organised community, he believed in mobilisation. Only by applying democratic pressure and threat would Trade Unions, politicians and eventually governments change policy. It was, for him, the responsibility of every individual to confront Nazism, not to delegate responsibility and rely on the rectitude of the state. Everyone, for him, had a moral and political imperative to attack Nazism.

Gollancz's influence within the community was considerably muted both by his complicated and (even at this stage of his life) christological theology, and perhaps more importantly by his rejection of the Anglo-Jewish taboos regarding loyalty to Britain. For many British Jews any criticism, even implied, of Britain or the British smacked of ingratitude and might indeed lead to hostile reaction. A good example of this was the *Jewish Chronicle*'s virulent review, written significantly by the Secretary of the Board of Deputies' Defence Committee, Sidney Salomon, of Gollancz's pamphlet 'Shall our Children Live or Die?', published in 1942. The review referred to the book as 'puerile', 'formless', the product of 'pseudo-pacifists, the parlour communists, the false preachers'. Indeed it was 'a disservice' where 'the past imperial policy of this country is again used as an argument'.[4]

Strictly Orthodox Jewry was another exception to the communal rule. This group had fewer problems concerning conflicting British and Jewish identities than most in the community. Their lives and motivations derived wholly from their understanding of Torah. Dual loyalty was not their problem; indeed they did not much care for the emancipation, which they saw as the harbinger of heretical religious reform. European Jewry, the heartland of traditional Jewish scholarship, was very much part of their world. To them, the Jews of Vilna and Warsaw were closer than the non-Jews amongst whom they lived. They had looked to the Yeshivot of Eastern Europe for religious guidance – it was there that great Talmudic minds had produced their work. More than this, the concept of *Klal Yisrael* – the community of Israel – was central to their thinking. The importance of each individual Jew within Israel was paramount and no effort should be spared to save them.

The activities of Rabbi Solomon Schonfeld, both in his efforts for refugees before the war and his attempts to lobby Parliament during the war, have already been mentioned. Another Orthodox Jewish leader, Harry Goodman, the Political Secretary of the World Agudah, travelled to obtain visas from the Irish and Mexican governments and was in constant contact with diplomats and representatives regarding the fate of European Jewry.[5] Chief Rabbi Hertz was also, to some extent, in this category, for he too was centrally concerned with the religious milieu of Europe. However, it would be wrong to exaggerate this group's exceptionality. Hertz was obviously pivotal in the communal life, while Goodman was the Agudah deputy at the Board of Deputies, and both were heavily involved (on the Anglo-Jewish Association side) in the conflict over Zionism.

A third group included those few university academics and intellectuals who expressed an abiding interest in Jewish concerns. Cecil Roth, the Reader in Post-Biblical Jewish Studies at the University of Oxford, though one of the main proponents of the politics of liberalism, eventually came to see Nazism in its exceptional historical context. He realised the severity of the calamity before most in Britain and railed against what he saw as the disunity, corrupted values and ignorance of British Jewry in the face of it. Cecil Roth was a paradoxical figure in British Jewry, one who combined an almost slavish pandering to English ways and loyalties (by no means atypical of British Jews) with a great knowledge of and commitment to Jewish nationalism.

Other academics merged into the fourth category – the more extreme Jewish nationalists. This was by no means a united group. Some, like the Zionist Revisionists or the historian Lewis Namier (then holder of the Chair in History at Manchester University and the only leading British Jew at this time to give up his employment to work full time for the Jewish cause) were Palestinocentric Zionists, often for different reasons and with different dreams. Others, like the journalist Joseph Leftwich or the novelist Louis Golding, derived more from the traditions of Yiddish nationalists or Jewish culturalists. Yet others, like the politician John D. Mack, were influenced by a variety of cross-currents.

All of these, as well as many involved in the World Jewish Congress (such as Professor Morris Ginsberg of the LSE), a body predicated on the idea of a global Jewish unity, were more willing to accept the concept of a supra-national Jewry and of a co-ordinated international Jewish response to crisis. As a result they rebelled against what they considered the supine lack of self-assertion which they saw as typifying Anglo-Jewry, as well as the resulting emphasis on philanthropy. A few of them, such as Glasgow Zionist M. Friedlander, were even prepared to sound the death-knell of one of Anglo-Jewry's most cherished notions. In his view the world was 'today witnessing the funeral of the idea that the world was civilised. Along with the physical destruction of so many thousands of Jews we are also witnessing the death of a precious idea born in the last two centuries, that the world was moving towards a humane liberation where fraternity, liberty and equality would be the rule of the day'.

He went on to refer to the 'bankrupt idea of liberalism'. For him the 'only sensible and safe step for the Jew to take is to rely entirely on himself. This is exactly what Zionism has been and is proposing to do.'[6] Whilst it was certainly true that the Zionists in particular devoted their attentions largely to Palestine, all those in this fourth category were more aggressive than most in the community with regard to their politics concerning the Jews of Europe.

As we have seen, most in these four categories of non-conformists were individuals operating independently, although some had affiliations to one or other Jewish institution. Only the non-Zionist, theocratic Agudah and the Revisionist New Zionist Organisation can be viewed as wholly nonconformist political institutions. Both were small in number,[7] often ridiculed[8] and, in the case of the New Zionist Organisation, anathematised by the mainstream communal bodies. The Agudah, however, did manage to maintain its connections within the normative communal leadership. This was due in part to the diplomatic skills of Harry Goodman and in part to the familial connection between Schonfeld and Chief Rabbi Hertz. As a result their contributions, along with the other independent non-conformists like Gollancz, Laski, Namier, Roth and others, who had involved themselves however reluctantly in the mainstream debate, have been included and analysed in the main body of the book.

It is, however, worth concluding with a brief look at the completely ostracised New Zionist Organisation.[9] Its political outlook was almost wholly divergent from that of the normative community, and this no doubt accounts for its exclusion. Revisionist politics, in direct contrast with those of the mainstream, can legitimately be described as the politics of defiance. The Revisionists were sharply critical of the politics of fear so dominant in the community. They saw the main Jewish organisations as

still operating with an ancient paraphernalia of camouflage in which the complete concealment of Jewish identity and separate purpose is the sign of final triumph. And so it is that Jewry has made no separate or concerted effort to face the problem of their own people in Europe ... of opening doors for escape, or of moving the governments of the U.N. to consider definite plans presented by Jews and for Jews ... Their first and most dominating aim is to ensure that the Jewish label will be absent.[10]

They were similarly critical of the prevailing preference for philanthropic approaches to political problems. A. Abrahams, their main ideologue, maintained that philanthropic measures 'ease pain for a moment but have never led anywhere'. This was particularly true of the immense crisis in Europe. Realising that '[i]n terms of money any project for rescuing anything like large masses of European Jews ... would call for sums far beyond the means of world Jewry', the Revisionists openly declared their policy. The 'rescue of the Jewish nation cannot be achieved by philanthropic means. Only political means and a clear programme can achieve it.'[11] This programme was clearly enunciated. As a first step the Revisionists made serious efforts to effect communally co-ordinated action with regard to the Jews of Europe. In a balanced *Jewish Standard* editorial of 25 December 1942, marked by its unusual politeness towards Brodetsky, the Revisionists argued that it was imperative

that a demand should be put to the Jewish leaders in this country to meet in order to appoint ... a responsible personality freed from other tasks and other labours, who will devote his full time, day and night, to the single job of heading a Co-ordinating Committee which would deal with the whole problem of organising the salvage and transfer of European Jewry ... who will pledge himself to engage on nothing but the sole task of co-ordinating and unifying all Jewish bodies.[12]

This appeal came against the background of their increasing despair at the disunity of British Jews. In a fierce article appearing in the *Jewish Standard* on 11 December 1942, Abrahams calculated that 'Some fifteen separate Jewish organisations are at present engaged in the job of publicising the pogroms, conducting diplomatic work for intervention, raising money, and proposing plans ... they have thrown themselves into their task with the verve and abandon which can in no circumstances go hand in hand with considered action.' He felt that the competition between the different groups and egos had reached such an extent that 'Each organisation, each body and committee, is bent on outwitting and outdistancing the other.' Acutely aware that his stance might be viewed as polemic, he ends his article with a desperate plea that the situation be rectified. '[T]his is no mere jeremiad, but the bitter truth.'[13]

The Revisionists' frustration with the existing communal structures is clear. These structures were organisationally deadlocked and inadequately led. The organisations represented on the relatively short-lived Board of Deputies' Consultative Committee 'continued their chaotic action, calling upon governments, addressing Parliament, issuing communiqués without previous consultation among themselves'.[14] This conflict obstructed effective and unified

action. The various organisations represented on the committee had
'not put their contacts and machinery'[15] at its disposal. Furthermore
its chairman, Professor Brodetsky, added this activity to his numerous
other duties. He 'came to London only twice a week, and during that
time had to attend to the work of the Jewish Agency, the Board
of Deputies and its various committees and the World Jewish
Congress'.[16]

The Board's Consultative Committee passed swiftly into abey-
ance but the Revisionists kept up their demands. Pointing to President Roosevelt's establishment of the War Refugee Board in 1944,
the *Jewish Standard* averred:

[W]hile it is thus generally realised that rescue work requires the special
full-time attention of a body able to concentrate exclusively on this vital
human task, the Board of Deputies considers the rescue question as one of
the problems with which the Foreign Affairs Committee and the Executive
are dealing among many others, and the demand to set up a special rescue
committee has been constantly refused in the past. Yet such a committee
must be established if British Jewry is to have an instrument exploring
every single possibility of rescue and throwing all its influence and capacity
into the balance to make possible a constant flow of Jews from Europe
wherever humanly possible. Be it an independent committee or a sub-
committee, it should be headed by a chairman unburdened by any communal responsibility but by this special duty.

The call for co-ordinated action was sincere and anguished. 'The
rescue task transcends all party divisions ... In any case, Anglo-
Jewry must make its own contribution to the task, if it is to have a
clear conscience before itself and before history.'[17] The perceived
inaction of the communal leadership led to their bitterest plea.

The Board of Deputies of British Jews represents the only free Jewry in the
neighbourhood of Europe, the only organised body of the Jewish people
that is able to meet, consult, draw up plans and proceed to attempt their
realisation. As such there rests on it a stupendous responsibility for which
they will have to render an account to their less fortunate brethren when the
time comes. It were well that they bethought themselves of the excuses they
may hereafter have to give to the tortured and plundered Jews of Europe
when hostilities cease, for their passivity and their failure to use the freedom
and power that was in their hands. Will it suffice for British Jewry to explain
that there was a quarrel between the Board and the Anglo-Jewish Association and that nothing could be done before their bickering had ceased?[18]

Revisionist demands for autonomous action by the Anglo-Jewish
community were fuelled by their assessment, almost unique in the

community, that the ultimate fate of European Jewry did not depend upon the outcome of the military conflict between the Axis and the Allies. There were, in effect, two separate wars taking place.

These two wars have since 1939 proceeded side by side, one hardly affecting the other. While the armies of the Democracies were locked in battle with the Nazis, the other struggle proceeded with even greater ferocity, a struggle in which the weapons were all on one side. But this latter war was in some ways almost an independent affair, barely touching the thoughts and actions of the Democracies engaged in that struggle with the same assailant.[19]

In other words, winning the military conflict was not merely not the only way of saving the Jews, it was in fact not a way of saving them at all. As this book has tried to show, both the dominant philosophies of hope and fear had led to a belief that a victory on the fields of battle was the best way to save the Jews of Europe. It was only because the Revisionists rejected both these prevailing philosophies outright that they could reach the conclusions they did.

The detailed structure the Revisionists repeatedly called for envisaged the co-ordination of all the Jewish world organisations, the establishment of rescue agencies at key places armed with money and skill, the creation of information-collecting centres, and the installation of an adequate and permanently functioning machine for rescue work with a full-time chairman to lead the work.[20] In particular the Revisionist assessment of the Holocaust as separate from the World War had led them to understand the opportunity for pressuring the Axis satellites on the question of Jews under their jurisdiction. On 25 December 1942, shortly after the Allied Declaration, the *Jewish Standard* published two prominent articles on this subject. The first, by Abrahams, under the headline 'What Can Be Done', discussed a wide-ranging plan to attempt the saving of European Jewry. Realising that satellite leaders were much swayed by the changing of Germany's military fortunes – when Germany was succeeding they tended to toe the Berlin line more than when it was failing – he noted that 'it appears that Hungary and others of the Balkan countries are beginning to look around for alibis in the event of a collapse of the Axis position in South-East Europe'.[21] He believed that 'here there has emerged a likely area for diplomatic operations'. On the same page the *Standard*'s diplomatic correspondent, in an article entitled 'Axis Satellites are Weakening', similarly saw the likelihood of 'some of the satellite States seeking means and opportunities of dissociating themselves from the Axis whenever military developments should make it possible . . . All these developments combine to form a general European situation which might be used for setting in motion measures designed to press for evacuating Jews from areas abutting on Eastern Europe.'[22] In an editorial which had appeared two weeks previously, the *Standard* had already argued that 'there are at present in parts of Bulgaria, Rumania and Hungary over a million and a half of Jews whose departure might be conceivably negotiated, provided a united effort is made by the Jews of this country and America'.[23] By 25 December both Abrahams and the diplomatic correspondent had seen a glimmer of hope in 'the speech delivered a few days ago by the Hungarian Prime Minister, practically rejecting German demands regarding the Jews in Hungary'. Abrahams believed that an opportunity existed for the Jewish leadership 'to explore the possibility of an arranged transfer of Jews from Hungary'. He urged them to approach the Foreign Offices of the United Nations to discuss the possibility of 'excluding certain of the high-placed officials of the Hungarian Government from post-war retribution if they took the step of risking their present position by approving a large-scale departure of the Jewries that have become massed in their cities'.[24]

The Revisionists maintained this stance throughout the war. In 1943 they urged that 'countries like Bulgaria, Rumania and Hungary could in present circumstances be pressed to alleviate the treatment of Jews in their area, and maybe also to facilitate their departure'.[25] And in 1944, pointing out that the 'Soviet Government maintains diplomatic relations with Bulgaria, and so does the US Government in regard to Finland',[26] they reiterated their call for more diplomatic pressure and action for the Jews of Europe.

The New Zionist Organisation was not entirely alone in these thoughts. Others, such as Agudah leader Harry Goodman, Victor Gollancz (through his involvement in the co-drafting with Eleanor Rathbone of the twelve-point plan proposed by the National Committee for Rescue from Nazi Terror[27]) and Chief Rabbi Hertz, also advocated and attempted to implement similar policies. But as we have seen, all these individuals can be viewed in one way or another as nonconformists within the context of Anglo-Jewry's prevailing political arena. The New Zionist Organisation remained a small political force, with less than 2,000 members at the height of the war.[28] Its representatives were excluded from communal meetings devoted to the catastrophe in Europe even at the most tragic moments,[29] and they were further prevented from circulating their proposals at such gatherings.[30] The Board of Deputies and the Zionist Federation refused to participate in, or indeed even to acknowledge, groups involving the Revisionists. Both had remained conspicuously absent from the list of prominent Jewish groups (which included the Agudah, the Chief Rabbi's Religious Emergency Council and a number of organisations representing Polish and Czechoslovak Jewish emigrés in addition to the New Zionist Organisation) which had come together to form the United Jewish Emergency Committee in August 1942 to organise action to assist European Jewry. As a result the committee had little sustained effect on the general communal scene.[31]

The opprobrium in which the New Zionist Organisation was held was due to its rejection of the firmly held communal philosophies of hope and fear. So central were these to Anglo-Jewry's world view that any attempt to explore them, and the inconsistencies which lay within them, posed such acute problems to the community that the Revisionists were marginalised with a ferocity reserved only for them. The majority of Anglo-Jewry considered the strident nationalism of Revisionist Zionism, its call for a Jewish state on both sides of the Jordan River and in particular its rejection of liberal democracy as very dangerous indeed.

Though it is undoubtedly true to say that the Revisionists were as contentious as any within the community, particularly where the issue of Palestine was concerned, they did maintain a consistent, well-argued and responsible attitude with regard to the tragedy of European Jewry. Their anguished pleas cannot be dismissed as mere rhetoric. They, alongside the other nonconformists of this chapter, rejected in whole or in part the prevailing communal philosophies of liberalism and the emancipation contract. This rejection is the key to an understanding not only of their response to the Holocaust but also of that of the mainstream community.

The magnitude and horror of the Holocaust are so great, and the event itself has become so central in the sensibilities of the post-war Jewish world, that any attempt at studying Jewish onlookers runs the risk of being accused of insensitivity. Without power and without the ability to exercise any direct military, diplomatic or financial pressure on Germany or its satellites, British Jews obviously could not stop the Final Solution. Allied governments did, however, have limited opportunities to help some Jews at various stages of war. Their failure to exercise these opportunities has been the subject of numerous works.[32] Whether British Jews could have succeeded in pushing the British government into meaningful action relating to the Jews of Europe is a matter which must be left to historians of British politics, rather than those of British Jews. What certainly can be said is that notwithstanding the urgings of some of its non-conformist members Anglo-Jewry mounted no effective or popular campaign to pressurise the government in any way. Indeed the Holocaust was not very high on the Anglo-Jewish agenda. The British Jewish community lived by its own values, shaped by its perceptions of the world around. These values might seem wrongly premised but their existence was real enough. In the end they left Jewry weak, disunited and isolated.

Why was it that the Holocaust made such little impact on Anglo-Jewry; why in hindsight do British Jews appear insensitive? It was because British Jews had neither collective self-esteem nor a sense of being in control of their own lives. As a result they had no inclination to take risks. Anglo-Jewry had a phobia about anti-semitism – a neurosis which at times verged on self-hatred. Thus there could be no self-assertion in the face of adversity, rather paralysis marked by a series of absorbing and debilitating conflicts. British Jews could thus feel no confidence in the competence of their communal organisation – there was no unified, supportive network with regard to their European Jewish brethren. Why were they timid when with hindsight we feel they should have been more daring? Because it simply was not evident to most British Jews that they could act any differently, even though every day news of the killing of Jews on a massive scale reached these shores. They were, to this extent, trapped by their own values. The response of the British Jewish community to the extermination of the Jews of Europe must thus be seen in its own terms, as proclaimed daily from its pulpits, organisational platforms and newspaper columns.

Notes

Abbreviations used in the notes:
BD   Board of Deputies Archives
JC   *Jewish Chronicle*
PRO   Public Record Office
CAB   Cabinet Papers
FO   Foreign Office Files
PREM   Office of the Prime Minister

INTRODUCTION

1 For American Jewish response see Bibliography entries for Bauer, Berman, Davidowicz, Feingold, Friedman, Kranzler, Laqueur, Lookstein, Medoff, Penkower, Syrkin and Wyman. S. M. Finger edited the report of the American Jewish Commission on the Holocaust chaired by former Supreme Court Justice Arthur Goldberg (see Bibliography). For British government, press and popular response see Bibliography entries for Gilbert, Kushner, Wasserstein and Sharf. British Jewish response is considered *inter alia* by Wasserstein in his book *British and the Jews of Europe, 1939–1945* (Oxford, 1979) and in his article 'The Myth of Jewish Silence' (*Midstream*, 26, No. 7, August/September 1980), 10–16, and in more detail in his article 'Patterns of Jewish Leadership in Great Britain during the Nazi Era', in Braham, R.L. (ed.), *Jewish Leadership during the Nazi Era* (New York, 1985). Sompolinsky's 1977 thesis *Ha-Hanhagah ha-Anglo-Yehudit, Memshelet Britannia Veha-Shoah* (Bar-Ilan University, 1977) has been neither published nor translated into English. His article 'Anglo-Jewish Leadership and the British Government: Attempts at Rescue 1944–45' was published in *Yad Vashem Studies*, 13 (1979), 211–47.

2 As Cecil Roth rightly observed, the *Chronicle* provided 'a week to week picture of everything that was happening in the Jewish world, at home and overseas, in the fullest detail. For the research worker it is invaluable' (*The Jewish Chronicle 1841–1941: A Century of Newspaper History*

(London, 1949), p. 116). It is hard to overstate the usefulness of the *Chronicle* as a thorough compendium of Anglo-Jewish activities and attitudes. Moreover, in addition to its role as a national paper for Anglo-Jewry its coverage of world events was generous. Though the newspaper had opinions of its own (and where it has I show it), it reported the full range of Anglo-Jewish thinking. The *Jewish Chronicle* reflected well what was known by British Jews and what the different segments of British Jewry were thinking and doing. Its conception of Anglo-Jewry was very broad – though its editors were predominantly London-based and middle-class, the newspaper did not by any means ignore provincial centres or East End London Jewry. (Indeed it is interesting to note that there seems no evidence to suggest a different response to the Holocaust on the part of provincial or working-class Jews from that of other sections of the community. Even the Communist Party, which had mobilized many Jews during the 1930s in the fight against Mosley, did not concentrate very much effort on a consideration of Hitler's Final Solution. The lack of Communist Party response to the Holocaust is one of the most surprising features of the period.) The *Chronicle* covered, as far as was possible, all sections and strata within British Jewry and took account of cultural as well as political discourses. It printed the public statements of all the many organisations within the community, thereby reflecting in sum the views of every major group. As a result it provides the historian with a near-complete picture of all the public activities and statements of the period under review.

3 For pre-war East End political life see Cesarani, D. (ed.), *The Making of Modern Anglo-Jewry* (Oxford, 1990); Gerwitz, S., 'Anglo-Jewish Responses to Nazi Germany 1933–39: The Anti-Nazi Boycott and the Board of Deputies of British Jews', *Journal of Contemporary History*, 26, No. 2 (April 1991), 255–76; and Krikler, B., 'Anglo-Jewish Attitudes to the Rise of Nazism' (unpubl. manuscript at the Wiener Library, London).

4 *Jewish Standard*, 4 May 1945, p. 4. Though the statement contains an element of exaggeration it points to the general impression that the East End was no longer having any distinctive impact on Anglo-Jewry.

5 Alderman has shown that Phil Piratin's election as MP for Stepney in 1945 is not evidence of a mass Jewish Communist presence in the East End. By that time 'Hitler's bombs had ... already changed the face of the Jewish East End for good.' See Alderman, G., *The Jewish Vote in Great Britain since 1945*, Centre for the Study of Public Policy, University of Strathclyde (Glasgow, 1980), p. 6 and 24, and *The Jewish Community in British Politics*, (Oxford 1983), p. 118.

PART I: KNOWING AND BELIEVING

1 In particular, Walter Laqueur's authoritative work *The Terrible Secret: Suppression of the Truth about Hitler's 'Final Solution'* (London, 1980) explores these topics. In connection with Britain at a general informational level, Andrew Sharf's *The British Press and Jews under Nazi Rule* (London, 1964) offers detailed information on the reporting by British newspapers (excluding Jewish ones). Of secondary relevance, but nonetheless an important document, is Jan Karski's *Story of a Secret State* (London, 1945), a personal memoir on the main conduit of information from Europe to London – the Polish Underground. See also Martin Gilbert, *Auschwitz and the Allies* (London, 1981) and Arthur Morse, *While Six Million Died* (London, 1968).

2 Sharf, *British Press*, pp. 113, 193. See also McLaine, I., *Ministry of Morale: Home Front Morale and the Ministry of Information during World War II* (London, 1979), p. 169.

3 Gilbert, *Auschwitz*, pp. 13–14.

4 BD, C11/2/35/3.

5 *JC*, 9 January, p. 1.

6 Laqueur, *Terrible Secret*, p. 73.

7 See Bauer, Y., *The Holocaust in Historical Perspective* (Washington, 1978), p. 20; Laqueur, *Terrible Secret*, p. 74.

8 Laqueur, *ibid.*, p. 74.

9 *Ibid.*, p. 75.

10 Gilbert, *Auschwitz*, p. 51.

11 PRO, FO 371/30917 (Norton (Berne) to Foreign Office containing message from Dr G. Reigner to S. S. Silverman, MP).

12 Laqueur, *Terrible Secret.*, p. 178.

13 *JC*, 11 September 1942, p. 1; Laqueur, *ibid.*, p. 76.

14 Gilbert, *Auschwitz*, p. 68.

15 Laqueur, *Terrible Secret.*, p. 118; Hearst, E., 'The British and the Slaughter of the Jews', *Wiener Library Bulletin*, 21, No. 1 (1966–7) p. 34.

16 *JC*, 2 October 1942, p. 1.

17 Sharf, *British Press*, p. 99; Wasserstein, *Britain and the Jews of Europe, 1939–1945*, p. 170; Gilbert, *Auschwitz*, pp. 73, 85; Fox, J. P., 'The Jewish Factor in British War Crimes Policy in 1942', *English Historical Review*, 92, No. 362 (1977), p. 95; Watts, F. (ed.), *Voices of History, 1942–43* (New York, 1943), pp. 507–25.

18 PRO, FO 371/30923, C11923, folios 122–4. See also Gilbert, *Auschwitz*, pp. 96–97.

19 Fox, 'Jewish Factor', p. 101.

20 *JC*, 11 December 1942, p. 1.

21 Wasserstein, *Britain*, pp. 172–4.

22 Gilbert, *Auschwitz*, p. 111.

23 Morse, *While Six Million Died*, p. 54.

24 Gilbert, *Auschwitz*, p. 131.

25 Sharf, *British Press,*, p. 111.

26 Gilbert, *Auschwitz*, p. 161.

27 BD, file 543; *JC*, 14 June 1944, p. 1.

28 Gilbert, *Auschwitz*, p. 265.

29 *JC*, 18 August 1944, pp. 1, 7.

30 See Penkower, M. N., *The Jews were Expendable: Free World Diplomacy and the Holocaust* (Illinois, 1983), p. 234.

31 Sharf, A., 'The British Press and the Holocaust', *Yad Vashem Studies*, 5 (1963), p. 190.

32 Gollancz, V., *What Buchenwald Really Means* (London, 1945), pp. 2–3.

33 Brodetsky, S., *Memoirs: From Ghetto to Israel* (London, 1960), p. 218.

34 *Jewish Year Book* (1948), p. 299.

35 *Ibid.*, p. 297. These out-of-date figures are not, of course, evidence of what British Jews knew or did not know, but are rather a reflection of their moral sensibilities.

36 Sharf, *British Press*, p. 201.

37 Engel, D., 'Bibliographical Essay: The Western Allies and the Holocaust', (unpublished), p. 14; Jewish Historical Society of England, Lucien Wolf Memorial Lecture: *The Jews in the Post-War Settlement*, Prof. Selig Brodetsky (London, 1942), p. 18.

38 Bauer, *The Holocaust in Historical Perspective*, p. 19.

39 Wasserstein, *Britain*, pp. 356–7.

40 Quoted in Trevor-Roper, H., 'The Germans and The Jews', *The Listener*, 1 January 1981, pp. 19–20. See also Laqueur, *Terrible Secret*, p. 203.

41 Katz, J., 'Was The Holocaust Predictable?', in Bauer, Y. and Rotenstreich, N. (eds.), *The Holocaust as Historical Experience* (London, 1981), p. 23.

42 Laqueur, *Terrible Secret*, p. 204.

43 Koestler, A., *The Yogi and the Commissar* (London, 1945), p. 97.

44 Syrkin, M., 'What American Jewry Did During the Holocaust', *Midstream*, 28, No. 8 (1982), p. 6.

45 Irving Howe, letter in *Commentary*, 76, No. 3 (1983), p. 5.

46 *JC*, 3 July 1942, p. 8.

47 Katz, 'Was the Holocaust Predictable?', p. 33.

48 Bauer, Y., *American Jewry and the Holocaust: The American Joint Distribution Committee, 1939–1945* (Detroit, 1981), p. 190.

49 *JC*, 3 July 1942, p. 8.

50 Wasserstein, B., 'Patterns of Jewish Leadership', p. 34. (The implication in Wasserstein's observation is revealing: would any leader making such a forecast have been irresponsible?)

51 Trevor-Roper, 'The Germans and the Jews', pp. 19–20.

52 Syrkin, 'American Jewry', p. 6.

53 Friedman, S. S., *No Haven for the Oppressed: United States Policy Toward Jewish Refugees 1938–1945* (Detroit, 1973), pp. 137–8.
54 Friedlander, S., 'On the Possibility of the Holocaust: An Approach to a Historical Synthesis', in Bauer and Rotenstreich (eds.), *The Holocaust as Historical Experience*, p. 9.
55 Penkower, *The Jews Were Expendable*, pp. vii–viii.
56 Trevor-Roper, 'The Germans and the Jews', pp. 19–20.
57 Reading, Eva, Marchioness of, *For the Record*, (London, 1973), p. 175.
58 Trevor-Roper, 'The Germans and the Jews', pp. 19–20.
59 Baron, S. W., 'The Modern Age', in Schwarz, L. (ed.), *Great Ages and Ideas of the Jewish People* (New York, 1956), p. 348. See also Kushner, T., *The Persistence of Prejudice: Antisemitism in British Society during the Second World War* (Manchester, 1989), p. 180.
60 Hertz, J. H., 'Sermon – The Tragedy of Vienna 1st Day Shavous, 5th June 1938', quoted in Hertz, J. H., *Early and Late: Addresses, Messages and Papers* (London, 1943), p. 59.
61 Bauer, Y., *The Jewish Emergence from Powerlessness* (London, 1971), p. 61. Namier, J., *Lewis Namier: A Biography* (London, 1971), p. 246.
62 Penkower, M. N., 'Believe the Unbelievable', *Midstream*, 27, No. 4 (1981), p. 35.
63 Bauer, *The Holocaust in Historical Perspective*, p. 25.
64 *Ibid., American Jewry and The Holocaust*, p. 456.
65 Wasserstein, B., 'The Myth of Jewish Silence', *Midstream*, 26, No. 7 (1980), 10–16. The *Jewish Echo* reported on the inquest into Zygielbojm's death, giving details of his suicide note as well as noting Hannen Swaffer's revelation, in the *Daily Herald* of 18 May 1943, that Zygielbojm had proposed that Jewish leaders should go to Downing Street in a body to protest against the inactivity of the Government in the face of the Jewish tragedy in Europe and commit suicide on the steps of Number 10. 'Then and only then', Zygielbojm had said, 'will the world see what the slaughter of a people means' (*Jewish Echo*, 21 May 1943, p. 6). The *Jewish Standard* reported Zygielbojm's death but initially made only a veiled reference to his suicide, saying that he had found that 'he could not go on living because Jews in Poland were being systematically exterminated, while a silent world looked on but without any attempt to intervene, or even any real effort to open a way of escape for those who still remained alive' (*Jewish Standard*, 21 May 1943, p. 3). A month later the paper did publish the coroner's verdict but refrained from further comment. Likewise there was no explicit reference to suicide in the *JC* reports on Zygielbojm's death or in its obituary (see *JC*, 21 May 1943, p. 11). Aside from a Memorial Meeting at the largely emigré Polish Jewish Centre, there seems to have been no noticeable effect of his death on the community.
66 Bauer, *The Holocaust in Historical Perspective*, p. 24.
67 Hertz, J. H., *Out of the Depths I Cry unto Thee. Sermon by the Chief Rabbi at*

The Service of Prayer and Intercession on behalf of the Jews in Germany. Royal Albert Hall, Sunday 9th July 1933 (London, 1933), p. 4.

68 Gollancz, V., *Let My People Go* (London, 1942), p. 11.

69 Katz, 'Was the Holocaust Predictable?', p. 53.

PART II: INTRODUCTION

1 See *JC*, 12 May 1944 p. 14 in the context of a proposed discussion on Polish anti-semitism. Such thinking was not confined to the United Synagogue. Federation, Reform and Liberal synagogues were similarly silent. There were likewise few calls to action from congregational rabbis. The Jewish press notes only one, Harry Swift of the St John's Wood Synagogue, who appealed to his flock to urge their MPs to impress upon the Government the need for immediate action (see *Jewish Standard*, 18 December 1942, p. 3). For the Hertz–Waley Cohen conflict see V. D. Lipman's comments in *Encyclopedia Judaica*, Vol. 5, p. 684 and references to Hertz in R. Henriques, *Sir Robert Waley Cohen* (London, 1966).

2 Hyamson, A. M., 'A Letter from London', *Contemporary Jewish Record*, 6, No. 5 (1943), p. 482.

3 World Jewish Congress, *World Jewish Congress Facts* (London, undated), p. 1.

4 From 1940–5 Neville Laski served as an alternative Director for David Kessler. Both he and Stein seem to have been important forces acting on editor Ivan Greenberg. Greenberg was a Revisionist and Laski and Stein were both now firmly in the Anglo-Jewish Association camp opposed to the Zionist Caucus. The checks and balances inherent in the editor–board relationship thus ensured that the *Chronicle* steered a steady course. After the war when Greenberg's revisionism became more strident, Stein and Laski were among the primary movers to have him dismissed.

1   COMMUNAL PRIORITIES: CONFLICT AND DOMESTIC ANTI-SEMITISM

1 Feingold, H., *Did American Jewry Do Enough During The Holocaust?* (Syracuse, 1985), p. 11.

2 Cohen, S. A., 'Selig Brodetsky and the Ascendancy of Zionism in Anglo-Jewry: Another View of his Role and Achievements', *Jewish Journal of Sociology*, Vol. 24, No. 1, June 1982, p. 25.

3 See Bermant, C., *The Cousinhood: The Anglo-Jewish Gentry* (London, 1971).

4 For detailed background see Shimoni, G., 'From Anti-Zionism to Non-Zionism in Anglo Jewry 1917–1937', *Jewish Journal of Sociology*, 28, No. 1 (1986), 19–48.

5 Brodetsky, *Memoirs* p. 243.

6 Stein to Weizmann, 5 November 1944, Weizmann Archives. See also Cohen, S. A., 'Same Places, Different Faces: A Comparison of Anglo-Jewish Conflicts over Zionism during World War I and World War II', in Cohen, S. A. and Don Yehiya (eds.), *Comparative Jewish Politics* , Vol. II, *Conflict and Consensus in Jewish Political Life* (Tel-Aviv, 1986), p. 77.

7 *JC*, 4 February 1944, p. 8.

8 See Cohen, S. A., 'Israeli Sources for the Study of Anglo-Jewish History', *Jewish Historical Society of England Transactions*, 27 (1982), p. 130 and p. 146 n. 58.

9 Cohen, 'Same Places, Different Faces', p. 73.

10 *Ibid.*, p. 65.

11 PRO, FO 371/36741, 371/20825.

12 Isaiah Berlin, then attaché at the British Embassy in Washington, went further and asserted in 1944 that the Congress was 'wholly Zionist and rather bogus'. See PRO, FO 371/42798; *JC*, 14 January 1944, p. 1 and 9 April 1943, p. 11; Shimoni, G., 'The Non-Zionists in Anglo-Jewry, 1937–1948', *Jewish Journal of Sociology*, 28 No. 2 (1986), 89–115 and 'Selig Brodetsky and the Ascendancy of Zionism in Anglo-Jewry, 1939–1945', *Jewish Journal of Sociology*, 22 No. 2 (1980), 125–61.

13 PRO, FO 371/20825. At the setting up of the World Jewish Congress branch in Birmingham, Rev. Dr Cohen was reported by the *Chronicle* to have cynically observed, 'Many Jews in Birmingham held themselves aloof from the movement because they averred that the leaders of Anglo-Jewry were antagonistic. This he regarded as the highest testimonial that could be offered for the existence of the World Jewish Congress' (*JC*, 17 December, p. 12).

14 Minutes of the First World Jewish Congress, p. 157.

15 Report of Executive Officers, World Jewish Congress British Section, 23 and 24 October 1943, p. 3.

16 *Contemporary Jewish Record*, 7 (1944), p. 289.

17 Finestein, I., Epilogue to Picciotto, J., *Sketches of Anglo-Jewish History. Revised and Edited, with a Prologue, Notes and an Epilogue by Israel Finestein, M.A.* (London, 1956), p. 423.

18 *Ibid.*, p. 419.

19 Cohen, S. A., *English Zionists and British Jews: The Communal Politics of Anglo-Jewry, 1895–1920* (Princeton, 1982), p. 267. See also Finestein, Epilogue to *Sketches of Anglo-Jewish History*, p. 419. The degree to which the basis of the dispute rested on a clash of cultures can be seen in the comment of Robert Waley Cohen's biographer, R. Henriques, who is also a scion of a leading Cousinhood family. 'Thus in Britain there was arrayed against Bob as against nearly all British Jews of his tradition and background, an alliance of alien dogma, custom and superstition which had never before been any part of Judaism except in dark corners deep inside the ghettoes of Eastern Europe' (*Sir Robert Waley Cohen* (London, 1966), p. 386).

20 *JC*, 29 January 1943, p. 5.

21 *JC*, 5 February 1943, p. 6.

22 Fischer, Lord S., *Brodetsky – Leader of the Anglo-Jewish Community* (Leeds, 1976), p. 24.

23 Brodetsky at a meeting of the Board, *JC*, 9 April 1943, p. 11.

24 *JC*, 5 February 1943, p. 6. Schonfeld's actions should not be interpreted as an attempt to thrust the Agudah into a leadership role in England during the war. The Agudah was a self-contained, even élitist, group confined solely to the ultra-Orthodox, which had no wish to widen its constituency. Schonfeld's actions during the war, like his refugee trains bringing Jewish children to Britain as war loomed, were conceived wholly in a spirit of genuine rescue.

25 Committee for a Jewish Army, Publication No. 1, *Towards a Jewish Army* (London, 1942), p. 4.

26 *JC*, 4 August 1944, p. 5.

27 *Ibid.*, 18 June 1943, p. 1.

28 *Ibid.*, 25 June 1943, p. 3.

29 *Ibid.*, 14 June 1944, p. 12.

30 *Ibid.*, 7 January 1944, p. 6 and 14 January 1944, p. 12. On Waley-Cohen and Hertz, see above, p. 162 n. 1.

31 *JC*, 29 January 1943, p. 13.

32 A few Orthodox religious organisations were created, such as the Machzike Ha-dath, but they remained small and enclosed groupings. The Federation of Synagogues, though primarily designed for the 1881–1914 immigrants, was organised by Sir Samuel Montagu, very much an Anglo-Jewish grandee. (By 1926, however, control of the Federation had passed to the immigrants. See Cesarani, D., 'Communal Authority in Anglo-Jewry, 1914–1940' p. 123 in his *The Making of Modern Anglo-Jewry* (Oxford, 1990)). Jewish Trade Unions were certainly creations of the immigrants but died out after two generations. Outside these limited spheres no lasting central institutions emerged. The Zionist Federation of Great Britain and Ireland did benefit largely (though by no means exclusively) from the support of 1880–1914 immigrants or their descendants. Nevertheless, as Cesarani demonstrates, the Federation, far from seeking to secede from the central communal bodies, actively sought to enter and control them. See 'Communal Authority', pp. 115–40.

33 Brodetsky, *Memoirs*, p. 244.

34 *JC*, 11 August 1944, p. 10.

35 *Ibid.*, 5 March 1943, p. 10.

36 Hertz, J. H., *A Book of Jewish Thoughts – New and Revised Edition, Selected and Arranged by the Chief Rabbi* (London, 1941), p. 97.

37 Hertz, 'Jews – 1939', in *Early and Late*, p. 298. After 1941 Anglo–Jewry spent much time rallying to the cry of the Jewish Anti-Fascist Committee in Moscow, donating money to the Soviet War Appeal (for which

there was a separate British Jewish organisation) and hailing Soviet Russia for having saved Jews and for deeming anti-semitism illegal. Such an ideological switch towards Russia was, of course, not confined to the Jewish community in Britain at this time. Before 1941, there had indeed been divergent opinions within the community regarding the Soviet Union. These were a testimony to the strength of Anglo-Jewry's formula of the condition of Jewry as the barometer of liberation. Some, such as Brodetsky and Hertz, stressed the subjugation of Jewish religious culture, whilst others, like Bentwich and Gollancz, stressed the outlawing of anti-semitism, the constitutional guarantee of religious freedom and the existence of the autonomous region in Biro-bidjan.

By 1941, though obviously still worried about Soviet communism and its anti-religion and anti-Zionist policies, Hertz was urging British Jews to sublimate these anxieties until victory had been achieved. '[T]he lives of millions of Jews in Europe depend on the victory of the Soviet Forces. They alone can secure to those millions of Jews in Eastern Europe the Freedom to *live*, and rescue them from extermination by the hell-hounds of Hitler.' At a mass meeting for the visiting actor-director Shloime Mikhoels and the poet Itzik Feffer in October 1943, Hertz noted, with considerable justification, that 'If Russia had not made her immortal stand, Jews in this country would by now have been led off in "death trains".' Though Hertz remained a convinced anti-Bolshevik, the destruction of European Jewry had necessitated a change in the attitude to Soviet Russia.

In all civilised lands there is a universal chorus of sympathy with the doomed [Jewish] victims, but so far well-nigh universal inaction as regards rescue. It is the hope of all good men that victory of the Soviet Armies will strengthen the forces of Liberalism and Humanity that seem to be paralysed at this moment – with fatal results to the multitudes of Jewish men, women and children who might still be saved from torture and butchery.

The use of capital letters (Liberalism and Humanity) seems a deliberate mimicry of Soviet rhetorical sloganism – maybe the more pragmatic radicalism implied within the Soviet terms of these Enlightenment concepts would yield less ambivalent results than their Western, liberal counterparts.

Hertz had another, secondary, reason for supporting the Soviet cause. A palpable British Jewish financial contribution to the Soviet war effort might persuade the Soviet leadership to soften its policies regarding Jewish religious life and Zionism and release Soviet Jewry from its isolation from the rest of the Jewish world; 'if we do our full duty, we not only help to smash Hitlerism, *but bring back Russian Jewry to the fold of Israel*'. See Jewish Fund for Soviet Russia, *Calling All Jews to Action*, (London, 1943), p. 14; *Daily Worker*, 18 October 1943, p. 4.

38 Hertz, *Book of Jewish Thoughts*, p. 6.

39 Brodetsky, *Jews in the Post-War Settlement*, p. 11.

40 *JC*, 8 December 1944, p. 12. Glasgow's Rabbi Kopul Rosen was one of the few British Jews to challenge the assumptions that lay behind these statements, arguing that 'the anti-semite does not object to Jewish behaviour – he objected to Jewish existence' (*Jewish Echo*, 23 February 1945, p. 7).

41 *JC*, 1 October 1943, p. 3.

42 *Ibid.*, 1 October 1943, p. 10.

43 *Ibid.*, 22 May 1942, p. 8.

44 *Ibid.*, 22 May 1942, pp. 8–9.

45 *Ibid.*, 3 April 1942, p. 14.

46 Brodetsky, *Jews in the Post-War Settlement*, pp. 22–3.

47 Brodetsky, 'The Balfour Declaration: Its Political Significance', in Goodman, P. (ed.), *The Jewish National Home; The Second November 1917–1942* (London, 1943), p. 257.

48 See Alderman, G., *The Jewish Community in British Politics*, p. 122, and Salamon, S., 'The Jewish Defence Committee', p. 8 in the Neville Laski Papers, Mocatta Library, UCL AJ33/158. These tactics were employed against Fascist candidates at the Leeds North East, Middleton and Prestwich by-elections of 1940.

49 *JC*, 2 October 1942, p. 1.

50 Brodetsky, *Memoirs*, p. 219.

51 Henriques, *Sir Robert Waley Cohen*, p. 382.

52 *JC*, 23 January 1942, p. 19.

53 *Ibid.*, 11 February 1944, p. 12.

54 Henriques, *Sir Robert Waley Cohen*, p. 382.

55 *Ibid.*, pp. 383–4.

56 *JC*, 31 July 1942.

57 Harold Laski in the *New Statesman and Nation*, 25, 13 February 1943, p. 108. Laski, H., *Reflections on the Revolution of our Time* (London, 1943), p. 31, and p. 83, n. 143.

58 See Ainsztein, R., 'The Failure of the West. How Many More Could Have Been Saved?', *Jewish Quarterly*, 14, No. 4 (1966/7), pp. 13–14. For the community's selectivity regarding immigrants, see the detailed study by Louise London, 'Jewish Refugees and British Government Policy, 1930–1940', in Cesarani, *The Making of Modern Anglo-Jewry*, especially pp. 185–6.

59 Sherman, A. J., *Island Refuge: Britain and Refugees from the Third Reich 1933–9* (London, 1973), pp. 175–6. See also Cabinet Conclusions 55(38)5, November 16 1938, PRO, CAB 23/29.

60 See Wasserstein, *Britain*, p. 92.

61 Schiff to Brotman, 4 May 1943, BD C2/2/51. See also Wasserstein, *Britain*, p. 120

62 Sherman, *Island Refuge*, p. 219. See also Stent, R., *A Bespattered Page?:*

The Internment of His Majesty's 'Most Loyal Enemy Aliens' (London, 1980), p. 67.
63 M. Gordon Liverman to A. G. Brotman, 14 May 1940, BD, C2/3/3/10/2. See also Wasserstein, *Britain*, p. 92, and Holmes, C., review of Wasserstein, in *Jewish Journal of Sociology*, 22, No. 1 (1980), 59–72.
64 Letter from B. Marguiles, *JC*, 20 August 1943, p. 17.
65 *JC*, editorial, 26 June 1942, p. 8. Marion Berghahn cites J. Rudolf Bienenfeld as noting, in a August 1942 talk to mark the foundation of the Jacob Ehrlich Society, that although the refugees constituted about 20 per cent of Anglo-Jewry they were 'nowhere represented in English-Jewry associations and organisations'. See Berghahn, M., *Continental Britons: German-Jewish Refugees from Nazi Germany* (Oxford, 1988), p. 155; Bienenfeld, R. J. R., 'Die Aufgabe der Jacob Ehrlich Society', Lecture, 22 August 1942, London.
66 *JC*, 7 May 1943, p. 5.
67 *Ibid.*, 2 January 1942, p. 18.
68 Gollancz, *Let My People Go*, p. 9; *Jewish Standard*, 8 January 1943, p. 5; and *Daily Herald*, 6 January 1943, Laski's article, 'Failure to Act is Connivance'.
69 Kushner, T., *The Persistence of Prejudice* chapters 1 and 5, and 'The Paradox of Prejudice: The Impact of Organised Antisemitism in Britain during an Anti-Nazi War', in Kushner, T. and Lunn, K. (eds.), *Traditions of Intolerance: Historical Perspectives on Fascism and Race Discourse in Britain* (Manchester, 1989), p. 85.

2 THE INSTITUTIONAL RESPONSE TO THE HOLOCAUST

1 See Cohen, S. A., 'Same Places, Different Faces'; Cohen, S. A., 'Selig Brodetsky and the Ascendancy of Zionism in Anglo-Jewry: Another View of his Role and Achievements', *Jewish Journal of Sociology*, 24, No. 1 (1982), 25–38; Shimoni, G., 'The Non-Zionists in Anglo-Jewry'; Shimoni, G., 'Selig Brodetsky and the Ascendancy of Zionism in Anglo-Jewry'; Wasserstein, B., 'Patterns of Jewish Leadership'.
2 The Holocaust was not to divert Zionists from their course. As Barnett Janner said when presiding at the opening session of the Zionist Federation's Annual Conference in January 1943 – one month after Eden's Commons Declaration – 'There is no need for me in opening this conference to bear at length upon the terrible calamity that has befallen the Jewish people in Europe. It is our business as Zionists to continue with the work in which we have been engaged from the establishment of our Federation' (*Zionist Review*, 22 January 1943, p. 6).
3 *Ibid.*, 3 November 1944, p. 7.
4 Cohen, L., *Some Recollections of C. G. Montefiore* (London, 1940), p. 253.

5 *JC*, 17 September 1943, p. 12; see also BD/E1/111. Selig Brodetsky was elected to the Presidency of the Board in December 1939 and continued to hold the office throughout the rest of the war. His claim to fame in the communal eye was that he had been the first Jewish Senior Wrangler at Cambridge. In addition to his considerable intellectual abilities in the fields of mathematics and physics, he also at times showed great insight into the condition of world Jewry, although his writings on this subject did not attract Anglo-Jewry's attention with quite the same tenacity. His essay on the political significance of the Balfour Declaration, written in late 1942, was as cogent an analysis as had been penned by an English-speaking Jew. Despite his continuing commitments and involvement in the Zionist cause he was, like the vast majority of British Jews, intensely loyal to England.

6 *JC*, 30 July 1943, p. 9.

7 *JC*, 2 April 1943, p. 5.

8 *Contemporary Jewish Record*, 6 (1943), p. 20.

9 *JC*, 21 January 1944, p. 10.

10 Shimoni, 'Selig Brodetsky and the Ascendancy of Zionism in Anglo-Jewry', p. 150.

11 Bentwich, N., *My Seventy-Seven Years: An Account of My Life and Times, 1883–1960* (London, 1962), p. 191.

12 *JC*, 2 April 1943, p. 5.

13 Bentwich, *My Seventy-Seven Years*, p. 192.

14 Hyamson, A. M., 'British Jewry in Wartime', *Contemporary Jewish Record*, 6, No. 1 (1943), p. 19.

15 *JC*, 4 February 1944, p. 1.

16 *Ibid.*, 11 September 1944, p. 9.

17 *Ibid.*, 17 April 1942, p. 10.

18 *Ibid.*, 18 December 1942, p. 10, and 25 December 1942, p. 10.

19 *Ibid.*, 4 August 1944, p. 10.

20 *Ibid.*, 29 May 1942, p. 8.

21 *Ibid.*, 8 September 1944, p. 8. This was the one issue on which the *Chronicle* was subjected to sustained criticism, albeit from an expected and partisan source, namely the Zionist Caucus and its supporters. The *Zionist Review*, the journal of the Zionist Federation, frequently aired these strictures, most prominently in a full-page article by Rebecca Sieff on 12 March 1943. Her argument was marked by considerable hyperbole and drew on the established fears of British Jewry. Sieff was unabashed in her claim that the Zionist Federation had been the subject of unprecedented treatment. 'No institution has ever been assailed with such a ferocity as that which the "Jewish Chronicle" metes out to that fine body.' Such an assault, she argued, carried great danger:

If Jewish life were not so precarious, every responsible-minded Jew would feel a sense of shame that the unthinking non-Jew should be led to accept the 'Jewish Chronicle' as a true mirror of Jewry, a mirror distorting difficulties to look like chaos. But Jewish life is all too precarious and to depict Jewry through the grotesque glass of irresponsibility is to do a disservice to the Jewish people and to those who lead them.

The *Chronicle*'s reporting of non-conformist Jewish groups (or 'freak' bodies, as Sieff called them) such as the New Zionist Organisation, the Jewish Army Committee and Rabbi Schonfeld came in for particular attack. It was not that the *Chronicle*'s owners had an entrenched ideological or partisan bias – a common accusation against newspapers. Rather, Sieff found fault in the fact that few of the *Chronicle*'s shareholders 'take any active part in Jewish affairs and some none at all. Only one of the directors is conspicuous in Jewish affairs in this country and prominently connected with an important Jewish organisation.' Now that the Caucus controlled the community's central body, the Board of Deputies, all power was to be vested in it and dissident and outside groups should be starved of publicity.

The other main newspaper supporter of the Caucus was the Glasgow *Jewish Echo*. It too attacked the *Chronicle* on this issue, accusing it of being 'the mouthpiece of the Yahudist [i.e. assimilationist] policy' and a 'full-bloodied anti-Zionist organ'. In truth these were nonsensical charges, but passions ran high, especially among those members of the Caucus still haunted by the 1917 debacle surrounding Alexander and Montefiore's letter to the *Times* regarding the Balfour Declaration. See the *Zionist Review*, 12 March 1943, p. 8, and the *Jewish Echo*, 16 July 1943, p. 3.

22 *JC*, 3 September 1943, p. 8. Sometimes this demoralisation affected the *Chronicle* itself. An 11 August 1944 editorial on the surfeit of communal committees reflects the search for a model of the Jewish fighting model (see chapter 5 above) by taking an approach which might now seem ironic, but was in fact a sign of desperation: 'It is not, of course, without its healthy aspects, if only because it testifies to a vitality in a people reeling under the most devastating blows – blows which would have quenched the creative appetite of any nation less essentially healthy under God's providence, a people vigorous and inured to fighting without respite for its life and honour.'

23 *JC*, 26 March 1943, p. 5.

24 *Ibid.*, 17 April 1942, p. 10, and 7 January 1944, p. 5.

25 *Sunday Times*, 23 February 1986, p. 21.

26 See Laqueur, *Terrible Secret*, p. 208. It would be wrong to suggest that these policy alternatives were totally ignored. On 18 June 1944 a Board of Deputies resolution 'urged that all measures be taken to impress upon the peoples of German Satellite nations the importance of helping

Jews escape from the Nazis (*Contemporary Jewish Record*, 7, p. 406). The World Jewish Congress was, however, the only frequent exception to the rule of lack of policy of investigation. Sydney Silverman, its chairman, issued a statement on 18 December 1942, published in the *Manchester Guardian*, pointing out that 'satellite rather than Axis Powers might well be pressurised to "let the Jews out".' However, these were exceptions.

27 *JC*, 6 August 1943, p. 13.
28 Brodetsky, *Memoirs*, p. 229.
29 *Ibid.*, p. 231.
30 *JC*, 18 February 1944, p. 14.
31 *Ibid.*, 11 February 1944, p. 11.
32 *Ibid.*, 14 August 1942, p. 11.
33 *Ibid.*, 31 July 1942, p. 4.
34 *Ibid.*, 2 April 1943, p. 5. A letter to which, incidentally, only one reply appeared in the following issues: 'The excellent letter, on a very important subject, which Rabbi Dayan I. Abramsky, addressed to your columns prompts me to ask, now that he has occupied his distinguished position for nearly eight years, when will he begin to preach in the English language?' *JC*, 16 April 1943, p. 13.
35 *Ibid.*, 10 December 1943, p. 13; *Di Vochenzaitung*, 30 July 1943, p. 4.
36 *JC*, 16 July 1943, p. 12.
37 *Ibid.*, 10 September 1943, p. 5.
38 Hertz, J. H., 'Service of Prayer and Intercession', 9 July 1933, in Hertz, J. H., *Sermons, Addresses and Studies* (London, 1938), Vol. 1, p. 369.
39 Hertz, *Out of the Depths I Cry unto Thee*, p. 8.
40 *Ibid.*, p. 11.
41 *JC*, 24 April 1942, p. 1.
42 *Ibid.*, 24 July 1942, p. 1. See also BD Minute Book 32, July 1942 to April 1945, minutes to meeting of 19th July 1942. Of the seventy-seven deputies present seven (including Brodetsky) took part in the debate regarding the synagogue. Following this debate the next item was the report of the Executive Committee (in which there was no reference to events in Europe), followed by the report of the Law, Parliamentary and General Purposes Committee (again no mention). The matter was finally discussed in the next agenda item, the report of the Joint Foreign Committee.
43 *JC*, 28 August 1942, p. 5.
44 *Ibid.*, Editorial, 18 December 1942, p. 8.
45 *Ibid.*, 29 January 1943, p. 15.
46 *Ibid.*, 5 March 1943, p. 13.
47 *Ibid.*, 12 February 1943, p. 13.
48 *Ibid.*, 17 March 1944, p. 13.
49 *Jewish Standard*, 30 October 1942, p. 8.

50 *JC*, 3 December 1943, p. 12.
51 *Ibid.*, 11 June 1943, p. 15.
52 *Ibid.*, 4 February 1944, p. 8.
53 *Ibid.*, 8 September 1944, p. 12.
54 *Ibid.*, 17 March 1944, p. 11.
55 *Ibid.*, 26 May 1944, p. 1, and *Jewish Standard*, 2 June 1944, p. 3.
56 PRO, FO 371/30914/487. See also Fox, 'Jewish Factor' p. 87.
57 PRO, FO 371/30914/2009, A. L. Easterman to Eden, and Fox, *ibid.*, p. 87.
58 PRO, FO 371/30915/2263, and Fox, *ibid.*, p. 87.
59 PRO, FO 371/30917, and Gilbert, *Auschwitz*, p. 52.
60 Brodetsky, S., *Memoirs*, pp. 219–20.
61 PRO, FO 371/30923; also Gilbert, *Auschwitz*, pp. 93–5 and Fox, 'Jewish Factor', p. 98.
62 PRO, FO 371/30923; also Fox, *ibid.*, p. 101 and Wasserstein, *Britain*, pp. 170–1.
63 BD, C11/7/2/6. See also Wasserstein, *Britain*, p. 170, and his 'Patterns in Jewish Leadership', pp. 38–9.
64 Wasserstein, *Britain*, p. 171. Winant to State Department, 7 December 1942, United States National Archives, 740.00116, European War 1939/660.
65 *JC*, 11 December 1942, p. 1 and 18 December 1942, p. 1.
66 PRO, FO 371/32682 (WI 7401/4555/48).
67 Wasserstein, 'Patterns of Jewish Leadership', pp. 38–9.
68 Brodetsky, *Memoirs*, p. 220.
69 Account of meeting by Brodetsky in minutes of Zionist Executive, 23 December 1942, Central Zionist Archives, 24/302/26. See also Wasserstein, *Britain*, p. 176, and his 'Patterns of Jewish Leadership', p. 39.
70 BD, C10/2/8/20/2, and Wasserstein, *Britain*, p. 177.
71 PRO, PREM 4/51/8/556. See also Wasserstein, 'The Myth of Jewish Silence', p. 11, and his 'Patterns of Jewish Leadership', p. 40.
72 *Hansard*, House of Lords, 23 March 1943. See also Wasserstein, 'The Myth of Jewish Silence', p. 11, and his 'Patterns of Jewish Leadership', p. 40.
73 PRO, PREM 4/51/8/472 and 3.
74 PRO, FO 371/42790/42 and 8, and Gilbert, *Auschwitz*, p. 181.
75 See Sompolinsky, 'Anglo-Jewish Leadership and the British Government', p. 212.
76 PRO, PREM 4/31/8/448 and PRO, CAB 95/15, 8 May 1944. See also Wasserstein, *Britain*, p. 227, and his 'The Myth of Jewish Silence', p. 11; Gilbert, *Auschwitz*, p. 208; Sompolinsky, 'Anglo-Jewish Leadership and the British Government', p. 224.
77 See Penkower, *The Jews were Expendable*, p. 197.
78 *Ibid.*, p. 205.
79 *Ibid.*, p. 206.

80 Hertz, J. H. 'A Moral Challenge to British Jewry, 6th April 1934', in *Sermons, Addresses and Studies*, Vol. 1, pp. 157–8.
81 Hertz, J. H., 'National Protest Against Nazi Persecution, Albert Hall, 1st December 1938', in *Early and Late*, p. 59.
82 Letter from Bernard Bockon, *JC*, 31 December 1943, p. 13.
83 Sherman, A. J., *Island Refuge* (London, 1973), p. 266.
84 *Ibid.*, p. 30; memorandum by Home Secretary, 7 April 1933.
85 Bentwich, N., *They Found Refuge: An Account of British Jewry's Work for Victims of Nazi oppression* (London, 1956), p. 41; Sherman, *Island Refuge*, p. 271.
86 PRO, FO 371/24078/233 (WI 4035/45/48), Home Office memorandum, 20 September 1939; Wasserstein, *Britain*, p. 82.
87 PRO, CAB 98/1/262: memorandum by Home Secretary for Cabinet Committee on the Refugee Problem, December 1939; Wasserstein, *ibid.*, p. 82.
88 Wasserstein, *ibid.*, p. 82.
89 PRO, CAB 98/1/92 ff. Minutes of meeting of Cabinet Committee on the Refugee Problem, 8 December 1939; Wasserstein, *ibid.*, p. 83.
90 Wasserstein, *ibid.*
91 Bentwich, *They Found Refuge*, p. 120; Wasserstein, *ibid.*, p. 83.
92 Central British Fund for Jewish Relief and Rehabilitation. *Report for 1933–1943* (London, 1944), p. 5; Wasserstein, *ibid.*, p. 83.
93 Bentwich, *They Found Refuge*, pp. 46 and 120; Wasserstein, *ibid.*, p. 83.
94 *JC*, 4 February 1944, p. 6.
95 *Ibid.*, 11 August 1944, p. 5.
96 See Bentwich's letters in *JC*, 16 March 1943, p. 9 and again on 24 September 1943, p. 14.
97 *JC*, 31 December 1943, p. 12.
98 *JC*, 22 September 1944, p. 11.
99 United Synagogue File No. 1931, 'Concentration Camps – 1945', and also letter in similar vein from Dollis Hill and Gladstone Park District Synagogue, 10 May 1945, in same file. There were, in addition, anguished pleas from non-conformist Jewish leaders following the liberation of Nazi death camps in response to reports that not enough supplies were getting to the survivors. The Agudah leader Harry Goodman, targeting the concentration on post-war planning and Zionism which we shall investigate in chapter 5, pronounced bitterly: 'It almost appeared as if Anglo-Jewry had "written off" Jews on the continent. They had been concerning themselves with magnificent post-war plans, with Biltmore and San Francisco, but in the meantime Jews were dying in hundreds in Bergenbelsen and Teresienstadt. We might have been able to save them' (*Di Vochenzaitung*, 13 April 1945, p. 4). The Revisionist weekly, the *Jewish Standard*, attacked what it considered to be the lack of understanding and efficiency of the mainstream Jewish leadership:

Despite the fact that about a month had passed since the liberation of Buchenwald – since when other camps have been overrun – no co-ordinated and effective action has been undertaken by the Anglo-Jewish community for dealing with the grave situation. The Board of Deputies has taken no decision, established no machinery, and still deals with the problem as though it had years to spare. (*Jewish Standard*, 11 May 1945, p. 1)

100 Ginsberg, M., *The Jewish Problem* (World Jewish Congress British Section, London, February 1943), p. 3.
101 *Ibid.*, pp. 3–4.

PART III: INTRODUCTION

1 Cohen, S. A., *English Zionists and British Jews* (Princeton, 1982), p. 178. Though this book deals with a slightly earlier period of Anglo-Jewish history, it is clear that the communal structure was not substantially different during the period under review. See also Cohen, *English Zionists*, pp. 161–78, particularly the views of Lucien Wolf. For further background see Bibliography entries for Endelman, Gilam, Alderman, Salbstein, Cesarani, Cohen, S. A., Finestein, Gartner, Shimoni and Williams.
2 *Jewish Standard*, 26 November 1943, p. 5.
3 Cohen, *English Zionists*, pp. 113–14.
4 *Ibid.*, pp. 224–5.

3 THE POLITICS OF HOPE

1 Hertz, J. H., 'A Moral Challenge to British Jewry' (7th Day of Passover Sermon, Central Synagogue, 6 April 1934), in Hertz, *Sermons, Addresses and Studies*, Vol. 1, p. 157. Hertz was by no means the most extreme advocate of this view. According to the *Jewish Echo* one Glasgow rabbi, at a meeting of mourning for the victims of Nazi persecution, 'almost proclaimed Hitler as the messenger of God Almighty to punish the children of Israel because some Jewish men are alleged to be not scrupulous enough about the dietary laws, and some women do not frequent the Mikvah ritual bath'. Such views, however, were rare, and when, as in this case, they were uttered they were heartily condemned. See *Jewish Echo*, 22 January 1943, p. 3.
2 Hertz, 'The Great Synagogue will Rise Again' (7 September 1941), in *Early and Late*, p. 68.
3 Hertz, *Readings from Holy Scriptures (Annotated) – for the Jewish Members of His Majesty's Forces, selected by the Chief Rabbi* (London, 1942), p. 338. 'And Haman said unto King Ahasuerus, There is a certain people scattered abroad and dispersed among the people in all the provinces of

thy Kingdom; and their laws are diverse from all people; neither keep they the King's laws; therefore it is not for the King's profit to suffer them' (Esther, 3:8).

4   Brodetsky, *Jews in the Post-War Settlement*, p. 22.

5   *JC*, 28 August 1942, p. 6; Hosea, 6:1.

6   See letter by D. Hammond, *JC*, 17 July 1942, p. 9; letter by H. Binstock, *JC*, 8 October 1943, p. 16; Psalms, 20:8.

7   Hertz, J. H., *Out of the Depths I Cry unto Thee*, p. 5.

8   Hertz, *Sermons, Addresses and Studies*, Vol. 2, pp. 263–4.

9   Laski, N., *The Jews of Greater Germany. Address by President of a Special Meeting of the Board of Deputies of British Jews on Sunday 17 July 1938* (London, 1938), p. 16.

10 *JC*, 17 July 1942, p. 8; Isaiah, 54:17. For a further example of secular journals turning to religion at times of great crisis, see the front pages of the *Zionist Review* for 4 December 1942 and 11 December 1942, where Psalm 94 and Isaiah, chapter 14 respectively are reprinted prominently in boldface and without comment. The *Review* similarly marked the destruction of Hungarian Jewry with Jeremiah, chapters 50 and 51 on 9 June 1944 and VE Day with Isaiah, chapter 14, Zephaniah, chapter 3 and Jeremiah, chapter 23 (4 May 1945, p. 1).

11 Hertz, *A Book of Jewish Thoughts*, p. 33.

12 Roth, C., *A Short History of the Jewish People* (2nd ed. London 1943, section written 1942–3), p. 430. In a section written in 1936 Roth had commented, 'the people who had survived the Crusades could survive National Socialism' (pp. 420–1).

13 Hertz, *A Book of Jewish Thoughts*, p. 98. See Psalm 126:5 included in the Sabbath and Festivals Grace after Meals.

14 Hertz, 'The Tragedy of Vienna', *Early and Late*, p. 53.

15 Roth, C., Vote of thanks to the Chair of 5th Lucien Wolf Memorial Lecture: 'Humanity and the Refugees', the Jewish Historical Society of England, Wednesday 1 February 1939 (London, 1939), p. 32.

16 Roth, Address to Cambridge University Jewish Society; *JC*, 8 May 1942, p. 11.

17 *JC*, 9 April 1943, p. 12.

18 *Ibid.*, 1 October 1943, p. 12.

19 Hertz, *Sermons, Addresses and Studies*, Vol. 1, Preface, p. vii.

20 *Jewish Gazette*, 24 July 1942, p. 1.

21 Statement of the Anglo-Jewish Association General Meeting, 17 February 1944 (in *Contemporary Jewish Record*, 7 (1944), p. 301).

22 Bowle, J., *Viscount Samuel: A Biography* (London, 1957), p. 309, on a speech in favour of appeasement, 23 November 1937, discussion with Lord Halifax, Foreign Secretary.

23 Wasserstein, B., letter in *Midstream*, 27, No.2 (1981), p. 63.

24 *Jewish Year Book*, 1939, p. 356.

25 Roth, *Short History of the Jewish People*, pp. 420–1.

26 Laski, *The Jews of Greater Germany*, p. 15.

27 Hertz, J. H., 'Conference of Anglo-Jewish Preachers, 1938', in *Early and Late*, p. 172.

28 Hertz, *Out of the Depths I Cry unto Thee*, p. 2.

29 Laski, *The Jews of Greater Germany*, p. 15.

30 Hertz, J. H., at 5th Lucien Wolf Memorial Lecture, Jewish Historical Society of England, Wednesday 1 February 1939 (London, 1939), p. 5.

31 Hertz, *Out of the Depths I Cry unto Thee*, p. 2.

32 Hughes, E., *Sidney Silverman: Rebel in Parliament* (London, 1969), p. 83, on Silverman's comment in an article which appeared in 1942.

33 *JC*, 10 April 1942, p. 8.

34 Hertz in *Sermons, Addresses and Studies*, Vol. 2, pp. 259–60.

35 Hertz, *In Ancient Egypt and Present-Day Germany: A Passover Sermon – April 11th, 1933* (London, 1933), pp. 12 and 13.

36 Laski, *The Jews of Greater Germany*, p. 16.

37 *JC*, 4 August 1944, p. 17.

38 Hertz, *Out of the Depths I Cry unto Thee*, pp. 10–11.

39 Office of the Chief Rabbi, *A Service of Prayer and Intercession on behalf of the Sufferers from the Renewed Attack on Religion and Human Freedom: 17th Tammuz, Sunday 17th July 1938* (London, 1938), p. 6. See also Hertz, 'Palestine Victory Campaign', Grosvenor House, 8 July 1941, in *Early and Late*, p. 196, and his *Nazi War: Prayer of Supplication to be read every Sabbath and Festival after the Prayer for the King and the Royal Family, Office of the Chief Rabbi* (London, 1940).

40 Hertz, 'Intercession Service, 23rd March 1941', in *Early and Late*, p. 63.

41 *Ibid.*, p. 64.

42 Hertz, in *JC*, 10 April 1942, p. 4.

43 Hertz, Broadcast BBC African Service, 6 April 1942, 'Passover and the Peasant Crisis', in *Early and Late*, p. 12.

44 Hertz, *JC*, 10 April 1942, p. 4.

45 Laski, H., *Reflections on the Revolution of our Time* (London, 1943, p. 231).

46 Hughes, *Silverman*, p. 84 – cited from Silverman's 1942 newspaper article, 'Plea for the Jews'.

47 *JC*, 26 June 1942, p. 12.

48 *Ibid.*, 24 July 1942, p. 5.

49 Roth, C., in Jewish Historical Society of England, *Miscellanies*, (London, 1942), p. viii.

50 Bentwich, N., *Wanderer Between Two Worlds* (London, 1941), pp. 225 and 338.

51 Brodetsky, S., 'The Balfour Declaration: Its Political Significance', pp. 265–6.

52 Bentwich, N., *Judaea Lives Again* (London, 1944), p. 6.

53 Brodetsky at the Inter-University Jewish Federation 23rd Annual Conference in Manchester; *JC* 9 January 1942, p. 6.
54 Paneth, P., *Guardian of the Law – The Chief Rabbi, Dr J. H. Hertz* (London, 1943), p. 97.
55 Hertz, J. H., 'England Awake', in *Early and Late*, p. 83.
56 Hertz, *Early and Late*, p. 210.
57 Hyamson, A. M., 'British Jewry in Wartime, February 1943' *Contemporary Jewish Record*, 6, No. 1 (1943), pp. 21–2.
58 *JC*, 24 April 1942, p. 5.
59 BD, C14/16; Brodetsky to Eden, 18 December 1942.
60 Hertz, 'The Great Synagogue will Rise Again', p. 69
61 Brodetsky, *The Jews in the Post-War Settlement*, p. 23.
62 *JC*, 25 June 1943, p. 8.
63 Berlin, Sir I., 'Lewis Namier: A Personal Impression', in Gilbert, M. (ed.), *A Century of Conflict, 1850–1950* (London, 1966), p. 222.
64 Hertz on the Balfour Declaration at meeting on 25th anniversary; *JC*, 6 November 1942, p. 6.
65 Hyamson, A. M., 'A Letter from London', 25 June 1944, in *Contemporary Jewish Record*, 7, No.4 (1944), p. 372.
66 *JC*, 12 January 1940, p. 14.
67 See Wasserstein, *Britain*, and Sharf, 'The British Press and the Holocaust'. Both indicate that it was the civil service, not the press that suppressed reactions to the Holocaust.
68 Hertz at Albert Hall meeting, 29 October 1942. See Hearst, E., 'The British and the Slaughter of the Jews', pp. 34–5.
69 Hertz, *Early and Late*, p. 63.
70 *JC*, 17 April 1942, p. 15.
71 *Ibid.*, 24 November 1944, p. 8.
72 Hertz, quoted in '70th Birthday message to Churchill', *JC*, 8 December 1944, p. 5.
73 Bauer, Y., 'The Goldberg Report', *Midstream*, 31, No.2 (1985), p. 28, and Feingold, H. L., 'Who Shall Bear Guilt for the Holocaust: The Human Dilemma', *American Jewish History*, 68, No.3 (1979), p. 263.
74 *JC*, 17 September 1943, p. 5.
75 *Ibid.*, 5 February 1943, p. 4.
76 World Jewish Congress British Section, *Report of the W.J.C. (British Section) – A Note on Bermuda and After* (London, 1943), p. 10.
77 *JC*, 6 November 1942, p. 8. A demonstration which effected no change in Nazi policy regarding the Jews in Europe was even on the home front hardly 'a commendable success'. Eden had replied to the invitation to attend the protest meeting thus: 'It will be recalled that the Prime Minister sent a message on this subject both on the occasion of the Centenary of the Jewish Chronicle last year and on that of the demonstration organised by the American Jewish Congress in New York last July.' In the circumstances, therefore, he continued, he was very sorry

that he did not feel able to comply with the request even to send a
message to the meeting. See *JC*, same issue, p. 5.
78 *JC*, 22 October, 1943, p. 13.
79 Gollancz, *Let My People Go*, p. 9.
80 Gollancz, *What Buchenwald Really Means*, p. 10.
81 Berlin, 'Lewis Namier', p. 219.
82 Hertz, 'Palestine Victory Campaign', Grosvenor House, 8 July 1941, in
Early and Late, p. 196.

4 THE POLITICS OF FEAR

1 Brodetsky, *Jews in the Post-War Settlement*, p. 9.
2 *JC*, 31 July 1942, p. 4.
3 Brodetsky, *Memoirs*, p. 238.
4 *Jewish Year Book*, 1940, p. 345. Further on in the same review it
implicitly records Dutch Jewry's adherence to the same conception of
emancipation. Reporting on the Queen's drive through Amsterdam on
the 40th anniversary of her accession, it comments that 'her Jewish
subjects ... had vied with their fellow citizens in decorating their houses
and public buildings as a demonstration of their loyalty and affection'
(p. 360).
5 Brodie, I., 'British and Palestinian Jews in World War II', *American
Jewish Year Book*, 1947, pp. 51–3.
6 *Ibid.*, p. 53. Similar statements had been expressed during the First
World War.
7 Office of the Chief Rabbi, *Memorial Prayer for those Fallen in Battle*
(London, 1940).
8 See Office of the Chief Rabbi, *The Nazi War; Prayer of Supplication to be
read every Sabbath and Festival after the Prayer for the King and the Royal
Family* (London, 1940); *Early and Late*, p. 69, and *JC*, 9 June 1944, p. 1.
9 Office of the Chief Rabbi, *The Nazi War Intercession Prayer*, 26 May 1940
(London, 1940).
10 Cohen, I., *The Jews in the War* (London, 1942), p. 7.
11 Cohen's booklet goes on to declare,

the Jews have always been ready to play their part in defence of their
native or adopted country, but never before were they so eager to make
every sacrifice as now ... They are to be found in the fighting forces of
all the Allied Democracies, and on land, in the air, and on sea they have
displayed a daring, skill and valour at least equal to those of their
comrades in arms. (p. 57)

12 *JC*, 11 February 1944, p. 8.
13 Brodetsky, *Memoirs*, p. 221. Further on he records that

after the war, when Hitler's Black List was discovered and published, containing the names of 2,300 people who were to be arrested and shot immediately the Germans landed in Britain, I found, quite naturally, I suppose, that my name was there. I was rather proud to find myself of the finest people in the land, among them my close friends and colleagues, Jews and non-Jews. (*Memoirs*, p. 202)

14 Hyde, H. M., *Strong for Service: The Life of Lord Nathan of Churt* (London, 1968), p. 188.
15 *JC*, 3 December 1943, p. 5.
16 *Ibid.*, 21 May 1943, p. 5. Geoffrey Alderman notes that 'Lipson had been Mayor of Cheltenham when a by-election occurred there in June 1937. The local Conservative Association refused, against all expectations, to adopt him, because he was Jewish. He ran as an Independent Conservative against the official candidate and narrowly won the seat; but in 1945 his majority was much increased' (Alderman, G., *The Jewish Vote in Great Britain since 1945*, p. 33, n.20). Lipson, a staunch anti-Zionist, was particularly sensitive to the dual loyalty issue.
17 *JC*, 12 June 1942, p. 5. British Jews, though they obviously preferred non-Jews to intercede on their behalf (as opposed to their own intervention), preferred rather mediocre, compliant Gentiles who could be instructed as how to act. James Parkes, one of the leading pro-Jewish Christian clerics, resigned from the Council of Christians and Jews realising that what was needed was a more powerful and intellectually impressive group to promote the Jewish cause. This was not what the Jewish leadership wanted at all. Indeed, when forceful non-Jewish personalities such as Parkes, Driberg or Lords Wedgwood and Strabolgi spoke on Jewish issues (often with a frankness that the British Jewish establishment found embarrassing), the Jewish organisations kept their distance. See Kushner, *The Persistence of Prejudice*, p. 184.
18 *JC*, 24 July 1942, p. 4.
19 Driberg, T., *Ruling Passions* (London, 1977), p. 202–3.
20 *JC*, 28 April 1944, p. 14.
21 *Ibid.*, 24 December 1943, p. 15. 'Malchus' (Yiddish), 'the powers that be'.
22 *Ibid.*, 31 July 1942, p. 5.
23 *Ibid.*, 14 August 1942, p. 8.
24 *Ibid.*, 31 December 1943, p. 8. One exception to this rule was John Mack, who was to contrast the vigorous championship of Jewish causes by Gentile parliamentarians such as Wedgwood, Eleanor Rathbone, Commander Lock Lampson and Major Cazalet 'with the apologetic attitude of some Jewish Members'. *Jewish Echo*, 12 March 1943, p. 8.
25 *Hansard*, House of Lords, 23 March 1943.
26 Wasserstein, 'Patterns of Jewish Leadership', p. 40.
27 Hertz, *A Book of Jewish Thoughts*, p. 98.

28 See Lehmann, R. P., *Nova Biblioteca Anglo-Judaica* (London, 1961), pp. 198–200. Prayers included:

A Service of Prayer and Intercession on Behalf of the Sufferers from the Nazi Attack on Religion and Human Freedom, Sunday 17 July 1938.

The Nazi War, Intercession Prayer, Sunday 26 May 5700–1940.

The Nazi War, A Service of Prayer and Intercession in connection with the Anniversary of the Outbreak of Hostilities, Sunday 8 September 5700–1940.

A Service of Prayer, Intercession and Thanksgiving in connection with Britain's Fight for Freedom, Sunday 23 March 5701–1941.

A Service of Prayer and Intercession in connection with the Second Anniversary of the Outbreak of Hostilities, Friday 7 September 5701–1941.

Order of Service for the National Day of Prayer and Dedication on the Fourth Anniversary of the Outbreak of Hostilities, Friday 3 September 5703–1943.

Order of Service for the National Day of Prayer and Dedication on the Fifth Anniversary of the Outbreak of Hostilities, Sunday 3 September 5704–1944.

The World War. Service of Praise and Thanksgiving for the Victories of the Allied Nations, 1945.

29 Bentwich, *Judaea Lives Again*, p. 180. Glasgow leader Fred Nettler was one of the very few to lay blame for the Holocaust on Christian thought. The victims, he said, were 'but a part of the blood sacrifices extracted from Jews during the birth and growth of the Christian World'. Views such as this were rarely enunciated, for they ran so counter to the two prevailing communal political philosophies. Jewish leaders went out of their way to proclaim Christianity as one of the mainstays of liberal morality, and criticism of such an integral part of the British societal fabric would have been unthinkable to a community so wedded to the idea of an emancipation contract. See *Jewish Echo*, 3 December 1943, p. 10.

30 *JC*, 10 April 1942, p. 4.

31 *JC*, 3 July 1942, p. 7.

32 Paneth, *Guardian of the Law*, p. 98.

33 Henriques, E. F. Q., 'Aryanisation', *Anglo-Jewish Association Review*, 1 (1944), pp. 18–19.

34 Hertz, *Out of the Depths I Cry Unto Thee*, pp. 6–8. The *Contemporary Jewish Record* reported that 'a warning that people must face the reality of anti-semitism in this country was contained in Chief Rabbi Hertz's New Year Letter 5704. "Foremost among those who have been willing to do so are the heads of Churches."' *Contemporary Jewish Record*, 7 (1944), p. 642.

35 *JC* Editorial, 16 October, 1942, p. 8.

36 Hertz, 'Demonstration Against Nazi Massacres, Albert Hall, 29th October, 1942', in *Early and Late*, p. 76. See also *JC*, 6 November, 1942, p. 5.

37 *JC*, 3 March 1944, p. 7.

38 Brotz, H., 'The Position of the Jews in English Society', *Jewish Journal of Sociology*, 1, No. 1 (1959), p. 94.

39 PRO, PREM 4/51/7/359; Stein to Martin.

40 Tumin, M. M., 'The Cult of Gratitude', *Judaism*, 13 (1964), 131–42, and Fein, H., *Accounting for Genocide: National Responses and Jewish Victimization during the Holocaust* (New York, 1979), p. 185.

41 *JC*, 25 December 1942, p. 5. When it came to expressing gratitude Jewish parliamentarians evidently felt they could speak more easily *qua* Jews. But when it came to pressing claims for the Jews of Europe the constraints of the emancipation contract won out and the MPs were not nearly so forthright.

42 *JC*, 25 December 1942, p. 12.

43 *Ibid.*, 1 January 1943, p. 9.

44 Hearst, E., 'The British and the Slaughter of the Jews – II', *Wiener Library Bulletin*, 21, No. 2 (1967), p. 40; *JC*, 25 December 1942, p. 8.

45 *JC*, 31 March 1944, p. 10.

46 *Ibid.*, 7 July 1944, p. 5.

47 *Ibid.*, 16 February 1943, p. 13.

48 *Ibid.*, 11 June 1943, p. 5.

49 *Ibid.*, 4 August 1944, p. 6. The inherent tension between the platitudes involved in the gratitude and honour strategies and the realities of the situation are clearly evidenced by this Board of Deputies debate. Brodetsky opened the debate on saving the Jews of Hungary from deportation by expressing 'his appreciation to all those bodies, both Jewish and non-Jewish, which were interesting themselves on this question and for the manner in which they had co-operated'. Victor Mischon followed with similar sentiments, saying, 'it was good to see this unity'. Harry Goodman, however, sounded a discordant note, pointing out that 'at this moment at least four, perhaps five, different organisations were doing the same thing in their own way, approaching the same people, and could not co-operate with each other'. In replying to the debate Brodetsky, contrary to the optimism of his opening, conceded that 'he was constantly trying to obtain the fullest consultation between the various Jewish bodies, but unfortunately co-operation between all the organisations had been found impossible'. See BD Minutes Book, 32, July 1942 to April 1945, Minutes to meeting of 26 July 1944, and *JC*, 4 August 1944, p. 6.

50 PRO, FO 371/32682 (WI, 7401/4555/48), 16 December 1942, Note by Law.

51 *JC*, 14 May 1943, p. 17.

52 Gollancz, *Let My People Go*, p. 7.

53 Hughes, *Silverman*, p. 82.

54 Laski, H. J., 'A Note on Anti-Semitism', p. 107.

55 Tumin, 'Cult of Gratitude', expanded version in Rose, P. I. (ed.), *The Ghetto and Beyond: Essays on Jewish Life in America* (New York, 1969), p. 81. British non-Jewish society had, by this time, abandoned any notion of the emancipation contract. Indeed it is to be doubted very much whether any non-Jews, apart maybe from a few liberal thinkers, had ever understood the emancipation of the Jews as a contract obligating non-Jews to keep one side of a bargain and dictating a specific form of action which each side must perform. In fact, as Kushner observes, popular British attitudes 'caught Jews within a vice, demanding that Jews assimilate yet denying them free access to Gentile preserves'. To this extent Cesarani is correct when he depicts Anglo-Jewry as being in a 'no-win situation'. The activities of the Jews during the war did not seriously affect British attitudes towards the Jews. Thus there was in fact no contract. But British Jews still very much believed in its existence, and continued to feel that they were validated not on the grounds of their Jewish identity, but on the basis of their conforming to the values and manners óf respectable English society. The emancipation contract thus existed only in the minds of British Jews; it was in this sense a delusion albeit based on an interpretation of some statements of nineteenth-century British political thinkers.

Historians of the period of the emancipation of the Jews in Britain, such as Gilam and Endelman, do not believe that a contract was envisioned at that time. Gilam says explicitly that 'in England emancipation was unconditional ... Jews were accepted for what they were', and approvingly quotes the great German Jewish historian, Heinrich Graetz: 'You English Jews had not to give solemn assurance that you are good patriots, that you love your native country as much as your fellow citizens. The honours you have received have been granted to you sans phrase as the descendants of Jacob, as the guardians of your ancient birthright' (Gilam, A., 'The Emancipation of the Jews in England 1830–1860', unpublished Ph.D. thesis, Washington University, 1979, p. 271). Bill Williams thinks otherwise, arguing that the emancipation contract was an intrinsic part of liberalism, the 'Anti-Semitism of Tolerance', as his classic article on the subject calls it. What certainly can be said is that following the large turn-of-the-century immigration, the succession of Aliens Acts and the First World War, Anglo-Jewry began to believe that such a contract did indeed exist. It was a desire to counteract this growing belief that prompted Harry Sacher to write his pamphlet *Jewish Emancipation: The Contract Myth* in 1917. However the belief persisted.

The timing of Sacher's article does not seem to lend support to Williams's contention that the contract emerged as an intrinsic part of British liberalism. After all, the crisis of the First World War coincided, so far as the Gentile world was concerned, with the end, not the beginning, of the self-confident Victorian era with its dominant liberal philosophy. It was within the Jewish world that the liberal outlook remained influential after this time. To arrive at their formulation of the contract British Jews had collapsed two co-existent yet ambivalent philosophies prevailing in British society, namely liberalism and anti-semitism, into one. This was a fundamentally mistaken redaction by British Jews, but one which grew out of their attempts to understand the new form of systematic, ideological anti-semitism which emerged during and after the First World War. In all probability the emancipation contract never existed in non-Jewish Britain. At no time did British Gentiles envisage a contract which entailed them in certain obligations.

See Endelman, T. M., *Radical Assimilation in English Jewish History, 1656–1945* (Bloomington, 1990); Kushner, *The Persistence of Prejudice*, pp. 195, 198; Endelman, T., 'The New Anglo-Jewish History', *Jewish Quarterly*, 137 (1990), 53–5; Cesarani, D., 'An Embattled Minority: The Jews in Britain during World War One', in Kushner, T. and Lunn, K. (eds.), *The Politics of Marginality* (London, 1990); Williams, B., 'The Anti-Semitism of Tolerance: Middle-Class Manchester and the Jews 1870–1900', in Kidd, A. J. and Roberts, K. W. (eds.), *City, Class and Culture: Studies of Social Policy and Cultural Production in Victorian Manchester* (Manchester, 1985), p. 94.

56 *JC*, 10 November 1944, p. 10, and *Jewish Standard*, 24 November 1944, p. 1. The killing of Lord Moyne went to the heart of the Yishuv's debate regarding policy toward the British, a debate anxiously followed by British Jews, who felt particularly vulnerable on this score. The motivations for, and the vehemence of, Samuel's comments were thus of a peculiarly Anglo-Jewish variety.

57 *JC*, 24 November 1944, p. 5.

5   THE JEWISH FIGHTING MODEL

1 *JC* editorial, 18 December 1942, p. 8; *ibid.*, 3 September 1943, p. 8.

2 Gollancz, V., *Nowhere to Lay Their Heads – The Jewish Tragedy in Europe and its Solution* (London, 1945), p. 3.

3 *JC*, 26 March 1943, p. 5.

4 *Ibid.*, 4 June 1943, p. 5, Brodetsky in a speech in the East End of London to the Mantle and Costume Branch of the National Union of Tailors and Garment Workers (30 May).

5 Gollancz, V., *Shall Our Children Live or Die? A Reply to Lord Vansittart on The German Problem* (London, 1942), p. 64.

6 *JC*, 18 December 1942, p. 1. It is interesting to note that even on the Day of Mourning and Prayer, the community maintained its religious divisions and there were separate Sephardi and Liberal services in addition to the Ashkenazi Orthodox service in Bevis Marks.

7 *JC*, 10 April 1942, p. 1.
8 *Ibid.*, 10 April 1942, p. 12.
9 *Ibid.*, 10 April 1942, p. 8.
10 Dr R. N. Salamon seconding vote of thanks to the Chair at the 5th Lucien Wolf Memorial Lecture, the Jewish Historical Society of England, 1 February 1939 (London, 1939), p. 32.
11 Cohen, *The Jews in the War*, p. 57.
12 *JC*, 1 November 1944, p. 11.
13 *Ibid.*, 27 August 1943, p. 1.
14 *Ibid.*, 21 July 1944, p. 1.
15 *Ibid.*, 7 August 1942, p. 8.
16 *Ibid.*, 11 December 1941, p. 8.
17 *Ibid.*, 4 February 1944, p. 5.
18 *Ibid.*, 22 September 1944, p. 5.
19 See Patterson, Lt. Col. J. H., *With the Judaeans in the Palestine Campaign* (London, 1922).
20 *JC*, 21 August 1942, p. 6.
21 *Contemporary Jewish Record*, 7 (1944), p. 182.
22 *JC*, 3 July 1942, p. 8.
23 *JC* editorial, 14 August 1942, p. 8.
24 Committee for a Jewish Army, *Jewish Legion – Jewish Army* (London, 1943), p. 19; Speeches at Conway Hall, 12 April 1943; Committee for a Jewish Army Publication, No.3. Though Revisionists were certainly prominent in the search for a model of the Jewish fighting spirit, they were by no means alone. More mainstream organisations such as the Board of Deputies and the Zionist Federation allied themselves in some degree to the cause. Indeed the Committee often made a point of distancing itself from the main Revisionist body, the New Zionist Organisation, in order to emphasise its cross-community appeal. The New Zionist Organisation occasionally complained about this strategy of the Committee. See *Jewish Standard* article, 'Rushing in where Angels Fear to Tread', 18 December 1942, p. 6 and also 20 August 1943, p. 4.
25 See full-page advertisement of the Anglo-American Committee for a Jewish Army, *JC*, 5 February 1943, p. 5.
26 *Manifesto and Proclamation of the Anglo-American Committee for a Jewish Army* (London, 1943; no page numbers).
27 *Ibid.*
28 *Jewish Legion – Jewish Army*, pp. 11–13.
29 Committee for a Jewish Army, Publication No.4, February 1944.
30 *JC*, 23 June 1944, p. 5.
31 *Jewish Legion – Jewish Army*, p. 11.
32 Committee for a Jewish Army, Publication No.4, p. 2.
33 *JC*, 14 August 1943, p. 3.
34 *Ibid.*, 9 July 1943, p. 6.
35 *Ibid.*, 29 September 1944, p. 6.

36 Leftwich at the Yiddish Pen Club, at a meeting to mourn Yiddish and Hebrew writers murdered in the Warsaw ghetto, *JC*, 16 July 1943, p. 5.

37 Laski, H. J., *Faith, Reason and Civilisation: An Essay in Historical Analysis* (London, 1944), p. 19.

38 *JC*, 13 August 1943, p. 1. See also Flavius Josephus's description of Masada printed in bold on the front page of the black border issue of the *Zionist Review* on 28 May 1943 and headlined 'Heroism in the Warsaw Gheto'.

39 Brodetsky, *Memoirs*, p. 217.

40 Bauer, Y., *From Diplomacy to Resistance: A History of Jewish Palestine 1939–45* (New York, 1973), p. 399, no. 18.

41 Committee for a Jewish Army, Publication No. 4, p. 2.

42 *JC*, 29 December 1944, p. 6.

43 *JC*, editorial 5 June 1942, p. 10.

44 *JC*, 5 June 1942, p. 10.

45 *Ibid.*, 6 March 1942, p. 8. The Keren Hayesod was the main fund-raising arm of the Jewish Agency.

46 *Times*, 5 December 1942, p. 14.

47 *JC*, 9 January 1942, p. 6.

48 Brodetsky, 'The Balfour Declaration', p. 254.

49 *Ibid.*, p. 269.

50 See *JC*, 29 May 1942, p. 11.

51 Brodetsky to Board of Deputies, *JC*, 2 January 1942, p. 7.

52 *JC*, 23 January 1942, p. 8.

53 *Ibid.*, 24 July 1942, p. 6.

54 *Ibid.*, 14 August 1942, p. 6.

55 *Ibid.*, 29 January 1943, p. 1.

56 *Contemporary Jewish Record*, 7 (1944), p. 406.

57 *JC*, 7 January 1944, p. 16.

58 Brodetsky, *Memoirs*, p. 215.

59 *JC*, 22 May 1942, p. 1.

60 *Ibid.*, 22 January 1943, p. 1.

61 For similar events in the United States, see Penkower, M. N., 'Believe the Unbelievable', in *Midstream*, 27, No. 4 (1981), p. 35.

62 *JC*, 11 August 1944, p. 6.

63 *Ibid.*, 30 June 1944, p. 10.

64 *Ibid.*, 10 March 1944, p. 6.

65 *Ibid.*, 2 July 1943, p. 7.

66 Nazi Extermination of the Jews. Speeches by Prof. S. Brodetsky and Dr Chaim Weizmann and Resolution Adopted by Board of Deputies of British Jews (London, 18 June, 1944). See Sompolonsky, M., 'Anglo-Jewish Leadership and the British Government', p. 218. Brodetsky, in replying, followed the traditional Anglo-Jewish pattern. He reassured the public, justifying the paucity of assistance and warning against over-emphasising the sufferings of the Jews.

67 *Contemporary Jewish Record*, 7 (1944), p. 68.
68 *JC*, 8 December 1944, p. 6.
69 *Manchester Guardian*, 16 November, 1943, p. 6.
70 Brodetsky, 'The Balfour Declaration', pp. 225–6.
71 *Ibid.*, p. 269.
72 *JC*, 7 July 1944, p. 6.
73 *Ibid.*, 6 November 1942, p. 5.
74 Goodman, *The Jewish National Home*, p. xxii.
75 *Ibid.*, p. xix.
76 *JC*, 13 October 1944, p. 7.
77 Bentwich, *Wanderer*, p. vii.
78 *Ibid.*, p. 296.
79 *Ibid.*, p. 349.
80 Bentwich, *My Seventy-Seven Years*, p. 190.
81 Bentwich, *Judaea Lives Again*, p. 5.
82 *Ibid.*, p. 174.
83 Reading, Eva, Marchioness of, *For the Record*, pp. 176–7.
84 See Rose, N., *Lewis Namier and Zionism* (Oxford, 1980), pp. 113–14.
85 *JC*, 1 October 1943, p. 12.
86 *Ibid.*, 18 August 1944, p. 3.
87 Brodetsky, p. 21.
88 Hertz, 'Address to Anglo-Jewish Preachers, 1935', in *Sermons, Addresses and Studies*, Vol. 2, p. 14.
89 Hertz, 'Palestine Victory Campaign', in *Early and Late*, p. 196.

CONCLUSION

1 Laski, H. J., *Reflections on the Revolution of our Time* (London, 1943), p. 97.
2 *Ibid.*, p. 83.
3 *Ibid.*, p. 31.
4 *JC*, 3 April 1942, p. 14.
5 In 1943 he secured 100 immigration visas from the Irish government and saw the Apostolic Delegate concerning the fate of Italy's Jews. In 1944 he obtained 500 Irish and 400 Mexican visas for Hungarian Jews. See *Di Vochenzaitung*, 14 May 1943, pp. 1 and 3, and Penkower, *The Jews Were Expendable*, pp. 250 and 255. Penkower comments that these were 'impressive but limited achievements'. For the emotional link between Agudah and the Jews of Europe, see *Jewish Standard*, 18 September 1942, p. 7; see also readers' proposals on assistance to Jews of Europe. *Di Vochenzaitung*, 22 January 1943, p. 4.
    The Agudah, like all Jewish bodies, was, however, drawn into the pettiness of communal conflict even at the most inappropriate of times. See the flippant articles 'My Friend the "Jewish Echo"', 'Celebrations in These Days?' and 'Bouquets All Round' in the 25 December 1942

edition of *Di Vochenzaitung*, immediately following the Allied Declaration and the Bevis Marks Service of Mourning.

6 M. Friedlander was Headmaster of the Glasgow Talmud Torah and Director of Education to the Glasgow Board of Jewish Education. *Jewish Echo*, 24 December 1943, p. 7.

7 See *ibid.*, 28 August 1942, p. 3 and 26 February 1943, p. 10 (letter from Hirshke Binyomins); *Jewish Standard*, 31 December 1943, p. 1.

8 *Jewish Echo*, 28 August 1942, p. 3 and 19 February 1943, p. 3. The Agudah is said to be the repository of 'ill-chosen jokes, Batlonic witticism [i.e. with intellectual pretensions but half-baked ideas] and public denunciation'. Not 'everyone who has the gift of the gab and a store of distorted Midrashim and antiquated jokes should be allowed to establish new funds and carry on new campaigns'.

9 See notes 29, 30 and 31 below.

10 *Jewish Standard*, 22 January 1943, p. 5.

11 *Ibid.*, 1 October 1943, p. 4.

12 *Ibid.*, 25 December 1942, p. 3.

13 *Ibid.*, 11 December 1942, p. 4.

14 *Ibid.*, 9 April 1943, pp. 5 and 7.

15 *Ibid.*, 9 April 1943, p. 7; 25 December 1942, p. 3.

16 *Ibid.*, 9 April 1943, p. 5.

17 *Ibid.*, editorial, 2 June 1944, p. 3; 28th January 1944, p. 4.

18 *Ibid.*, 17 December 1943, p. 3.

19 *Ibid.*, editorial, 8 September 1944, p. 3.

20 *Ibid.*, 9 April 1943, pp. 4 and 5.

21 *Ibid.*, 25 December 1942, p. 3.

22 *Ibid.*

23 *Ibid.*, 11 December 1942, p. 4.

24 *Ibid.*, 25 December 1942, p. 3.

25 *Ibid.*, 24 November 1943, p. 4.

26 *Ibid.*, 2 June 1944, p. 3.

27 For the twelve-point plan, see Minutes of National Committee for Rescue from Nazi Terror, Parkes Papers 15/057, University of Southampton Archives: first published draft drawn up by Eleanor Rathbone in April 1943 and amended slightly by Gollancz, and a revised edition published in January 1944. See the Committee's pamphlet *Continuing Terror* (London, 1944) for detailed exploration of the feasibility of the plan.

28 *Jewish Standard*, 31 December 1943, p. 1.

29 The Joint Foreign Committee of the Board of Deputies called a special meeting to be held on 8 December 1942 in connection with the reports of the massacres in Poland. Two members of the Presidency of the New Zionist Organisation, A. Abrahams and the Irish T. D. Robert Briscoe, were invited, but only in a personal capacity. However, so acute was the conflict between the mainstream and the Revisionist Zionists, even

at this tragic moment, that on arrival at Woburn House (the home of the Board) 'it was sought by Dr Brodetsky, at the last moment, to avoid their presence at the meeting. Subsequently, however, Mr Robert Briscoe was admitted to the meeting, with Mr A. Abrahams waiting outside.' *Jewish Standard* article, 'While Jews Die …', 11 December 1942, p. 1. Briscoe had, no doubt, been exonerated due to his eminent position in Irish public life.

30 *Jewish Standard*, 9 April 1943, p. 4.
31 *Ibid.*, 14 August 1942, p. 7.
32 See Wasserstein, *Britain*, Gilbert, *Auschwitz*, and Kushner, T., 'Rules of the Game: Britain, America and the Holocaust in 1944', *Holocaust and Genocide Studies*, 5, No.4 (1990), 381–402.

Bibliography

PRIMARY SOURCES

Archives

Archives of the United Synagogue, Adler House, London.
Board of Deputies of British Jews, Woburn House, London.
Jewish Committee for HM Forces, Woburn House, London: Minute Books.
Public Record Office.

Printed materials: books and pamphlets

Abramsky, C. (ed.), *Calling All Jews To Action!* (London, 1943)
Anglo-Jewish Association Year Book, 1951 (London, 1951)
Aronsfeld, C. C., 'British Jewry seen through Nazi Eyes', *Jewish Monthly*, 1, No. 2 (1947), 46–52
Association of Jewish Ex-Servicemen, *Anglo-Jewry in Battle and Blitz*, 2nd and 3rd issues entitled *British Jewry in Battle and Blitz* (London, no dates)
Barou, N., *The Jews in Work and Trade: A World Survey* (London, 1945)
Bartoszewski, N. and Lewin, Z., *Righteous Among Nations* (London, 1969)
Ben-Gurion, D., 'Before the Tribunal of History', *Zionist Review*, 4, No. 38 (1944), 3, 7
Ben-Jacob, J., *The Jewish Struggle* (London, 1942)
Bentwich, N., *Judaea Lives Again* (London, 1944)
    My Seventy-Seven Years: An Account of my Life and Times, 1883–1960 (London, 1962)
    Wanderer Between Two Worlds (London, 1941)
Board of Deputies of British Jews, *The Jews in Europe: Their Martyrdom and their Future* (London, 1945)
Brodetsky, S., 'The Balfour Declaration: Its Political Significance', in Goodman, P. (ed.), *The Jewish National Home: The Second November 1917–1942* (London, 1943), pp. 253–72
    The Jews in the Post-War Settlement, Lucien Wolf Memorial Lecture, Jewish Historical Society of England (London, 1942)

188

Memoirs: From Ghetto to Israel (London, 1960)

Brodie, I., 'British and Palestinian Jews in World War II'. *American Jewish Year Book* (1947), 51–72

Burger, F., *Gollancz's Buchenwald Never Existed* (London, 1945)

Burnett, R. G., *These My Brethren* (London, 1946)

Casper, B. M., *With The Jewish Brigade* (London, 1947)

Central British Fund for Jewish Relief and Rehabilitation, *Report for 1933–1943* (London, 1944)

Cohen, I., *The Jews in the War* (London, 1942)

Cohen, Sir J. B. B., *Count your Blessings* (London, 1956)

Cohen, L., *Some Recollections of C. G. Montefiore* (London, 1940)

Committee for a Jewish Army, *Behind the Near Eastern Front: Arabs and Jews* (London, 1942)

Jewish Legion – Jewish Army (London, 1943)

Manifesto and Proclamation of the Anglo-American Committee for a Jewish Army (London, 1943)

Publications, Nos. 1–5 (1942–5)

Repatriated Palestine Jews (London, 1944)

Souvenir Booklet Closing Ball (London, 1945)

Towards a Jewish Army (London, 1942)

Driberg, T., *Ruling Passions* (London, 1977)

Easterman, A. L., *King Carol, Hitler and Lupescu* (London, 1942)

Eden, Sir A., Earl of Avon, *The Eden Memoirs: The Reckoning* (London, 1965)

Emden, P. H., *Jews of Britain: A Series of Biographies* (London, 1944)

Epstein, I., Levine, E. and Roth, C. (eds.), *Essays in Honour of the Very Rev. Dr J. H. Hertz on the Occasion of his 70th Birthday – September 25th 1942* (London, 1942)

Geyer, C. and Loeb, W., *Gollancz in German Wonderland* (London, 1942)

Ginsberg, M., *The Jewish Problem* (World Jewish Congress, British Section) (London, 1943)

Gollancz, V., *Let My People Go* (London, 1942)

Nowhere to Lay their Heads: The Jewish Tragedy in Europe and its Solution (London, 1945)

Reminiscences of Affection (London, 1968)

Shall our Children Live or Die? A Reply to Lord Vansittart on the German Problem (London, 1942)

What Buchenwald Really Means (London, 1945)

Goodman, P. (ed.), *The Jewish National Home: The Second November 1917–1942* (London, 1943)

Guedalla, P., *Mr Churchill: A Portrait* (London, 1945)

Harris, Sir P., *Forty Years in and out of Parliament* (London, 1947)

Henriques, E. F. Q., 'Aryanisation', *Anglo-Jewish Association Review*, 1 (1944), 17–19

Hertz, J. H., *Anti-Semitism – A Sermon* (London, 1922)

A Book of Jewish Thoughts – New and Revised Edition, Selected and Arranged by the Chief Rabbi (London, 1941)

Early and Late: Addresses, Messages and Papers (London, 1943)

In Ancient Egypt and Present-Day Germany: A Passover Sermon – April 11th 1933 (London, 1933)

Out of the Depths I Cry unto Thee. Sermon by the Chief Rabbi at The Service of Prayer and Intercession on behalf of the Jews in Germany. Royal Albert Hall, Sunday 9th July 1933 (London, 1933)

Readings from Holy Scriptures (Annotated) – for the Jewish Members of His Majesty's Forces, selected by the Chief Rabbi (London, 1942 and 1944)

Sermons, Addresses and Studies, 3 vols. (London, 1938)

Horowitz, P., *The Jews, the War and After* (London, 1943)

Hyamson, A. M., 'British Jewry in Wartime'. *Contemporary Jewish Record*, 6, no. 1 (1943), 14–22

'A Letter from London', *Contemporary Jewish Record* 6, No. 5 (1943), 480–5; 7, No. 2 (1944), 164–7; 7, No. 4 (1944), 369–74

Palestine: A Policy (London, 1942)

Jabotinsky, V., *The Jewish War Front* (London, 1940)

The Jewish Chronicle 1841–1941: A Century of Newspaper History (London, 1949)

Jewish Fund for Soviet Russia, *Beaver Hall Conference* (London, 1944)

Calling All Jews to Action (London, 1943)

Jewish Historical Society of England, *Lucien Wolf Memorial Lectures: The Hebrew University and its Place in the Modern World*, by Professor Leon Roth (London, 1944)

Humanity and the Refugees, by the Bishop of Chichester (London, 1939)

The Jews in the Post-War Settlement, by Selig Brodetsky (London, 1942)

Minorities and the Democratic State, by Jan Masaryk (London, 1943)

Toleration and Democracy, by Dr A. D. Lindsay, Master of Balliol College, Oxford (London, 1941)

Jewish Historical Society of England, *Miscellanies IV* (London, 1942)

Karski, J., *Story of a Secret State* (London, 1945)

Koestler, A., *Arrival and Departure* (London, 1944)

Scum of the Earth (London, 1941)

The Yogi and the Commissar (London, 1945)

Laski, H. J., *Faith, Reason and Civilisation: An Essay in Historical Analysis* (London, 1944)

The Germans – are they Human? A Reply to Sir Robert Vansittart (London, 1941)

'A Note on Anti-Semitism', *New Statesman and Nation*, 25 (13 February 1943), 107–8

'On a Jewish Soldier's Letter', *New Statesman and Nation*, 26 (9 October 1943), 229–30

Reflections on the Revolution of our Time (London, 1943)

The Strategy of Freedom: An Open Letter to Students, especially American (London, 1942)

Laski, N., *Jewish Rights and Jewish Wrongs* (London, 1939)
  The Jews of Greater Germany. Address by President at a Special Meeting of the Board of Deputies of British Jews on Sunday 17th July 1938 (London, 1938)
Locker, B., *Palestine and the Jewish Future* (London, 1942)
Montefiore, L. G., *The Jews in Germany: Facts and Figures* (London, 1934)
Namier, L. B., *Conflicts: Studies in Contemporary History* (London, 1942)
  'The Jewish Problem Reargued: A Palestine State the Only Solution', *Manchester Guardian*, 16 November 1943, pp. 4, 6
National Committee for Rescue from Nazi Terror, *Continuing Terror* (London, 1944)
Newman, C. (ed.), *Gentile and Jew* (London, 1945)
Office of the Chief Rabbi, *Memorial Prayer for the Victims of the Mass Massacres of Jews in Nazi-occupied Lands. To be recited on Tisha B'Av after the Reading of the Law and on succeeding Sabbaths after the Prayer for the King and the Royal Family* (London, 1942)
  Memorial Prayer for those Fallen in Battle (London, 1940)
  The Nazi War Intercession Prayer (London, 1940)
  The Nazi War: Prayer of Supplication to be read every Sabbath and Festival after the Prayer for the King and Royal Family (London, 1939 and 1940)
  Order of Service for the National Day of Prayer and Dedication on the 4th Anniversary of the Outbreak of the Hostilities, 3rd September 1943 (London, 1943)
  Order of Service for the National Day of Prayer and Dedication on the 5th Anniversary of the Outbreak of the Hostilities, 3rd September 1944 (London, 1944)
  A Service of Prayer and Intercession for the Jews in Germany, 20th November 1938 (London, 1938)
  A Service of Prayer and Intercession on behalf of the Sufferers from the renewed attack on Religion and Human Freedom: 17th Tammuz Sunday 17th July 1938 (London, 1938)
  Supplication for the Success of HM Forces and the Safety of the Civilian Population and Memorial Prayer for those fallen in Battle and for Civilian Victims of the War. To be recited every Sabbath and Festival after the Prayer for the King and the Royal Family (London, 1941)
  The World War – Service of Praise and Thanksgiving for the Victories of the Allied Nations (London, 1945)
Paneth, P., *Guardian of the Law – The Chief Rabbi, Dr J. H. Hertz* (London, 1943)
Patterson, Lt. Col. J. H., *With the Judaeans in the Palestine Campaign* (London, 1922)
Political and Economic Planning, *Are Refugees an Asset?* (London, 1944)
Presland, J. [pseud. of Gladys Bendit], *A Great Adventure: The Story of the Refugee Children's Movement* (London, 1944)
Raczynski, Count E., *In Allied London* (London, 1962)
Rathbone, E. F., *Falsehoods and Facts about the Jews* (London, 1944)

Reading, Eva, Marchioness of, *For the Record* (London, 1973)

Rofe, C., *Against the Wind* (London, 1956)

Roth, C., 'The Collapse of English Jewry', *Jewish Monthly*, 4 (1947), 11–17

  History of the Jews in England (London, 1941)

  'Italy's Jews', *Anglo-Jewish Association Review*, (February 1945), 10–12

  The Jewish Contribution to Civilisation (London, 1942)

  A Short History of the Jewish People (London, 1943)

Sacher, H., *Jewish Emancipation: The Contract Myth* (London, 1917)

  Zionism and the Jewish Future (London, 1916)

Salaman, R. N., *Whither Lucien Wolf's Anglo-Jewish Community?* (London, 1953)

Samuel, Viscount E. A., *Lifetime in Jerusalem* (London, 1970)

Samuel, Viscount H., *Memoirs* (London, 1945)

Samuel, M., *The Great Hatred* (London, 1943)

Schonfeld, S., *Message to Jewry* (London, 1959)

Shinwell, E., *I've Lived Through it All* (London, 1973)

  Lead with the Left – my First Ninety-Six Years (London, 1981)

Simpson, W. W., 'Jewish Christian Co-operation in Great Britain', *Contemporary Jewish Record*, 7 (1944), 641–5

Stein, L., 'A Decade in Anglo-Jewry 1940–1950', *Year Book of the Anglo-Jewish Association* (London, 1951), 10–17

Union of Hebrew and Religion Classes, *Order of Service for Children attending the Constituent Classes – New Synagogue, Lag Ba'Omer, May 7th 1939* (London, 1939)

Watts, F. (ed.), *Voices of History, 1942–1943* (New York, 1943)

Webber, G. J., 'The Present Position of Anglo-Jewry', *Jewish Forum* (October 1946), 75–85

Wedgwood, J. C., *Memoirs of a Fighting Life* (London, 1941)

Weizmann, C., 'Palestine's Role in the Solution of the Jewish Problem', *Foreign Affairs*, 20, No. 2 (1942), 324–38

  Trial and Error (London, 1949)

World Committee for the Victims of German Fascism, *Brown Book of the Hitler Terror* (London, 1933)

World Jewish Congress, *Unity in Dispersion – A History of the World Jewish Congress* (New York, 1948)

World Jewish Congress – British Section, *America's Great 'Stop Hitler Now Demonstration'* (London, 1943)

  The Atlantic City Conference of UNRRA (London, 1944)

  The Disease of Anti-Semitism: Diagnosis, Crisis and A Remedy by Prof. M. Ginsberg, Norman M. Littel, Julian Franklyn and Dr A. Steinberg (London, 1944)

  European Conference of the WJC London August 19th–23rd 1943: Summary of Proceedings (London, 1945)

  The Jewish Problem – by M. Ginsberg (London, 1943)

Memorandum on Post-War Relief and Rehabilitation of European Jewry submitted to the Council of UNRRA (London, 1943)

National Conference October 23rd and 24th 1943: Report of the Executive Officers and Proceedings (London, 1943)

The Problem of Statelessness (London, 1944)

Protection against Group Defamation – Present Law and its Extension (London, 1944)

Report of Executive Officers, October 23rd and 24th, 1943 (London, 1943)

Report on Activities of the WJC January–May 1945 (London, 1945)

Reports of the WJC (British Section) – A Note on Bermuda and After (London, 1943)

Report of the WJC: North Africa: Reports of the Jews in Algeria: Memorandum to the US Government (London, 1943)

Reports of the WJC: Starvation over Europe: Hunger as Hitler's War Weapon, Strategy of Jewish Extermination (London, 1943)

St James's Conference of the Allied Governments in London and Nazi Anti-Jewish Crimes (London, 1942)

Uniting the Dispersed: Report for 1945. Search Department (London, 1945)

War Emergency Conference of the WJC – Atlantic City, November 1944 Addresses and Resolutions (London, 1945)

World Jewish Congress Facts (London, no date)

The World Jewish Congress (London, no date)

The Yellow Spot (London, 1936)

Zelmanovits, L., *Origin and Development of the World Jewish Congress. An Historical Survey* (London, 1943)

Printed materials: newspapers and journals

Anglo-Jewish Association Review
Christians and Jews: An Occasional Review
The Circle – Official Organ of the Workers Circle
Contemporary Jewish Record
Jewish Bulletin
Jewish Chronicle
Jewish Echo
Jewish Gazette
Jewish Standard
Jewish Year Book
New Judaea
Di Vochenzaitung (The Jewish Weekly)
Zionist Review

SECONDARY WORKS

Agar, H., *The Saving Remnant: An Account of Jewish Survival since 1914* (London, 1960)

Ainsztein, R., 'Facing the Truth', *Jewish Quarterly*, 16, No. 1 (1968), 35–9
'The Failure of the West. How Many More Could Have Been Saved?' *Jewish Quarterly*, 14, No. 4 (52) (1966), 11–20

Alderman, G., 'Antisemitism in Britain', *Jewish Journal of Sociology*, 31, No. 2 (1989), 125–40
The Jewish Community in British Politics (Oxford, 1983)
The Jewish Vote in Great Britain since 1945 Centre for the Study of Public Policy, University of Strathclyde (Glasgow, 1980)

Avital, Z., 'The Polish Government in Exile and the Jewish Question', *Wiener Library Bulletin*, 28 (1975), 43–51

Balfour, M., *Propaganda in War: Organizations, Policies and Publics in Britain and Germany* (London, 1979)

Baron, S. W., 'The Modern Age', in Schwarz, L. (ed.), *Great Ages and Ideas of the Jewish People* (New York, 1956), 313–484
Modern Nationalism and Religion (New York, 1947)

Bauer, Y., *American Jewry and the Holocaust: The American Joint Distribution Committee, 1939–1945* (Detroit, 1981)
From Diplomacy to Resistance: A History of Jewish Palestine 1939–45 (New York, 1973)
'The Goldberg Report'. *Midstream*, 31, No. 2 (1985), 25–8
and Rotenstreich, Y. (eds.), *The Holocaust in Historical Perspective* (Washington, 1978)
The Jewish Emergence from Powerlessness (London, 1971)
'Jewish Foreign Policy during the Holocaust', *Midstream*, 30, No. 10 (1984), 22–5
Out of the Ashes – The Impact of American Jews on Post-Holocaust European Jewry (Oxford, 1989)
'Reply to Marie Syrkin', *Midstream*, 14, No. 5 (1968), 63–4
'When Did They Know?' *Midstream*, 14, No. 4 (1968), 51–8

Bauer, Y. and Rotenstreich, N. (eds.), *The Holocaust as Historical Experience* (London, 1981)

Beloff, M., 'The Social Politics of Anglo-Jewry', *Jewish Journal of Sociology*, 31, No. 2 (1989), 121–4

Bentwich, N., 'The Social Transformation of Anglo-Jewry, 1883–1960', *Jewish Journal of Sociology*, 2 (1960), 16–24
They Found Refuge: An Account of British Jewry's Work for Victims of Nazi Oppression (London, 1956)

Berghahn, M., *Continental Britons: German-Jewish Refugees from Nazi Germany* (Oxford, 1988)
German-Jewish Refugees in England: The Ambiguities of Assimilation (London, 1984)

Berlin, Sir I., 'Lewis Namier: A Personal Impression', in Gilbert, M. (ed.), *A Century of Conflict, 1850–1950* (London, 1966), 215–30

Berman, A., 'American Zionism and the Rescue of European Jewry: An Ideological Perspective', *American Jewish History*, 70 (1981), 310–30
Nazism, the Jews and American Zionism, 1933–1948 (Detroit, 1990)

Bermant, C., *The Cousinhood: The Anglo-Jewish Gentry* (London, 1971)
Troubled Eden – An Anatomy of British Jewry (London, 1969)

Bettelheim, B., 'Freedom from Ghetto Thinking', in *Recollections and Reflections* (London, 1990)

Blass, S., *The British Jewish Experience in the Second World War* (unpublished B.A. (Hons) thesis, Manchester Polytechnic, 1989)

Bowle, J., *Viscount Samuel: A Biography* (London, 1957)

Bracher, K. D., *The German Dictatorship: The Origins, Structure and Effects of National Socialism* (London, 1971)

Braham, R. L. (ed.), *Contemporary Views on the Holocaust* (Boston, 1983)
Jewish Leadership during the Nazi Era (New York, 1985)
The Politics of Genocide – The Holocaust in Hungary (New York, 1981)

Breitman, R., 'The Allied War Effort and the Jews, 1942–3', *Journal of Contemporary History*, 20, No. 1 (1985), 135–55

Breitman, R. and Kraut, A. M., *American Refugee Policy and European Jewry, 1933–1945* (Indiana, 1987)
'Who Was the "Mysterious Messenger"?', *Commentary*, 76, No. 4 (1983), 44–7

Brotman, A. G., 'Jewish Communal Organisation', in Gould, J. and Esh, S. (eds.), *Jewish Life in Modern Britain* (London, 1964), 1–17

Brotz, H., 'The Position of the Jews in English Society', *Jewish Journal of Sociology*, 1, No. 1 (1959), 94–113

Cesarani, D., 'An Embattled Minority: The Jews in Britain during World War One', in Kushner, T. and Lunn, K. (eds.), *The Politics of Marginality: Race, the Radical Right and Minorities in Twentieth Century Britain* (London, 1990), 61–81
(ed.) *The Making of Modern Anglo-Jewry* (Oxford, 1990)

Cohen, M. J., *Churchill and the Jews* (London, 1985)
Palestine, Retreat from the Mandate: The Making of British Policy, 1936–1945 (New York, 1988)

Cohen, S. A., 'Anglo-Jewish Responses to Anti-semitism: Suggestions for a Framework of Analysis', in Reinharz, J. (ed.), *Living with Anti-Semitism* (London, 1987), 84–103
English Zionists and British Jews: The Communal Politics of Anglo-Jewry, 1895–1920 (Princeton, 1982)
'Israeli Sources for the Study of Anglo-Jewish History', *Jewish Historical Society of England Transactions*, 27 (1982), 129–47
'Same Places, Different Faces: A Comparison of Anglo-Jewish Conflicts over Zionism During World War I and World War II', in Cohen, S. A. and Don-Yehiya, E. (eds.), *Comparative Jewish Politics Volume*

II: *Conflict and Consensus in Jewish Political Life* (Tel-Aviv, 1986), 61–78

'Selig Brodetsky and the Ascendancy of Zionism in Anglo-Jewry: Another View of his Role and Achievements', *Jewish Journal of Sociology*, 24, No. 1 (1982), 25–38

Cohen, S. A. and Don-Yehiya, E. (eds.), *Comparative Jewish Politics Volume II, Conflict and Consenus in Jewish Political Life* (Tel-Aviv, 1986)

Conway, J. S., 'Between Apprehension and Indifference: Allied Attitudes to the Destruction of Hungarian Jewry', *Weiner Library Bulletin*, 27, Nos. 30–1 (1973–4), 37–48

Cruickshank, C., *The German Occupation of the Channel Islands* (Guernsey, 1975)

Dawidowicz, L. S., 'American Jewry and the Holocaust', *New York Times Magazine*, 18 April 1982, pp. 47–8, 101–14

'Indicting American Jews', *Commentary*, 75, No. 6 (1983), 36–44

Doxat, J., *Shinwell Talking* (London, 1984)

Druks, H., *The Failure to Rescue* (New York, 1977)

Edwards, R. D., *Victor Gollancz: A Biography* (London, 1987)

Elazar, D. J. and Cohen, S. A., *The Jewish Polity* (Indiana, 1985)

Endelman, T., 'Anti-Semitism in War-Time Britain: Evidence from the Victor Gollancz Collection', *Michael* (The Diaspora Research Institute, Tel-Aviv University), 10 (1986), 75–95

'The Englishness of Jewish Modernity in England' in Katz, J. (ed.), *Toward Modernity – The European Jewish Model* (Oxford, 1987)

The Jews of Georgian England, 1714–1830 (Philadelphia, 1979)

'The New Anglo-Jewish History', *Jewish Quarterly*, No. 37, (1990), 53–5

Radical Assimilation in English Jewish History, 1656–1945 (Bloomington, 1990)

Engel, D., *Bibliographical Essay: The Western Allies and the Holocaust* (unpublished)

In the Shadow of Auschwitz: The Polish Government-in-Exile and the Jews, 1939–1942 (London, 1987)

Fein, H., *Accounting for Genocide: National Responses and Jewish Victimization during the Holocaust* (New York, 1979)

Feingold, H. L., 'Courage First and Intelligence Second: The American Jewish Secular Elite, Roosevelt and the Failure to Rescue', *American Jewish History*, 72 (1982/3), 424–60

Did American Jewry Do Enough During the Holocaust? (Syracuse, 1985)

The Politics of Rescue: The Roosevelt Administration and the Holocaust, 1938–1945 (New York, 1970)

Review of Morse, A. D., 'While Six Million Died: A Chronicle of American Apathy', *American Jewish Historical Quarterly*, 58 (1968), 150–5

'Stephen Wise and the Holocaust', *Midstream*, 29, No. 1 (1983), 45–9

'Who Shall Bear Guilt for the Holocaust: The Human Dilemma', *American Jewish History*, 68, No. 3 (1979), 262–82

Finestein, I., Epilogue to Picciotto, J., *Sketches of Anglo-Jewish History. Revised and Edited with a Prologue, Notes and an Epilogue by Israel Finestein,* M. A. (London, 1956)

Post-Emancipation Jewry: The Anglo-Jewish Experience (Oxford, 1980)

'Jews in British Society', *Jewish Journal of Sociology,* 26, No. 1 (1984), 53–9

Finger, S. M., *American Jewry during the Holocaust,* American Jewish Commission on the Holocaust (New York, 1984)

Fischer, Lord S., *Brodetsky – Leader of the Anglo-Jewish Community* (Leeds, 1976)

Fox, J. P., 'Great Britain and the German Jews 1933', *Wiener Library Bulletin* 26, No. 1/2 (New Series, Nos. 26 and 27; 1972), 40–6

'The Jewish Factor in British War Crimes Policy in 1942', *English Historical Review,* 92, No. 362 (1977), 82–106

Review of Wasserstein, B., *Britain and the Jews of Europe, 1939–45, European Studies Review,* 10, No. 1 (1980), 138–46

Review of Wasserstein, B., *Britain and the Jews of Europe, 1939–45, International Affairs,* 56, No. 1 (1980), 143–4

Review of Wasserstein, B., *Britain and the Jews of Europe, 1939–45, Jewish Historical Society of England Transactions,* 27 (1982), 165–7

Freedman, M., *A Minority in Britain* (London, 1953)

Frey, R. S. and Thompson-Frey, N., *The Imperative of Response: The Holocaust in Human Context* (London, 1985)

Friedlander, S., 'On the Possibility of the Holocaust: An Approach to a Historical Synthesis', in Bauer, Y. and Rotenstreich, N. (eds.), *The Holocaust as Historical Experience* (London, 1981)

Friedman, I., 'Dissensions over Jewish Identity in West European Jewry', in Katz, J. (ed.), *The Role of Religion in Modern Jewish History* (Cambridge, Mass., 1975)

The Question of Palestine, 1914–1918 (London, 1973)

Friedman, S. S., *No Haven for the Oppressed: United States Policy Toward Jewish Refugees 1938–45* (Detroit, 1973)

Review of Wesserstein, B., *Britain and the Jews of Europe, 1939–45, American Jewish History,* 69, No. 4 (1980), 529–32

Gannon, F. R., *The British Press and Germany, 1936–1939* (London, 1971)

Gartner, L. P., *The Jewish Immigrant in England, 1870–1914* (London, 1973)

Gelber, Y., 'Zionist Policy and the Fate of European Jewry, 1939–1942', *Yad Vashem Studies,* 13 (1979), 179–210

Gewirtz, S., 'Anglo-Jewish Responses to Nazi Germany 1933–39: The Anti-Nazi Boycott and the Board of Deputies of British Jews', *Journal of Contemporary History,* 26, No. 2 (1991), 255–76

Gilam, A., 'The Emancipation of the Jews in England, 1830–1860', (unpublished Ph.D. thesis, Washington University, 1979)

The Emancipation of the Jews in England, 1830–1860 (New York, 1982)

Gilbert, M., *Atlas of the Holocaust* (Jerusalem, 1982)

Auschwitz and the Allies (London, 1981)

(ed.) *A Century of Conflict, 1850–1950* (London, 1966)

Gillman, P. and L., *'Collar the Lot!' How Britain Interned and Expelled its Wartime Refugees* (London, 1980)

Ginsberg, M., *Essays in Sociology and Social Philosophy. Vol II: Reason and Unreason in Society* (London, 1956)

Goldman, A., 'The Resurgence of Anti-Semitism in Britain during World War II', *Jewish Social Studies*, 46 (1987), 37–50

Goldsmith, S. J. (ed.), *Joseph Leftwich at Eighty-Five: A Collective Appraisal* (London, 1978)

Goodman, J., *The Mond Legacy* (London, 1982)

Gorny, J., *The British Labour Movement and Zionism 1917–1948* (London, 1983)

'The Jewishness and Zionism of Harold Laski', *Midstream*, 23, No. 9 (1977), 72–8

Gould, J. and Esh, S. (eds.), *Jewish Life in Modern Britain* (London, 1964)

Grunfeld, J., *Shelford, the Story of a Jewish School in Evacuation, 1939–1945* (London, 1980)

Gutteridge, R. J. C., *The Churches and the Jews in England, 1933–1945* (Jerusalem, 1987)

Hearst, E., 'The British and the Slaughter of the Jews', *Weiner Library Bulletin*, 21, No. 1 (1966–7), 32–8; 21, No. 2 (1967), 30–40

Heilman, S. C., *Synagogue Life: A Study in Symbolic Interaction* (London, 1976)

Henriques, R., *Sir Robert Waley Cohen* (London, 1966)

Herman, S. N., *The Reaction of Jews to Anti-Semitism* (Johannesburg, 1945)

Hilberg, R., *The Destruction of the European Jews* (New York, 1973)

Hirschfeld, G. (ed.), *Exile in Great Britain: Refugees from Hitler's Germany* (Oxford, 1984)

Holmes, C., *Anti-Semitism in British Society, 1876–1939* (London, 1979)

Review article: Wasserstein, B., *Britain and the Jews of Europe, 1939–45*, *Jewish Journal of Sociology*, 22, No. 1 (1980), 59–72

Howard, M., *War and the Liberal Conscience* (Oxford, 1981)

Howe, I., Letter, *Commentary*, 76, No. 3 (1983), 4–6

Hughes, E., *Sidney Silverman: Rebel in Parliament* (London, 1969)

Hyde, H. M., *Strong for Service: The Life of Lord Nathan of Churt* (London, 1968)

Jewish Quarterly. 'One Hundred British Jews Gassed in Auschwitz', *Jewish Quarterly*, 4, No. 3 (1956–7), 31

Katz, J., 'Was the Holocaust Predictable?', in Bauer, Y. and Rotenstreich, N. (eds.), *The Holocaust as Historical Experience* (London, 1981), 23–41

The Role of Religion in Modern Jewish History (Cambridge, Mass., 1975)

(ed.), *Toward Modernity – the European Jewish Model* (Oxford, 1987)

Kenyon, J., 'Outsider Who Loved England', *Observer Magazine*, 19 December 1976, pp. 28–35

Kidd, A. J. and Roberts, K. W. (eds.), *City, Class and Culture: Studies of Social Policy and Cultural Production in Victorian Manchester* (Manchester, 1985)

Kochan, M., *Britain's Internees in the Second World War* (London, 1983)
   Prisoners of England (London, 1980)
Kranzler, D., Letter to the Editor, *Midstream*, 27, No. 3 (1981), 58
   Thy Brother's Blood: The Orthodox Jewish Response During the Holocaust
   (New York, 1987)
Kranzler, D. and Hirschler, G. (eds.), *Solomon Schonfeld* (New York, 1982)
Krausz, E., *Ethnic Minorities in Britain* (London, 1972)
   Leeds Jewry: Its History and Structure (Cambridge, 1964)
Krikler, B., 'Anglo-Jewish Attitudes to the Rise of Nazism' (unpublished
   manuscript for the Institute of Advanced Studies in Contemporary
   History at the Wiener Library, London)
Kushner, T., 'The British and the Shoah', *Patterns of Prejudice*, 23, No. 3
   (1989), 3–16
   'The Paradox of Prejudice: The Impact of Organised Antisemitism in
   Britain during an Anti-Nazi War', in Kushner, T. and Lunn, K.
   (eds.), *Traditions of Intolerance: Historical Perspectives on Fascism and Race
   Discourse in Britain* (Manchester, 1989), 72–90
   *The Persistence of Prejudice: Antisemitism in British Society during the Second
   World War* (Manchester, 1989)
   '"Rules of the Game": Britain, America and the Holocaust in 1944',
   Holocaust and Genocide Studies, 5, No. 4 (1990), 381–402
   and Lunn, K. (eds.), *The Politics of Marginality: Race, the Radical Right and
   Minorities in Twentieth Century Britain* (London, 1990)
Laqueur, W., 'Jewish Denial and the Holocaust', *Commentary*, 68, No. 6
   (1979), 44–55
   The Terrible Secret: Suppression of the Truth about Hitler's 'Final Solution'
   (London, 1980)
   'Zionism and its Liberal Critics, 1896–1948', *Journal of Contemporary
   History*, 6, No. 4 (1971), 161–82
Lebzelter, G. C., *Political Anti-Semitism in England, 1918–1939* (London,
   1978)
Levene, M., 'Jewish Diplomacy at War and Peace: A Study of Lucien
   Wolf 1914–1919' (unpublished D.Phil. thesis, Oxford University,
   1981)
Lipman, V. D., 'Anglo-Jewish Attitudes to the Refugees from Central
   Europe, 1933–1939', in Mosse, W. E. *et al.* (eds.), *Second Chance: Two
   Centuries of German-Speaking Jews in the United Kingdom* (Tubingen, 1991)
   Social History of the Jews in England, 1850–1950 (London, 1954)
Lipstadt, D. E., *Beyond Belief: The American Press and the Coming of the Holo-
   caust 1933–1945* (New York: 1986)
   'Witness to the Prosecution: The Allies and the Holocaust: A Review
   Essay', *Modern Judaism*, 3, No. 3 (1983), 319–38
Litvinoff, B., *A Peculiar People: Inside World Jewry Today* (London, 1969)
Loewe, L., *Basil Henriques: A Portrait* (London, 1976)
London, L., 'Jewish Refugees and British Government Policy, 1930–1940',

in Cesarani, D. (ed.), *The Making of Modern Anglo-Jewry* (Oxford, 1990), 163–90

Longmate, N., *If Britain Had Fallen* (London, 1972)

Lookstein, H., *Were We Our Brothers' Keepers? The Public Response of American Jews to the Holocaust, 1938–1944* (New York, 1988)

McLaine, I., *Ministry of Morale: Home Front Morale and the Ministry of Information in World War II* (London, 1979)

Martin, K., *Harold Laski – A Biographical Memoir* (London, 1953)

Matz, E., 'Political Actions vs. Personal Relations', *Midstream*, 27, No. 4 (1981), 41–8

Maugham, R. C. F., *Jersey under the Jackboot* (London, 1946)

Medding, P. Y. (ed.), *Studies in Contemporary Jewry II* (Indiana, 1986)

Medoff, R., *The Deafening Silence: American Jewish Leaders and the Holocaust* (New York, 1987)

Minney, R. J., *Private Papers of Hore-Belisha* (London, 1960)

Morse, A. D., *While Six Million Died* (London, 1968)

Mosse, G. L., *The Crisis of German Ideology: Intellectual Origins of the Third Reich* (New York, 1964)

Mosse, W. E. et al. (eds.), *Second Chance: Two Centuries of German-Speaking Jews in the United Kingdom* (Tubingen, 1991)

Namier, J., *Lewis Namier: A Biography* (London, 1971)

Neusner, J., *Stranger at Home* (Chicago, 1981)

Newman, A., *Lecture to Commemorate the Centenary of the Birth of Chief Rabbi Dr Joseph H. Hertz, C. H.* (London, 1973)
   The United Synagogue 1870–1970 (London, 1976)

Noy, D. and Ben-Ami, I., *Studies in the Cultural Life of the Jews in England*, Hebrew University Folklore Research Center Studies, 5 (Jerusalem, 1975)

Orbach, W. W., *The American Movement to Aid Soviet Jews* (Amherst, 1979)

Peck, S. E., 'The Campaign for an American Response to the Nazi Holocaust, 1943–1945', *Journal of Contemporary History*, 15 (1980), 367–400

Penkower, M. N., 'American Jewry and the Holocaust: From Biltmore to the American Jewish Conference', *Jewish Social Studies*, 47, No. 2 (1985), 95–114
   'Believe the Unbelievable', *Midstream*, 27, No. 4 (1981), 31–7
   'In Dramatic Dissent: The Bergson Boys', *American Jewish History*, 70, No. 3 (1981), 281–309
   The Jews were Expendable: Free World Diplomacy and the Holocaust (Illinois, 1983)
   'The Struggle for an Allied Jewish Fighting Force', in Braham, R. L. (ed.), *Contemporary Views on the Holocaust* (Boston, 1983), 47–75

Picciotto, J., *Sketches of Anglo-Jewish History. Revised and Edited, With a Prologue, Notes and an Epilogue by Israel Finestein, M.A.* (London, 1956)

Pollins, H., *Economic History of the Jews in England* (Oxford, 1982)

Porat, D., *The Blue and Yellow Stars of David: The Zionist Leadership in Palestine and the Holocaust, 1939–1945* (Cambridge, Mass., 1990)

Reinharz, J. (ed.), *Living with Anti-Semitism* (London, 1987)

Reitlinger, G., *The Final Solution: The Attempt to Exterminate the Jews of Europe, 1939–1945* (New York, 1961)

Rhodes James, R. (ed.), *Chips: The Diaries of Sir Henry Channon* (London, 1970)

Rose, N., *Lewis Namier and Zionism* (Oxford, 1980)

Rose, P. I. (ed.), *The Ghetto and Beyond: Essays on Jewish Life in America* (New York, 1969)

Roskies, D. G., *Against the Apocalypse: Responses to Catastrophe in Modern Jewish Culture* (London, 1984)

Sagi, N., 'Teguvot Hatziboriut HaYehudit BaBritaniah LeRedifat HaYehudim BeReich HaShelishi B'Shanim 1930–1939' (unpublished Ph.D thesis, Hebrew University of Jerusalem, 1982)

and Lowe, M., 'Pre-War Reactions to Nazi Anti-Jewish Policies in the Jewish Press', *Yad Vashem Studies*, 13 (1979), 387–408

Salbstein, M. C. N., *The Emancipation of the Jews in Britain: The Question of the Admission of the Jews to Parliament, 1828–1860* (London, 1982)

Schwartz, L. (ed.), *Great Ages and Ideas of the Jewish People* (New York, 1956)

Scult, M., 'Response to Friedman', in Katz, J. (ed.), *The Role of Religion in Modern Jewish History* (Cambridge, Mass., 1975)

Shamir, H., *Be Terem Shoah: Redifat Yehudei Germaniah ve Da'at hakahal be Ma'arav Eropa, 1933–39* (Tel-Aviv, 1974)

Shapira, A. (ed.), *Diyun al Britaniah ve Yehudei Eropa, 1939* (Tel-Aviv, 1983)

Sharf, A., *The British Press and Jews under Nazi Rule* (London, 1964)

'The British Press and the Holocaust', *Yad Vashem Studies*, 5 (1963), 169–91

Sharot, S., *Judaism: A Sociology* (New York, 1976)

Sherman, A. J., *Island Refuge: Britain and Refugees from the Third Reich, 1933–39* (London, 1973)

Shimoni, G., 'From Anti-Zionism to Non-Zionism in Anglo-Jewry 1917–1937', *Jewish Journal of Sociology*, 28, No. 1 (1986), 19–48

'The Non-Zionists in Anglo-Jewry, 1937–1948', *Jewish Journal of Sociology*, 28, No. 2 (1986), 89–115

'Poale Zion: A Zionist Transplant in Britain (1905–1945)', in Medding, P. Y. (ed.), *Studies in Contemporary Jewry II* (Indiana, 1986)

'Selig Brodetsky and the Ascendancy of Zionism in Anglo-Jewry, 1939–1945', *Jewish Journal of Sociology*, 22, No. 2 (1980), 125–61

Smith, E. R., 'Jewish Responses to Political Antisemitism and Fascism in the East End of London, 1920–1939', in Kushner, T. and Lunn, K. (eds.), *Traditions of Intolerance; Historical Perspectives on Fascism and Race Discourse in Britain* (Manchester, 1989), 53–71

Sompolinsky, M., 'Anglo-Jewish Leadership and the British Government: Attempts at Rescue 1944–5', *Yad Vashem Studies*, 13 (1979), 211–47

Ha-Hanhagah ha-Anglo-Yehudit, Memshelet Britannia Veha-Shoah (unpublished Ph.D thesis, Bar-Ilan University, 1977)

Srebrnik, H., 'The British Communist Party's National Jewish Committee and the Fight Against Anti-Semitism During the Second World War', in Kushner, T. and Lunn, K. (eds.), *The Politics of Marginality: Race, the Radical Right and Minorities in Twentieth-Century Britain* (London, 1990)

'Communism and Pro-Soviet Feeling Among the Jews of East London, 1935–45', *Immigrants and Minorities*, 5, No. 3 (1986), 285–304

'The Jewish Communist Movement in Stepney: Ideological Mobilization and Political Victories in an East London Borough, 1935–1945' (unpublished Ph.D thesis, University of Birmingham, 1983)

Steinberg, B., 'Anglo-Jewry and the 1944 Education Act', *Jewish Journal of Sociology*, 31, No. 2 (1989), 81–108

Steiner, G., 'A Season in Hell', in *In Bluebeard's Castle – Some Notes Towards the Re-Definition of Culture* (London, 1971)

Stent, R., *A Bespattered Page ? The Internment of His Majesty's 'Most Loyal Enemy Aliens'* (London, 1980)

Strauss, H. A., 'Jewish Emigration from Germany – Nazi Policies and Jewish Responses', *Leo Baeck Institute Year Book*, 25 (1980), 313–61 and 26 (1981), 343–409

Syrkin, M., 'Reactions to News of the Holocaust', *Midstream*, 14, No. 5 (1968), 62–3

'What American Jewry Did During the Holocaust', *Midstream*, 28, No. 8 (1982), 6–12

Szajkowski, Z., 'Jewish Diplomacy', *Jewish Social Studies*, 12, No. 3 (1960), 131–58

Taylor, A. J. P., *English History, 1914–45* (London, 1965)

Trevor-Roper, H., 'The Germans and the Jews', *The Listener*, 1 January 1981, pp. 19–20

Troen, S. I. and Pincus, B. (eds.), *Organizing Rescue: National Jewish Solidarity in the Modern Period* (London, 1992)

Tumin, M. M., 'The Cult of Gratitude', in *Judaism*, 13 (1964), 131–42; also in revised form in Rose, P. I. (ed.), *The Ghetto and Beyond: Essays on Jewish Life in America* (New York, 1969), 69–82

Turkow, J., *Schmuel Zygelboim* (Buenos Aires, 1975)

Vago, B., 'The Horthy Offer: A Missed Opportunity for Rescuing Jews in 1944', in Braham, R. L. (ed.), *Contemporary Views on the Holocaust* (Boston, 1983), 23–45

Vital, D., Review of Wasserstein, B., *Britain and the Jews of Europe, 1939–45*, *Commentary*, 69, No. 2 (1980), 80–3

Wasserstein, B., *Britain and the Jews of Europe, 1939–45* (Oxford, 1979)

'The Myth of Jewish Silence', *Midstream*, 26, No. 7 (1980), 10–16

'Patterns of Jewish Leadership in Great Britain during the Nazi Era', in Braham, R. L. (ed.), *Jewish Leadership during the Nazi Era* (New York, 1985), 29–43

Wedgwood, C. V., *The Last of the Radicals* (London, 1951)

Weitz, Y., 'The Yishuv's Self-Image and the Reality of the Holocaust', *Jerusalem Quarterly*, 48 (1989), 73–87

Wiesel, E., *Zalman or The Madness of God* (New York, 1974)

Williams, B., 'The Anti-Semitism of Tolerance: Middle-Class Manchester and the Jews 1870–1900', in Kidd, A. J. and Roberts, K. W. (eds.), *City, Class and Culture: Studies of Social Policy and Cultural Production in Victorian Manchester* (Manchester, 1985), 74–102

The Making of Manchester Jewry 1740–1875 (Manchester, 1976)

Wischnitzer, M., *To Dwell in Safety – The Story of Jewish Migration Since 1800* (Philadelphia, 1948)

Wyman, D. S., *The Abandonment of the Jews: America and the Holocaust 1941–45* (New York, 1984)

Letter to the Editor, *New York Times Magazine*, 23 May 1982, p. 94

Paper Walls: America and the Refugee Crisis 1938–1941 (Massachusetts, 1968)

'Why Auschwitz was Never Bombed', *Commentary*, 65, No. 5 (1978), 37–46

Yad Vashem, *Rescue Attempts during the Holocaust: Proceedings of the Second Yad Vashem International Historical Conference* (Jerusalem, 1976)

REFERENCE WORKS

Jones, P., *Britain and Palestine, 1914–48* (Oxford, 1979)

Lehmann, R. P., *Anglo-Jewish Bibliography 1937–1970* (London, 1973)

Nova Biblioteca Anglo-Judaica (London, 1961)

Robinson, J. and Friedman P. (eds.), *Guide to Jewish History under Nazi Impact* (New York, 1960)

Index

World Jewish Congress 3, 9, 36, 39, 149
  attitude to Holocaust 57, 66–9
  British section 10, 12, 26–7, 31, 35, 36,
    99, 163n13, 170n26
  rescue of Jews 99

Zionism 3, 31–9, 54–6, 80–1, 146,
  149–50

  as response to war 132–43
Zionist Caucus 33–7, 54–6, 168–9n21
Zionist Federation 26, 34, 38, 155, 164n32,
  168n21
  and Jewish army 127
  post-war planning 136–7
Zionist Review 168n21, 174n10
Zygielbojm, Shmuel 18, 161n65